AMERICANS

Other Books by James C. Simmons

The Novelist as Historian: Essays on the Victorian Historical Novel
Truman Capote: The Story of His Bizarre and Exotic Boyhood (with Marie Rudisill)
The Secrets Men Keep (with Ken Druck)
Passionate Pilgrims: English Travelers to the World of the Desert Arabs
The Big Book of Adventure Travel: 500 Great Escapes

AMERICANS

THE
VIEW
FROM
ABROAD

JAMES C.
SIMMONS

HARMONY BOOKS
NEW YORK

GM

Published by Harmony Books, a division of Crown Publishers, Inc., 201 East 50th Street, New York, New York 10022. Member of the Crown Publishing Group.

Acknowledgments for permission to reprint previously published material are to be found on pages 232–239.

HARMONY and colophon are trademarks of Crown Publishers, Inc.

Manufactured in the United States of America

Library of Congress Cataloging-in-Publication Data

Simmons, James C.
    Americans : the view from abroad / by James C. Simmons.
    1. United States—Foreign public opinion. I. Title.
    E840.2.S56   1990
    973—dc20   89-27703
                                                     CIP

ISBN 0-517-57628-7

10 9 8 7 6 5 4 3 2 1

First Edition

For Mildred D. Davis, Lois Fish Fiedler, Oliver J. Gossard,
Donald F. Mahan, Anne Adams Messner, and Robert J. Miller—
all teachers of mine at Mariemont High School, Cincinnati.
They made a difference.

CONTENTS

*"Perhaps, after all, America has never been discovered.
I myself would say that it had merely been detected."*
Oscar Wilde, after his 1882 visit

INTRODUCTION

ALL of us long to know how others see us.

One hundred and fifty years ago Alexis de Tocqueville insisted that Americans live "in the perpetual utterance of self-applause, and there are certain truths which Americans can learn only from strangers." He proved that outsiders are sometimes the most perceptive interpreters of American society. If we are to understand clearly the advantages and disadvantages of life in America and the values that it provides, then we must see America through the eyes of the foreign observer.

Critic William Empson once defined the obvious as "what seldom gets said." And the obvious often eludes Americans when they look at their own country. Foreigners, however, are sufficiently detached to see clearly those things, obvious or otherwise, that Americans often take for granted or simply fail to notice about themselves.

"To penetrate American life—the real life—would require years—a genuine exploration," observed the French architect Le Corbusier. The first thing a foreigner must take into account about America—and it is not something automatically grasped even by Americans—is the enormous size of the country and the diversity of life that goes on inside it. No one view can capture more than a small aspect of

America's complexity. Yet each individual view can become a chip in a broad mosaic which as a whole can effectively make sense of the relentless sprawl that is the United States. The result is a fresh look at ourselves, both as a people and as a country. These personal observations by foreign observers can help us understand such important issues as: What is an American? What is American about the American experience? And what has happened to the American Dream?

"America is like life," English novelist E. M. Forster astutely observed after his 1947 visit here, "because you can usually find in it what you are looking for." As these hundreds of different interpretations make clear, America's strength lies not in its unity but its diversity. As a chaos of disparate realities, very different from the claustrophobic, centripetal societies of Europe, America alone in the history of the modern world has possessed the ability to revise itself for different people at different times. "The reality of America is selective, optional, fantastic: there is an America for each of us," the modern British scholar Peter Conrad declared in *Imagining America*. "Because America offers an incarnation of your most recondite and specialized fantasies, in discovering America you are discovering yourself."

"The people in the United States are like persons surrounded by mirrors," wrote American congressman Charles Sumner in 1838, noting the numerous books produced by English travelers to America. "They may catch their likeness from every quarter, and in every possible light, attitude, and movement. . . . Turn as we may, we catch our reflected features. The vista seems to lengthen at every sight."

Today, over 150 years later, the mirrors are still with us. And now, as then, the first question many Americans ask visiting foreigners continues to be, "Well, what do you think of us?"

AMERICANS

1. ★ AMERICA AS ★ SYMBOL

FILM *director Frank Capra likes to tell a story about a group of Japanese soldiers on a Pacific island near the end of World War II. They had fled to a cave after an American invasion and appeared determined to die rather than surrender. The situation looked bleak. "Finally some American GI had a bright idea," Capra recalls. "Promise them a trip to Hollywood. It worked. The Japanese soldiers surrendered, and after the war they eventually got their trip."*

Countries have a habit of becoming symbols. Whether as the Hollywood Dream Factory, the Golden Land, the New Eden, the Great Satan, the Wild West, or Crime City, America has stood for more things to more people than any other nation in history.

Alexis de Tocqueville struck a common chord after his 1831 visit when he called America "a laboratory of the future." We had left the old world because its preoccupation with the past precluded the possibility for a future. Although republicanism, democracy, and the industrial revolution did not begin here, America nonetheless was the first country given over entirely to new social ideas and technological innovation and, as such, was often the first to show the benefits and to suffer the shocks of change.

The Russian novelist Maxim Gorky's description in "The City of Mammon" of his arrival by ship in New York City in 1906 concluded with the classic symbol of America, one that continues to exert a powerful attraction to the peoples of the world:

The emigrants gathered to one side of the steamer. "Who is this?" asked a Polish girl in a tone of amazement, pointing to the Statue of Liberty. Someone from the crowd answered briefly: "The American Goddess." I looked at this goddess with the feelings of an idolater. . . . Here then is the land about which tens of millions of people of the Old World dream as the Promised Land. "The Land of Liberty!" I repeated to myself, not noticing on that glorious day the green rust on the dark bronze.

Arriving almost eighty years later, Australian Clive James, too, found in the Statue of Liberty the quintessential symbol for America and her promise:

Hegel defined history as the story of liberty becoming conscious of itself. In America it became self-conscious and eventually proud. But there is a lot to be proud of and if the statue boasts, it does so with some style. Indeed, the lady grows more elegant with time. The original shine of the untarnished copper was gradually overcome by a pale verdigris which protects the metal and makes her look soft against the sky, maternal for all her power. Though firmly anchored, she is flexible, though stronger than all the forces ranged against her she is light to the spirit—America as it would like to be, and at its best is. When night falls the big lights grouped around the eleven-pointed star-fort send up their coned beams to illuminate her as she strides seaward carrying her Declaration of Independence—the woman of liberation, *éclairant le monde* in a spike hat. Tricky to deal with but not unattractive if you like them tall.

From *Snakecharmers in Texas: Essays, 1980–87*

The best-known statue in the world, the Statue of Liberty has come to symbolize the American Dream, whose substance was pursued by the generations of emigrants processed on nearby Ellis Island from 1892 until 1954, when the federal immigration station there was finally closed. America as the Land of Opportunity is neatly summed up in this story of

a misplaced emigrant who discovered his pot of gold at the end of a Southern California freeway:

In Los Angeles we heard the story (well, *tall* story) of a Russian who bought himself a jumbo 1971 Ford LTD and learned to work the pedals well enough to get it going and lurch his way onto the Santa Monica Freeway. Afraid to change lanes and unable to read the signs, he drove straight ahead until the tank was empty. In the small California town where he ended up, he 1) found a job, 2) learned English, 3) got married, 4) bought a house, and 5) struck it rich. Now he is a big real estate honcho and tools around in a BMW.

From Vassily Aksyonov, *In Search of Melancholy Baby*

Raoul Lowery Contreras was born in Mexico City but now lives in San Diego, where he writes a syndicated column devoted to Hispanic-American themes. Two of his columns which ran in the San Diego Union *suggest the power of the American Dream, which sometimes turns into the American Nightmare. The first tells the story of a Mexican illegal who settled in San Diego and through hard work became a prosperous restaurateur:*

Dear Nacho: Twenty five years ago, I jumped the *cerca* [fence] between Tijuana and San Diego. It seems like yesterday. How scared I was the *migra* [immigration] might pick me up and send me back, but they didn't.

You know, Nacho, I walked into San Diego with $5 in my pocket. Today I own 18 restaurants. *Hay! Que suerte he tenido!* [Wow! What luck I've had!] But I get ahead of myself. My first job was washing dishes in a hotel restaurant, side by side with other *paisanos* [countrymen], who also worked as busboys.

They took me to their apartment which I shared with them, ten of them. We took turns sleeping on mattresses on the floor with others who worked during the day. We split the rent, $150 a month, eleven ways. Most sent money home to Mexico by money order.

You'll remember, cousin, I'm an orphan. I had no one to send money to, so I saved it. One day a cook didn't show up for work, so the boss asked if anyone could cook. I stepped forward saying, "*Patron* [boss], I can." Presto, I was a cook. I worked hard. These crazy Americans eat their steaks almost raw, Nacho, really. Making more money, I was able to save more; every week, $20 or $30.

In the meantime the *patron* told me I was a good worker, but I should learn more English. Asking around, I found, you're not going to believe this, free English classes in a public school. Free! On my nights off, I went to school. It was in class, Nacho, that I met the love of my life, Maria, who had jumped the *cerca,* also. She worked in a factory.

After a while, Maria and I married and rented an apartment. How nice it was not to sleep on a mattress on the floor. For ten years I worked at the hotel, working every minute, saving every penny we could, both learning English.

We bought a car, furniture; we even bought a television. The first of three children came quickly. Even with children, my savings grew to $5,000. *Hay! Que milagro!* [What a miracle!]

One day we drove to a hamburger stand, finding it closed. Standing outside was the owner, a little *chavala* [young lady] who made terrific hamburgers. She was crying because she had to close, as a new freeway a block away had taken away her traffic.

We consoled her, telling her hers were the best hamburgers. She hugged and thanked us, then tacked up a for-sale sign. Curious, we asked how much she wanted—$3,000, she responded.

My *esposa* [wife] looked at me. I looked back. Wordlessly, we nodded to each other, then told her, "Don't put the sign up. We'll buy it."

So we shook hands, went to the bank, wrote up a piece of paper, drew money from savings and handed it over. We were in business. We went to my *patron,* to tell him. Good man that he was, he suggested I keep my job, taking turns at the stand. He wrote down suppliers for us to call to buy meat, tortillas, and produce; cash, of course. We talked to our *paisanos* in the hotel and quickly lined up several to work with us.

We went to another *paisano* we knew, who painted signs announcing the grand opening of Pancho's Taco Stand. Another painted the stand bright red with yellow stripes. My wife made arrangements for gas and electricity, water, and everything. Thanks, public schools, for teaching us English.

I took my vacation from work and we opened the taco stand on a Friday. The first day we stayed open until 9 P.M. selling $22 worth of tacos and burritos. Rent was $10 a day; wages to my workers, $25; and supplies, $10.

We lost $23 the first day. The next day we stayed open until midnight and made $2. Within a month we stayed open all night and started making serious *masa* [dough], as much as $50 a day.

Oh, Nacho, business was good. Within a year we saved enough to buy another stand, hired a bookkeeper, paid our taxes, and bought a little house. Our food was so good, police and even Border Patrol (*la migra*) came to our stands every day to eat. It still tickles me to think about border patrolmen as customers.

Every year we added a stand. Nacho, I was making hundreds of dollars a day. We bought a larger house. No one ever asked us our citizenship. We made sure our children went to school every day and did their homework. We were determined they should be educated.

Nacho, I can't tell you how proud I was when my oldest boy came to me and told me he wanted to go to college. He told me he would work nights at one of the stands if he could have days free for school. I gave him my blessing. Nacho, he worked hard. He graduated from the state university with honors in business.

The day he did, he came to me with what he called a business plan. A business plan? He told me it was not wise to use savings to open up new stands, that we should borrow money to expand. I scoffed at the idea. Who would lend money to a *campesino* [peasant] like me? He made me dress in my best suit and we went to the bank.

Nacho, they took us into a private room, served coffee and offered us cigars, then thanked us for our business of many years. My son did all the talking. When he finished, the banker told us he would be happy to extend us a revolving line of credit for $100,000. A revolving line of credit? I didn't even know what that was. But with it we opened up four more restaurants that year and four more the next year. Now we have eighteen.

Then one day, Nacho, the Congress of the United States passed a law giving illegal aliens amnesty. Amnesty! Even though we had been in the country many years, paid taxes and our children were all born here, we never forgot. We were illegal.

On the first day of amnesty my wife and I gathered our papers and went to the Immigration office to apply. Imagine the surprise of the Immigration officer when he looked up and saw us. He was one of our best customers. He took our papers, laughing, and had us approved within a week.

Because we had been here so long and were, according to him, such good citizens, we were granted our *micas* [green cards] within a month. When a federal judge heard about us, he had us apply for citizenship right away. He, too, was one of our customers.

Nacho, we're now citizens of the United States. We will vote for president of the United States in a few weeks—the same day we open our nineteenth restaurant.

I have to go now. But let me say, *Primo mio, los Estados Unidos, que pais!* [My cousin, the United States, what a country!]

In another column Contreras explored how the traditional American promise of rebirth is sometimes corrupted to deliver death:

On the south levee of the Tijuana River channel, Jesus María Martínez Solarzano sits, already on American territory, waiting patiently for the sun to disappear into the Pacific Ocean.

(Mama, where's papa?)

He and hundreds of other Mexicans can begin the final leg of their journey, a journey which for Jesus María began in Huajuapan, State of Oaxaca, south of Mexico City. As darkness descends, Jesus María stands and prepares to wade across the sewage-choked river. So do hundreds of fellow Mexicans, watched by American border patrolmen through binoculars, guided by body-heat sensors scattered throughout the rural valley, incongruously part of the United States's sixth largest city, San Diego.

Experienced border jumpers tell Jesus María he stands only a one in three chance of being caught by the gringo Border Patrol, and if he is caught, he will be bused back to Tijuana and can try again. Once across the river, they tell him, he can steal a car, catch a bus or San Diego's Border Trolley, or join others and hire a taxi into downtown San Diego. From there he can make his way by freight train, by foot, or by cab—if he has the money. Most cab drivers, he's told, charge $100 per person to the agricultural fields of northern San Diego.

(Mama, I'm hungry.)

The valley's brush is thick, making it easy to hide from a Border Patrol helicopter flying above. Jesus María and two others from his village run, hide, run, and make their way through the brush until they come to a fence bordering a highway. They walk north until the fence stops. There they find a trolley station, read directions in Spanish on how to use the system, buy tickets from a machine, and wait.

(Shush, my little one, all we have is black beans.)

Jesus María and his friends leave the trolley before a skyscraper-dotted downtown San Diego and look for a restaurant where, they were told, they can eat cheaply and be told where there are jobs. They enter, order Oaxaca-style food, and start asking where they can find jobs. La Costa, they are told, just across from a posh resort. Field hands needed. Pay $40 a day, cash.

Forty dollars! Jesus María thinks. I can live on less than ten. I can send $30 a day, 70,000 pesos, home to María and the little ones. Oh, thank God for rich America!

Call a taxicab, they are told, and make a deal for the fare. Jesus María and his friends surreptitiously count their money. Jesus María has the most, a little more than $30; his friends, $20 between them. The cab comes. They grin when they see the driver is Mexican.

They ask, how much to La Costa? About $50. With a sigh of relief, they enter the cab. An hour later, the cab pulls off the interstate toward La Costa Resort with its $1,400-a-day suites, then takes a dirt road away from the resort and moves into the pitch-dark fields. No one knows where they're going.

(Mama, when's papa coming home?)

Jesus María fingers his Lady of Guadalupe medal and prays they find the workers' camp soon. He's tired; it's 3 A.M. He's fearful of the Border Patrol, *la migra,* who might swoop down on the cab any second. The driver stops as the dirt road crosses a ravine, steps out, looks around, then asks, *"Compañeros? Amigos?"* He repeats the calls, a little louder, several times. After several minutes and calls, a tiny Zapotec or Mixtec Indian steps out of the brush and asks, *"Quien llama?"* ["Who calls?"]

(Don't cry, little one. Tomorrow we will have milk.)

Jesus María and his friends step out of the cab and tell the Indian the name of their village. Good, the Indian replies, there are many from that area in camp. *"Bienvenidos."* ["Welcome."] The welcoming Indian leads them to an empty cave, where they can sleep and live.

The sun is hot. The work is hard. But, Jesus María thinks as he digs weeds from around tomato plants, tonight I will go to the store the other Indians patronize, buy a $30 money order and mail it to my family.

Later, leaving the store, he pridefully walks into the brush to make his way back to camp, can of beer in hand, happy with money on its way home.

(Papa went to the north to make money, my little one, so we can buy food, milk, clothes, and shoes. We'll be hearing from him soon.)

Unidentified male Mexican, about 30 years of age, stabbed five times, the San Diego County deputy sheriff writes on his report. No ID. Effects: a Guadalupe religious medal and a picture of a woman and eight kids. No money. Probably robbery, the deputy writes. No witnesses.

(Go find the mailman, my little one. See if there is anything from your father.)

One of the most common metaphors is that of de Tocqueville's—America as a laboratory for the future, promising either the salvation or damnation of mankind, as the three following observations suggest:

The future is to be read in the nature of America.

Italian editor and author Luigi Barzini,
Americans Are Alone in the World

America is where the mistakes are being made and made first; so we're going to get the answers first.

British novelist Christopher Isherwood, quoted by
Peter Conrad in *Imagining America*

One comes to America—always, no matter how often—to see the future. It's what life in one's own country will be like five, ten, twenty years from now.

An Israeli businessman, speaking to the author

Ihab Hassan was born in Egypt but came to the United States to teach as a professor of American literature. About America's "lack" of a past, he says:

Europe possesses a past. America makes one. But the past America makes becomes elsewhere in the world an optative future. That is, America, alembic of time, distills the future in the present, and so permits other nations to choose their destiny. This does not always win gratitude.

The historic role of America? Beyond language, nation, and clan, to create (precariously, violently) a new order of diversity. Neither "melting pot" nor "rubbish heap," neither sociolect nor idiolect, but the One and the Many mediated dangerously toward a uni-verse. The world's dream?

If America seems relatively apolitical, is it not because traditional politics (power and interest institutionalized in older forms) has become historically obsolete? More precisely: in what sense is an advanced technological country "post-political" rather than "apolitical"?

From Out of Egypt: Scenes and Arguments of an Autobiography

America as the Melting Pot impressed Polish writer Malgorzata Nieza-bitowska when she traveled across the country in the summer of 1986 on assignment for the National Geographic *magazine:*

We met a lot of people and heard many stories. All of them compose that extraordinary mosaic called America, but now as I get ready for my trip back to Poland, one memory keeps returning particularly often. One night during a sudden storm we stopped over in a small town in Nebraska. The motel was the only one in town, and we were the only guests. In the morning we discovered that the town had one paved street and about 300 inhabitants. It was called Lewellen.

For breakfast we went to the only cafe in town. The manager, three days' growth on his face, stood behind the counter. The customers, all men, were seated around the tables. In the middle stood a round, large and empty table. And that was where we sat to have our cinnamon rolls. Our entrance caused a sensation. All conversations died down, and everybody stared at us in silence. Finally a tall, red-bearded man brought over the coffeepot from the counter and offered to refill our cups, which were still full.

In a moment our table was teeming with people, all of them asking us questions and talking about themselves. It turned out that among these 15 or so Lewellen citizens there were a Greek, an Italian, an Irishman, a Hungarian, a German, and a Pole—if not in the first, then in the second or third generation. They teased each other good-humoredly about the supposed foibles of different nationalities, and we quickly joined in the fun.

Obviously life in Lewellen is no idyll, and everybody isn't always joking. Yet the image of this big table and the people gathered around it, whose ancestors came to a lost-in-the-prairie town from different parts of the world, has for me great charm and importance.

From "Discovering America," in *National Geographic*
magazine, January 1988

America has been called a melting pot, but it seems better to call it a mosaic, for in it each nation, people or race, which has come to its shores has been privileged to keep its individuality, contributing at the same time its share to the unified pattern of a new nation.

King Baudouin I of Belgium, as quoted
in *Reader's Digest,* October 1959

Americans are very nice, very human people. What a humane civilization and culture to have been created from a big melting pot.

Trinidad-born novelist V. S. Naipaul, as quoted in
The Illustrated Weekly of India, 1987

Jim Pinto, an Indian-born engineer who now lives in San Diego, has given new meaning to the term "American melting pot." In 1972 he founded Action Instruments, a measurement and instrument firm which has experienced some of the most rapid growth of any within the industry. He shares ownership of his company with the majority of his employees and reinvests virtually all profits in new production. The 51-year-old Pinto is quoted by business writer Joel Kotlin in the San Diego Union:

I guess I'm a bit of a new hybrid. My body was made in India, my science learned in England, and my management philosophy comes largely from the Japanese, but I'm putting it all together in California.

Other metaphors are more original, reflecting both the imaginations and the prejudices of the observers, as the following will suggest:

America—a land of boys who refuse to grow up.

Spanish author Salvador de Mardarcaga, quoted in
Olga Miller's The Perpetual Pessimist

The United States is the glory, jest, and terror of Mankind.

James M. Minifie, Canadian author, quoted in
The New Romans, edited by Al Purdy

The Great Satan.

Ayatollah Ruhollah Khomeini, Iranian leader

I like going there for golf. America's one vast golf course today.

Edward, Duke of Windsor, quoted in Newsweek,
January 24, 1970

A resident of the remote Marquesas Islands, where the most popular video rentals were Charles Bronson movies, and Dynasty *and* Dallas *were the favorite television shows, upon being asked by the author in 1985 what America meant to him:*

Boom, boom, fuck, fuck.

America's a hard school, I know, but hard schools make excellent graduates.

Oriana Fallaci, Italian journalist, in Penelope at War

11

America is a nation of obsessions.

Vassily Aksyonov, quoted in *U.S. News and World Report,*
August 17, 1987

America is a country that doesn't know where it is going but is determined to set a speed record getting there.

Canadian author Laurence J. Peter in *Peter's Quotations*

★

For South African bishop Desmond M. Tutu, fences become the controlling symbol for the differences between his country and America:

I am impressed with the openness of Americans symbolized by the lack of fences around most homes in contrast, to say, South Africa, a much fenced country in all kinds of ways. Also by their generosity. I am amazed at sophisticated people who can be so naive in their adulation of some of their presidents. But it is also an extraordinary country for all its faults. It is only in America that a black could actually be a serious candidate for the Presidency.

From a letter to the author dated August 3, 1988

★

Janusz Glowacki is the author of six plays, ten books, twenty radio plays, and four produced screenplays. Born in Poland, he came to the United States in 1982. Arthur Penn directed the Broadway production of his play, Hunting Cockroaches, *from which the following excerpt is taken:*

Anka's lying on the sheets. Jan's in a chair studying the map of America; nearby is a can of roach spray.
JAN: What a strange country. . . . Here's France, and Austria, and Germany, the Soviet Union, Poland. The boundary lines between all the countries twist and turn, and twitch like worms in a can. Messy. (*Points to American map.*) That's what you call a neat job. Look here. (*Points to states on the map.*) Montana, Wyoming, North Dakota, South Dakota, Missouri. (*He pronounced it "misery."*) This country was laid out by someone who had technical training. Buildings

(*traces rectangles in the air*), streets (*traces lines*), everything, even people are well made. That's what you call a good piece of work. Only the cockroaches seem not to have come out quite right . . . yet.

★

British novelist Anthony Burgess wrote in an essay in the New York Times *in 1971 about an American Eden corrupted by the Vietnamese war:*

When Europe, after millennia of war, rapine, slavery, famine, intolerance, had sunk to the level of a sewer, America became the golden dream, the Eden where innocence could be recovered. Original sin was the monopoly of that dirty continent over there; in America man could grow in an aura of natural goodness, driven along his shining path by divine reason. The Declaration of Independence itself is a monument to reason. Progress was possible, and the wrongs committed against the Indians, the wildlife, the land itself, could be explained away in terms of the rational control of environment necessary for the building of a New Jerusalem. Right and wrong made up the moral dichotomy; evil—that great eternal inextirpable enemy—had no place in America.

At last, with the Vietnam war and especially the Mylai horror, Americans are beginning to realize that they are subject to original sin as much as Europeans are. Some things—the massive crime figures, for instance—can now be explained only in terms of absolute evil. Europe, which has long known about evil and learned to live with it (*live* is *evil* spelled backwards) is now grimly pleased to find that America is becoming like Europe. America is no longer Europe's daughter nor her rich stepmother; she is Europe's sister. The agony that America is undergoing is not to be associated with breakdown so much as with the parturition of self-knowledge. . . .

But I ask the reader to note that I, an Englishman, no longer live in England, and I can't spend more than six months at a stretch in Italy—or any other European country, for that matter. I home to America as to a country more stimulating than depressing. The future of mankind is being worked out there on a scale typically American—vast, dramatic, almost apocalyptical. I brave the brutality and the guilt in order to be in on the scene. I shall be back.

★

General Secretary Mikhail Gorbachev, in his book Perestroika: New Thinking for Our Country and the World, *tried to refute Puritan John Winthrop's classic image of America as a "shining city atop a hill":*

I know that American propaganda—yes, propaganda—presents America as a "shining city atop a hill." America has a great history. Who will question the importance of the American Revolution in mankind's social progress, or the scientific-technological genius of America and its achievements in literature, architecture, and art? All this America has. But America today also has acute social and other problems, to which not only has American society not yet found an answer, but, even worse, it is looking for answers in places and in such a way that may lead to others having to pay.

The United States has a huge production potential and an enormous material wealth, but, at the same time, millions of unfortunate people. This is something to ponder. An almost missionary passion for preaching about human rights and liberties and a disregard for ensuring those same elementary rights in their own home. This also provokes thought. Endless talk about man's freedom and attempts to impose its way of life on others, wide-scale propaganda of the cult of force and violence. How are we to understand this? Arrogance of power, especially military power, constant growth in arms spending and gaps in the budget, an internal and now also an external debt. For what? What motivates the U.S.? We ask ourselves all these and many other questions, trying to grasp the American reality and to see the mainsprings behind U.S. policy.

I admit frankly that what we know does not support the idea of the United States of America as a "shining city atop a hill." With equal definiteness I can say that neither do we consider the U.S. an "evil empire." Like all countries America in reality casts both light and shadows.

For many years Britisher Trevor Fishlock served as the correspondent for The Times *of London in New York City. After a visit to the battlefield of Little Big Horn in eastern Montana, he penned a provocative essay in which he argued that General George Armstrong Custer had been transformed by defeat and death into an appropriate symbol for certain aspects of the American experience:*

Whether as hero or anti-hero, Custer serves a purpose as a national totem. He was neither a great man nor a good soldier. But nations must sometimes fashion heroes from inadequate clay. What is interesting about Custer is not so much the man himself, rather why he and the last stand exert enduring fascination. Though his reputation has been frequently assailed by historian demolition experts, he has not disappeared. On the contrary, he is a boulder of a legend lodged in the national memory. If one believes that societies derive a necessary stimulus from their myths and legends, like a secreted hormone, Custer has served his country well; better than he served it as a soldier. He is there to mean what people want him to mean: last of the cavaliers, martyr, exterminator, scoundrel, frontier hero, fool, an echo of a nation's rosily remembered adolescence, resident of the American pantheon.

From *The State of America*

Jane Walmsley, an American married to an Englishman, has lived in London since 1975. From her perspective on the other side of the Atlantic Ocean, she has decided that ice cream is the key to understanding American society:

Americans, for all their affluence and the distractions it can bring, know what really counts. ICE CREAM. More than allegiance to the flag, or a national newspaper, or Johnny Carson, or the microchip, it's mocha-chip (and peppermint crunch) that binds the nation together. Fail to appreciate this, and you've missed out on the quintessence of Ameri-culture. Ice cream is the Great Leveler . . . the Yank version of pubs. It is the fixed point in an otherwise mobile society, guaranteed to give pleasure to all. Americans will drive one hundred miles for the ultimate cone. Don't ask why. Debates about the MX missile are taken no more seriously than where you can find the best coffee flavor in Los Angeles. It's the American way of saying that, at bottom, stripped bare of affection, they know what life is about—and you can always appeal to them more successfully on that level. . . . If you can't come to grips with the Great American Dream, you can fall back on the Great American Cream. Mocha-chip is nice.

From *Brit-think, Ameri-think*

American author Jan Morris, who also expatriated herself to England, observed in Encounter:

I loved America the moment I set foot there. It is a country that will never be finished. Its natural state is seismic, or protean. Its citizens may pine for stability, order, permanence; but to live temporarily, from crisis to reappraisal, disillusionment to renewal, is the pride and penalty of being an American.

Nonna Rinck had been a respected librarian for 22 years in the Soviet Union, with, she says, "a good future, a good apartment, and a good life." She even had her own television talk show, on which she discussed the latest engineering books available. Today she is an émigré who lives in a tiny apartment in Long Island City.

Why did she leave such good prospects in her former country? "It's hard to explain," says Rinck. "It is why zoo animals that are well fed and well cared for walk out when the cage door is left open. At first I worked in an American factory for only a few dollars an hour. But I sang to myself because I was *free*."

William E. Geist, in the New York Times

★

Vu Thanh Thuy is a former war correspondent in South Vietnam. She now works as an editorial assistant for the San Diego Union. *A refugee from Vietnam, she sees the image of "boat people" as a controlling metaphor for the American experience:*

American just celebrated Thanksgiving. As I have come to understand it, it is the national holiday that commemorates the coming of the first "boat people" from Europe to America. How appropriate that almost four centuries later, we stand here, the most recently arrived boat people, this time from Asia, sharing this occasion with you and giving thanks to America.

This country opened its doors to us. It has been our shelter since 1980, and we have become a part of it.

America has given us so much to be thankful for. It is truly a land of possibilities, a land that can welcome the stranger in your midst and offer such warmth, acceptance, and hope. I can better understand why this country has been called a "permanently unfinished" society, so open and free, and with an unmatched capacity to absorb immigrants and refugees from all over the world. We will be forever grateful to you.

From the *San Diego Union*, January 31, 1988

Le Corbusier, the renowned French architect, found in America a hope for that portion of humanity committed to heroic action:

I shall come back to America. America is a great country. Hopeless cities and cities of hope at the same time. What an idea of the action between these two poles is thus expressed, what a battlefield is spread out between these two feelings which exist in the gasping heart of every man of action, of every man who believes enough in something to dare to attempt it, and who risks catastrophe for having wished to bring back trophies to the altar.

For, beyond the narrow limits of the average in human things, when magnitude enters into an undertaking (Assyrians, Hindus, Egyptians, Romans, and Gothic builders), the result becomes a public and civic thing and, like grace, makes a horror sublime.

All the French people whom I met on the ship going to New York, all those on this ship taking us back to Paris, resolve the question thus: "Once you have opened the door on America you cannot close it again."

From *When the Cathedrals Were White*

★

However, unlike Le Corbusier, the Chinese editor Liu Zongren was only too glad to return home after a two-year stay in the United States. He found in the film figure of E.T. an emblem of his feelings:

In Chicago everyone told me I should see *E.T.*, a highly popular science-fiction film. The general manager of China Books, Chris Noyes, and his family, took me to see it on the last night I was in the United States. I liked *E.T.* for a reason that most American kids might not think of: E.T. wanted to go home. He couldn't survive on earth, living with his new friends; he wanted to return to his own kind. The film didn't say anything about the planet E.T. lived on: we don't know if the planet had cars, refrigerators, color TV sets, or divorced parents. The film did show how excited E.T. was after he had "phoned home" and learned that his people were coming to take him home.

During my stay in the United States I had met many people, some of whom became very good friends. Many of them were like E.T.'s young friends; they had helped me in every way they could to understand American life. But few of them really understood me or knew why I couldn't feel comfortable among Americans, why I preferred to live a poorer and simpler life in China.

From *Two Years in the Melting Pot*

2 ★THE AMERICAN ★PEOPLE

BRITISH visitors to the United States 150 years ago thought us Americans a strange and inexplicable lot. They quickly perceived that we exhibited characteristics not shared by our cousins back in England. We have become virtually a different people. The Londoner who remarked, as many did, that he felt more at home in Paris than Chicago was only mirroring a belief that Americans had been transmuted into a different species from the British pioneers who had planted their civilization at Jamestown and Plymouth.

"The moment I set foot in the United States I felt that I had got amongst a new people," observed the Reverend David Macrae soon after his arrival in New York in 1867. "It is very remarkable that a country still in its infancy should already have produced so distinct a type of man. . . . An American is everywhere recognized. You know him by his speech; you know him by a certain ease and grandeur of manner, which is inspired by the greatness of his country and his personal share in its government; you know him by his features—the long sharp face, the eagle eye, and the pointed chin."

Why this transmutation? The more perceptive visitors in the last century understood that many of the national characteristics they branded as uniquely American were products of the generations of pioneering *needed to settle the continent. When Britisher Adam Nicolson made an extensive trip by automobile through the Western states in 1986, the impact of the pioneer experience on the shaping of the American character was everywhere evident to him:*

The history of America, or at least of the American West, consists of an indifference to history. The men and women, trappers and traders, later the farmers and settlers, who came up the rivers, who pushed their handcarts, who came in wagon trains, who eventually journeyed on the railroad, were doing what hadn't been done before. They were rejecting the restrained and enclosed life of Europe or the East Coast. It was a radical thing to do, based on a refusal to accept everything their ancestors had accepted in a world dominated by the inhumanities of repressive, seigniorial systems. That radical urge for individual freedom lies deep in the heart of America.

The Lewis and Clark expedition is, in a way, a great exception in the history of the discovery of the West. It was organised, sponsored, and financed by the President, a great reaching out by the federal government to the far Pacific coast. But from my perspective . . . it is not the expedition itself which is representative of America but a small incident that occurred on the way *back.* Three of its members, who—I would have thought with my European mind—would want nothing more than to return in triumph to St. Louis and to the settled East, decided to leave the Corps of Discovery and remain in the wilderness, living the life of mountain men, indifferent to their role in history as great pioneers. To my mind those three are essential Americans, the Americans I admire and envy. . . . Seeing themselves as individuals, they were doing their individual thing.

From *Two Roads to Dodge City*

British author T. H. White also reached a similar conclusion regarding Americans during a 1964 visit to the United States:

Americans . . . are essentially an *earnest* people. They have so much love and kindness and are so little blasé. But it is fatal to forget that they are all descended from *people who had the guts not to stay at home.* Americans are not English or Irish or Italian or anything else.

They are the children, in a melting pot, of adventurers who had this one thing in common, that they were individualists who had the courage, initiative, and vigor to break out of the Old World and conquer a continent. These joiners, like the joiners of that club at my private school, have joined the club of America. If somebody strikes against it, as happened at Pearl Harbor, they will always react with a blind, devastating energy. Americans are more likely to let off an atomic bomb than the Russians are. They are less old, less effete with history, more bred from strength, younger, more lovable, more terrible potentially.

From *America at Last*

★

Trevor Fishlock found the frontier spirit still strong among the inhabitants of Alaska when he traveled there on assignment. His report included the following observations on the people of that state:

In Alaska there is all the ambiguity of the frontier. The Last Frontier slogan is invested with self-consciousness and sadness. It is meant to sound robustly all-American and celebratory, but it has, too, a note of nostalgic longing, regret for vanishing youth. Otherwise, surely, Alaskans would have called their land, in a more forward-looking way, the New Frontier. Men still journey here to be frontiersmen. They grow their whiskers especially for the purpose. They ransack the trading post catalogues for thick wool shirts, thermal underwear, rifles, Bowie knives and books on how to build log cabins and bear-proof larders. They buy devices to get solar electricity "free from the midnight sun" and consider whether to invest in "the world's most powerful hand gun, 2000 foot-pounds of raw power! Alaska's answer to bear protection." Thus equipped they thrust their eager bushy faces towards the challenging wilderness—and are dismayed to find parking tickets on their windscreens. Anchorage and Fairbanks have traffic jams, parking congestion and severe carbon monoxide pollution. Even in distant Nome, population 2500, there are irksome regulations. *The Nome Nugget*, Alaska's oldest newspaper (the motto on its masthead states: There's no place like Nome), commented regretfully on the installation of the town's first traffic signal in 1984: "It doesn't make us do anything we weren't already supposed to do. So, no cause for alarm yet. It just makes one wonder who will get the first ticket and how long before the first bullet hole shows up. Big city life is creeping up on us."

From The State of America

Odile Fouchard, a gregarious Paris antique dealer, is an unabashed fan of the United States:

I like forcefulness. I like liveliness. I like liberty. I like Americans. *Voilà!*

Quoted in the Dallas Morning News, July 6, 1986

*The English actress Emily Lloyd (*Wish You Were Here, Cookie, *and* In Country*) was favorably impressed by Americans when she was an exchange student at a high school in Los Gatos, California, during 1986:*

Americans are much more open and frank than the British. By nature, almost all of them are optimists. I am too.

Quoted in Parade, September 27, 1987

Norwegian anthropologist Thor Heyerdahl sees the American capacity for achieving harmony out of diversity as an important characteristic of our people:

What strikes me most in America is the ethnic conglomeration of human beings who agree that their nation is the best in the world although they disagree about almost anything else. It strikes me by looking at America that a similar arrangement should be useful for the rest of the world. One day we may learn from the astronauts that this planet is the best in our solar system, and thus stop wasting our resources on offensive and defensive arms and refuge platforms in space.

From a letter to the author, dated October 6, 1988

The British journalist Alistair Cooke, an observer of America for almost forty years, agrees:

To watch an American on the beach, or crowding into a subway, or buying a theater ticket, or sitting at home with his radio on, tells you something about one aspect of the American character: the capacity to withstand a great deal of outside interference, so to speak; a willing acceptance of frenzy which, though it's never self-conscious, amounts to a willingness to let other people have and assert their own lively, and even offensive, character.

From *One Man's America*

The British soldier, explorer, and author Col. John Blashford-Snell remembers with fond appreciation the many Americans who have participated in his expeditions to the faraway regions of the world:

I have had large numbers of Americans working with me on expeditions. In general they are open, immensely friendly, and extremely generous—a great change from the more reserved British. At home they are overwhelmingly hospitable. If they have any fault in British eyes, it is perhaps that they tend to be more emotional, worrying about health and "relationships" far more than we do.

From a letter to the author, dated May 23, 1988

In 1980 the 23-year-old Spanish golfer Seve Ballesteros went into the record books as the youngest winner ever of the U.S. Masters Tournament. Of Americans he says:

It is clear that as a professional golfer my knowledge is concentrated more on an awareness of sports in America than on its traditions. Notwithstanding, the U.S.A. signifies for me the daily struggle where people constantly want to win, employing discipline, hard work, and consistency which should always be the tools to bring one luck in the end.

From a letter to the author, dated August 9, 1988

Allan Fotheringham is a Canadian journalist who spent four years on assignment in Washington. He found profound differences between the

Canadian and American national characters, best summed up by his observation that "Canadians cope; Americans conquer." His article appeared in the weekly Financial Post *of Toronto.*

There is a doctor in Toronto who has made a substantial reputation as an expert on back pain. He published a book, *How to Cope with Back Pain,* and it attracted the attention of a publisher in New York. The U.S. rights were acquired, and the publisher then explained that for the U.S. edition, there would be a slight change in the title. It would be called, *How to Conquer Back Pain.*

That is the difference. Canadians cope. Americans conquer. That is the main finding of a scribe returning to home soil after four years in Washington. . . . It is this "conquer" strain in the American character that shapes the country. The strong survive, and the weak are left to, well, cope. This rich nation's aversion to socialized medicine (the only industrialized country in the world without it) is based on the same attitudes. Aside from a germ called "socialism," Americans feel, deep down, that everybody should be able to take care of himself. . . .

Americans conquer. In Houston, they decided to conquer the oppressive summertime heat and so built the world's first domed stadium, so as to enjoy air-conditioned baseball. . . . Americans have an unlimited belief that anything is possible and anyone can rise to the top. They revel in the moneyed vulgarities of the Donald Trumps and the Mike Tysons. . . . Cope and conquer. That is the difference.

Katherine Whitehorn, a British journalist, was struck by American readiness to rush to divorce courts:

Americans, indeed, often seem to be so overwhelmed by their children that they'll do anything for them except stay married to the co-producers.

From *Observations*

The Italian editor and author Luigi Barzini finds Americans more difficult to understand than any other people:

The Americans' picture of themselves and of their ideals is always controversial and deceptive. They exalt exaggerated virtues, deplore partly imaginary sins, overpraise the nobility of the original hopes, cry over the present betrayal, denounce the imminent ruin of everything decent and honorable, and extol the perfect Utopia which is only a few inventions away—all this sometimes within the same political speech or essay.

The main obstacle to a foreigner's understanding of America is perhaps the Americans' descriptions of themselves. Travelers in the United States are at first pleasantly misled by the great wealth of oversimplified generalizations which have been fashioned in part to educate many Americans of different breed, blood, opinion, religion, and origin to a common pattern. After a while, travelers think they know everything and that everything is clear and logical. Later they discover that real things, events, and people can only with the greatest difficulty be fitted into the rigid pattern, that no two Americans are alike because most of them are better and worse than they describe themselves, and that, above all, they are more human and diversified than the model. Travelers are then completely baffled.

From *Americans Are Alone in the World*

For over forty years Harry Payne has been a doorman at London's elegant Hyde Park Hotel. He remembers some of the more famous Americans he has served over the years:

We have a very good class of American customer here. Very rarely do I get the arrogant types. There used to be some a few years ago, but they seem to have vanished. They've probably been killed by the people they've insulted.

Being the kind of place this is, I've seen a lot of famous people— the late Cary Grant, Frank Sinatra, Ava Gardner. They linger in memory. Sinatra, for example, when he was on the down. He was going with Ava Gardner, but she had some Spanish bullfighter as well. She was the most beautiful woman, without a doubt. . . . When President Nixon was here, I escorted him to his limo and got pushed out of the way by his Secret Service men.

The only guest I've asked for an autograph was Neil Armstrong, the first man on the moon. We had Yury Gagarin, the Russian, first man in space, but I didn't want his autograph.

Quoted in *Condé Nast Traveler*, February 1988

★

For the Australian critic Clive James, one of the most obvious traits of Americans is the hectic pace they often set for themselves:

It is an American characteristic not to stop running even after you have arrived.

Quoted in *The Observer*, 1981

★

*Italian semiotician and novelist (*The Name of the Rose*) Umberto Eco sees the comic-book character of Clark Kent as a typical American:*

Clark Kent personifies fairly typically the average reader who is harassed by complexes and despised by his fellow men; any accountant in any American city secretly feels the hope that one day there can spring forth a superman who is capable of redeeming years of mediocre existence.

Quoted in *Time*, March 14, 1988

★

British actor and wit John Cleese observed on "Good Morning America," July 29, 1988:

We need your openness, your honesty, and your French fries—especially your French fries.

★

Jean-Pierre Vidal, a salesman for a company that exports French technology to the United States, finds Americans likable but eccentric:

Americans are big kids. They're a new people, a young people. But they are too clean. I've read articles in the United States saying the French are too dirty. I say the Americans are too clean!

They have lots of cosmetics, soap, deodorants, all that. Their concern about cleanliness is pushed to an extreme. That's not bad; it's not negative. They're also a nation of consumers, so the more they wash, the more soap they buy, and it's good for the economy.

Quoted in the *Dallas Morning News*, July 6, 1986

However, French architect Le Corbusier saw the same emphasis on cleanliness in a different light:

Cleanliness is a national virtue in America. No filth, no dust. Sea breezes incessantly sweep through the limpid maritime sky. The offices are clean; the bath tubs, the shops, the glistening hotels; the dazzling restaurants and bars. The immaculate personnel, in shirt sleeves, in shining white. Food is wrapped up in bright cellophane. There is no more real dust than there is symbolic dust. Everything is new and spotless, including the collegiate Gothic of the universities.

Paris bistro, you disappointed me on my return, with your faded charm. It's too old, too old, saddening! Not even a nice little old, something neat and clean!

In contrast, there is style, a true style, in American cleanliness.

From *When the Cathedrals Were White*

★

For Jane Walmsley, who has lived in London since 1975, the American conviction that life is forever is our most important national characteristic:

The single most important thing to know about Americans—the attitude which *truly* distinguishes them from the British, and explains much superficially odd behavior—is that *Americans think that death is optional.* They may not admit it, and will probably laugh if it's suggested; but it's a state of mind—a kind of national leitmotiv if you like—that colors everything they do. There's a nagging suspicion that you can delay death (or—who knows?—avoid it altogether) if you really try. This explains the common preoccupation with health, aerobics, prune juice, plastic surgery, and education.

The idea is that you're given one life to live, and it's up to you to get it right. You should:

• use the time to maximize individual potential (have a nose job, get a college education) so as to ensure the highest quality life possible.
• take care of your body so it will last. If extended life span—or even immortality—proves possible, at least you're ready.

That's the secret of America's fundamental optimism; but it's not as cheery as it sounds. It imposes on the individual a whole range of duties and responsibilities. Your life is in your own hands . . . and the quality of that life as well. You owe it to yourself to be beautiful, clever, skinny, successful, and healthy. If you fail, it's because you're not trying hard enough. (You didn't jog regularly, you should've eaten more bran.) Death becomes your fault.

From *Brit-think, Ameri-think*

For a Russian commentator on the staff of Izvestia, *the big government daily, the rescue of three trapped gray whales in the Arctic ice in late 1988 suggested the best features of the American character:*

People's behavior was much more interesting than that of the whales. In just a few days, Americans rallied in pity for the Alaskan captives, displaying yet again what is one of the Americans' most important personality traits: the readiness to feel compassion and sympathy for whoever is in real trouble, whoever is powerless and cannot cope with misfortune alone. . . . There was no surprise at the number of people who looked after the captives and did so at their own expense and on their own time. True, there were those mainly after publicity, but they were by far a minority.

Quoted in *World Press Review*, December 1988

Alexander Chancellor, the Washington correspondent for the conservative London weekly The Spectator, *found in the televised Irangate congressional hearings important clues to understanding the American character:*

It is extraordinary how confident and articulate Americans are. I cannot recall ever meeting one who was at a loss for words or who gave the impression of being shy. They must all be educated from an early age in the arts of social intercourse and self-projection.

One is struck by this, watching the witnesses who appear before Congress, as in the current Iran-Contra hearings. Most British people, I imagine, would find this absolutely terrifying, but Americans seem to take it in their stride. Even those who have never been called upon to speak in public or appear on television look as if they have undergone special media training.

From "The Poise of Americans," in *The Spectator*, May 16, 1987

★

For Jane Walmsley the American insistence on choice is a major distinction setting us off sharply from our British cousins:

Choice—lots of it—is as dear to the American heart as newness. The point about choice is to exercise it as much as possible. That's why Yanks *elect* so many people: president, governors, judges, senators, congressmen, and dogcatchers.

Americans never like to commit themselves to anything for life. Leaders you can't change—like monarchs—make them nervous. They reserve the right to review decisions periodically; anything less is an attack on personal freedom, and reminds them of Communism. They even get edgy when fruit they like is out of season. Limited choice makes them think of Moscow matrons queuing hopelessly for goods. Nowhere do people view restrictions with more alarm. They mistrust package holidays and long-term investments. Contracts on employment must contain appropriate "get out" clauses. They plan vacations and shop for Christmas at the last minute, and make final decisions only when they've considered all possible choices. They conduct business by phone, and avoid committing anything to paper. They don't even like restaurants with set menus. The right to substitute a tossed salad for french fries is enshrined in the Constitution. Americans like to live life à la carte.

From *Brit-think, Ameri-think*

★

Despite two failed marriages to Americans, John Cleese retains a passion for American women:

I am fascinated by American women! And drawn to them. Someone once told me it's so I won't have to make up my mind where I fit into the British class structure. Americans are quite exotic in England; we can't quite place them. . . . I think American women do feel more of a need than English girls to prove themselves, so they're keener, more on the ball.

Quoted in the *San Diego Union*, July 31, 1988

American Friendliness

For many foreigners visiting our country, American friendliness is perhaps our most remarked national characteristic. American hospitality is legendary. "Americans do not hesitate to invite you into their homes, even though they may have just met you on the train or at the airport," asserts Dr. Mariana Milacic, a Yugoslavian mathematician at the University of Belgrade who often visits the United States. For Hanna Roditi, a director of a Tel Aviv school, this kindness shows itself in something as minor as an errand to the post office to mail a package home:

Americans seemed very open and very warm, and the services are always great. I went to the post office once in Miami to mail a package, and the clerk insisted on wrapping it for me. I couldn't believe it. Then I came back to my post office at home where they aren't very nice and they never do anything for you, and I wanted to cry.

Quoted in the *Dallas Morning News*, July 6, 1986

Christina Ruffini is a 23-year-old woman from Bologna, Italy, who spent a year in San Diego working as a governess and taking flying lessons toward her pilot's license. She remembers the time she hitchhiked up the California coast and what this experience taught her about Americans:

Americans can be very generous. Once a girlfriend and I hitchhiked from Los Angeles to San Francisco. What I liked was that the people who picked us up were very worried about us. They always wanted to help us. One couple asked us if we wanted money so that we could take a bus instead of hitchhiking. And they wanted nothing back. Later we hitched a ride to Salinas with a truck driver. He was also worried about our safety and tried over his CB radio to fix us up with a ride with another trucker from Salinas to San Francisco. When he could not, he told us, "I do not want to leave you on the streets, so I will take you up myself to make sure you get there safely." And then he drove us to San Francisco and dropped us off on Market Street where we were going to stay. And he didn't want anything back. He would not let us pay him. That was great! I think this sort of kindness is very much American, too. That trip was a highlight of my stay in America.

From an interview with the author, June 17, 1988

French author and philosopher Simone de Beauvoir was also impressed by the good humor of many Americans:

What makes daily life agreeable in America is the cordial good humor of the Americans. . . . This afternoon I went to cash a check. As soon as I entered the bank a uniformed employee advanced towards me and offered his services: I almost thought he was expecting me. He took me into a kind of hall where desks were arranged in rows; on each desk was a card with the name of a functionary. I sat down, showed my papers to a Mr. John Smith. He was not an anonymous cog in a machine, nor I an anonymous client, and he showed me courtesy addressed to me personally. He marked my check, and the cashier immediately paid me the money. At home my papers would have been verified on the other side of the counter, without consultation with me, and no doubt harshly; and I would have been treated as a mere number. I am not easily duped, and I know that this respect shown to individuals is quite formal. The polite smile which marks David Brown as an individual is also gratifying to the individual John Williams; nothing is more general than this singular trait which they all take so seriously. You sense a hoax, but it does not prevent the fact that, owing to this personal consideration, the American does not have to be stuck-up to feel his dignity; businesslike perhaps, but the friendliness of salesmen, employees, waiters, and porters is, though not disinterested, nonetheless never servile. They are neither sour nor stiff, and their pleasantness is real. We held the German soldiers responsible for the way in which they carried out their cruel orders. Indeed, man is never passive; in his obedience he sets limits to his liberty, and in submitting to evil accepts it; as a rule, this acceptance is carried out through invention and initiative which reveal the responsibility of the individual. And, in the same way, Americans do not submit passively to the propa-

31

ganda of smiles; in an atmosphere in which optimism is obligatory they gladly become cordial, trusting, and generous. A man's pleasant manner becomes less suspect the less interested he personally is in the success of the system; he is more hoaxed than hoaxer.

Whatever my view of American ideologies, I shall always have a warm feeling for the taxi drivers, the newspapermen, shoeshine boys, and all those people who suggest by their daily acts that men can be friends. For they create an atmosphere of trust, friendship, and gaiety. The man beside you is not a priori your enemy; even if he is wrong, he is not immediately guilty. With us, good will such as this has become uncommon.

From *L'Amérique au jour le jour*

★

Richard Ingrams, a reporter for the Illustrated London News, *enjoyed a memorable encounter with a street beggar near Washington:*

On our way down the hill from Monticello, Alexander remarked on another curious fact about Americans: "If you look at them, they always smile. I find that rather disconcerting." Personally, I said I found it rather nice, and a pleasant change from the dour and suspicious looks one gets from one's fellow countrymen.

In fact what is nice about America is not the scenery or the skyscrapers. . . . It is the smiling, open attitude of the American people. On my last morning in Georgetown I found myself confronted in the main street by a large, beaming, bearded man. "Good morning, sir," he cried. "I'm a bum! Would you give me some money?"

No cringing. No pretence about cups of tea. A frank, straightforward approach to the situation. I immediately fished in my pocket for all available change—something I would never do in England—and decided I would probably be back quite soon.

From "Stars and Gripes," in the *Illustrated London News*,
September 1987

★

Mark Grottel, a Soviet Jewish refugee who settled in Brooklyn, remembers the first important lesson he learned about his new country, the importance of the smile:

I have to tell you my favorite story about America. It was maybe one month after I began working at my first job in New York, at an engineering firm. Every day I sat at my desk, concentrating very hard. I was very serious. The problem was that I couldn't speak English and I was trying to learn new skills. My co-workers would pass back and forth in front of my desk. But I was concentrating so heavily that I didn't pay any attention to them.

One day a group of people came into the office. They just stood there looking at me. I didn't pay attention to them. One of these guys cried out very loud, "SMILE."

At first I didn't realize that he was talking to me. I looked up and saw everybody looking at me. He repeated, "SMILE."

My supervisor said to him, "Sir, this man just came from Russia. He has a problem with English." The man said, "Okay. He cannot talk. But, still, he can smile."

I understood what they were saying. So I started to smile. And everybody started to smile. When the group of men left the office, I was told that the man was a vice-president of our company.

I always think about this incident and laugh. Because in Russia if you smile during working hours, your boss will say, "You are not working. You are just wasting time." When a supervisor comes into the work area, suddenly everybody becomes very serious. Here it is just the opposite. The vice-president couldn't understand why I was so serious. He was trying to cheer me up.

For the first time I understood that in this country everybody has to smile.

Quoted by Al Santoli in *New Americans: An Oral History*

Abigail Van Buren ran the following letter from a Chinese-born woman in her advice column of November 17, 1988:

I am a Chinese woman who came to the United States fifteen years ago. I was in my late twenties and could not speak English very well. I read your column faithfully to learn the English language and more about the customs in my new country.

Lately I have read in your column that some people do not wish to be called "honey." May I relate my experience regarding the same?

When I first came here, I was especially nervous talking on the telephone because my English was so poor. Once I had to make a business call, so I dialed a number. A lady answered with a very sweet voice, and when I told her whom I was looking for, she said, "Honey, I'm afraid you dialed the wrong number." I said, "Oh, I am very sorry."

I dialed again, and the same lady answered the phone! I was very embarrassed, but the lady was very patient, and she said sweetly, "What number did you dial, honey?" I told her, and she said, "That is my number, but there is no such person here. I think you should check the number again."

Abby, fifteen years have passed. I do not remember whom I was looking for, but I will never forget the first time in my entire life someone—a total stranger whom I had bothered twice—called me "honey" twice! This would never happen in my country.

So why not keep the friendly American custom?

However, a British minister living in California had strong reservations about this aspect of the American scene which he expressed in his letter to "Dear Abby," April 11, 1989:

I know you meant well when you said, "Everybody could use a hug once in a while," but this advice can easily get out of hand.

I am an English-born clergyman who is presently living in California. I like my ministry and I love Americans. But one of the biggest culture shocks I've had to face in your country is the phenomenon of hugging.

Total strangers rush up and grab me as though I were a long-lost relative! Otherwise charming women will clasp me, impaling my cheeks on their flyaway diamond earrings. Even more alarming are the burly males who grip me in a bear hug from which there is no escape.

Abby, I am not a cold person, but such trespass bespeaks a false intimacy. As I had to put it to one clinging vine, "Madam, a handshake will do."

Alexandra Costa was the wife of the First Secretary of the Russian Embassy in Washington, D.C., on August 2, 1978, when she defected to the United

States. She is quick to contrast the importance and nature of friendship in America with that in her native Russia:

Friendship plays a special role in Russian life. In a country where an individual is powerless against the state and its satraps, where the state constantly intrudes on private life and any casual acquaintance may turn out to be a KGB informer, deep personal relationships of friendship and trust are cherished. Friends are the only protection against the facelessness of the bureaucracy, the only support network Soviet people have.

American culture that prides itself on the ability to provide an individual "space" and encourages people to stand alone seems cold and remote to Russians. Many defectors jump into hasty and ill-fated marriages just to avoid this sense of loneliness and isolation.

From *Stepping Down from the Stars*

The Violent American

"The best thing about Americans and their violence-oriented country is the fact that the Atlantic is between us," insists a retired British journalist. "American foreign policy perverts the advance of humanity and culture by creating a weapon-oriented life for all of us."

One aspect of American behavior which provokes numerous hostile comments from foreign observers is what they perceive as our tendency toward aggressive and violent actions. Dr. Hugo Molteni, a Buenos Aires physician, has never visited America but draws his conclusions from the newspapers, films, and television shows he has watched:

The information I have about the U.S. demonstrates that they are a people who are clearly aggressive. For example, in all the movies I see, violence predominates. Then there are the television series, police stories, crimes, assassination, drug deals. I think they have commercialized individual passions. The people of the United States [under President Reagan] have a wartime mentality.

Quoted in the *Dallas Morning News*, July 6, 1986

On May 22, 1988, Solomon Worku, twenty-five, a refugee from Ethiopia, was suddenly attacked by three members of a black gang and killed as he

sat smoking a cigarette in the yard of his San Diego apartment complex. He had recently completed a vocational course in auto mechanics. After sentencing the three gang members to eleven years each in state prison, the judge observed: "This was a vicious, unprovoked crime on a victim who was very vulnerable and who had come to this country for safety." His widow, Genet Teklu, who speaks no English, stated in a letter to the judge:

My husband and I arrived in the United States as refugees from Ethiopia in August 1986. . . . Now I am left in the dark with very young children and very little hope for me and my family. Why is an innocent family man's life so cheap? The criminals knew that Solomon was not one of their opposing gang members. They beat him out of their wanton desire and little regard for human life.

Quoted in the *San Diego Union,* September 1, 1988

★

The Russian comic Yakov Smirnoff has found in America's criminal violence a rich source for witticisms:

Police departments, like those in the United States, are created to protect you and keep you safe. As a matter of fact, thanks to them, Americans have many wonderful things we never had in the Soviet Union. Like warning shots. I think they're great. In Russia the police don't shoot up in the air. They shoot you! . . . and that's the warning for the next guy.

From *America on Six Rubles a Day*

★

English hiker Stephen Pern had the misfortune to sit next to a homicidal Texan on a bus from Southern California to Arizona:

I changed buses in San Diego and found myself beside a Texan with pink legs and a bicycle for which there was no room. I knew he was a Texan because he told me. The bicycle would be put on the next free coach.

"Goddamn fuckin' driver," said the Texan. "How come theah ain't no room? Fuckin' bike's worth five hundred fuckin' bucks."

The Texan bit his nails all the way through the first three towns, but he gradually calmed down. Within two hours he was rebounding a monologue. His opening line was pretty good.

"Ain't killed nobody in five years," he said. "Nossir, ain't no one died because of me in one long time."

I didn't know quite what to say, but the Texan seemed fairly self-contained. His remarks were made at intervals of roughly fifty miles. The next came as we whistled through El Centro.

"Evah go south, don't weah no yella suit," he said. "Yella's big trouble in Mexico. It's what theyah hoods all weah." Luckily most of my stuff was dull green, I told him, and in any case I wasn't going more than a token step south of the border.

We reached Yuma just after sunset. The Texan frowned.

"Know what a gargoyle is?"

"A what?"

"A gargoyle. Gargoyles're why I'm on this fuckin' bus. They fly round heah at night."

I fought down manic laughter. "Gargoyles fly round heah at night?"

"Right. Don't nevah ride this freeway after dark, not on no bike. You godda be so goddamn careful"—he leaned towards me—"because gargoyles ain't the only thing. Bigfoot's out theah too."

Bigfoot!

"You got any Bigfoot in Europe?"

"No," I said. "But there's a whole stack of gargoyles."

"No kidding?" said the Texan.

He got off the bus in Tucson, Arizona, though not before he'd mentioned that he wanted fifteen children. He also wanted to go fight the commies in Central America.

"Them fuckin' people think they own the fuckin' place," he said. "We give them fuckin' money, fight their fuckin' wars and they still screw up. Yeah, I'll be fuckin' down theah, you betcha."

But not down theah just yet, however, because the Texan was actually en route for his mother's house, his wife having kicked him out of their flat in Los Angeles. He said he'd soon find another girl.

"Young and dumb. I'll knock her up, divorce her, take the kid back to L.A. My Old Lady theah'll have me back when she sees I got a kid." It seemed a remarkably long-term plan. As he left the bus, I asked him his age.

"Nearly twenty," he said.

From *The Great Divide*

37

British author T. H. White sought to put the American propensity toward violence into a historical perspective:

Americans have a streak of lawlessness. . . . It is to be expected. In the first place, they are bred from parents who had enough individualism, anarchy, guts, or whatever you like to call it, to emigrate. They are not bred from stay-at-homes. They are bred from rebels who burst out. In the second place, in spreading over the relentless continent and winning the West, they have had to establish law as they pushed forward their boundaries by the individual law of the gun. In the third place, they are living in an actual Renaissance, a new birth of culture. People who live in Renaissances are apt to live with violence—like Marlowe or Webster or Ford. Here and now, with the cops and the gangsters and the outrages which suddenly explode, we are among the Borgias again and know the Duchess of Malfi.

From *America at Last*

American Provincialism

Recent polls which show over half the graduating American high school seniors cannot identify France, Italy, and Germany on a map of Europe only serve to underscore what is perhaps the most common complaint foreign observers have of Americans—the utter ignorance of countries and cultures beyond our shores. Australian actor Paul Hogan complained to the reporters assembled at a press conference to promote his film Crocodile Dundee II:

Americans have only recently discovered a sort of kinsman society on the other side of the planet. They're both melting pots, both new countries, with the same language. We knew about you, and you didn't know about us, and I found that sort of offensive.

Quoted in the *San Diego Union*, May 31, 1988

Christina Ruffini had much the same complaint about the Americans she met during her stay in Southern California:

Many Americans are much too provincial. They have no sense of what my Italy is like. I have had Americans ask me if we have freeways in Italy. This is crazy! I think this ignorance of a world beyond their borders is a big problem for many Americans.

From an interview with the author, June 17, 1988

Anita Mandrekar, who lives in Bombay, also found the ignorance of most Americans regarding her native India appalling on her recent trip to the United States.

Americans are generally ignorant on international matters. People there do not know much of the world outside. Even upper income groups still think that we in India live in jungles and have wild animals and snakes crawling all over.

From a letter to the author, dated August 7, 1988

This provincialism hurts American business abroad, as Edward B. Glick reported in the Los Angeles Times:

On a 1984 trip to West Germany I met a businessman who imports many items. Often, he said, the U.S. item is competitive with its foreign equivalents. Nevertheless, he usually buys from non-American firms. Why? "I am fluent in English, and I do like to speak it," he said. "But whenever the purely commercial considerations of price, quality, delivery date, and service are not at issue, I cannot ignore that your salesmen speak only English while theirs negotiate in excellent German."

From "English Only: New Handicaps in World Trade,"
in the *Los Angeles Times*, May 17, 1988

The pervasive provincialism of Americans also came as a major discovery for the Russian novelist Vassily Aksyonov upon his arrival here:

My greatest surprise was American provinciality. From a distance and through an iron curtain darkly, America of the open borders,

America the melting pot, America the global leader seemed like the crossroads of the world, the natural home of cosmopolitanism. We had the feeling that the TV weather report would give the temperature of the water at Nice and the depth of the snow cover on Kilimanjaro, that the news would report on King Carlos's new shoes, the latest intrigues in the central committee of the Chinese Communist party, and the penetration of Marxism into the depths of New Guinea. What we find is that if important international events do make it on the evening news, they are relegated to the end of the program and are glossed over as quickly as possible. The feature of the day is more likely to be a prim young miss telling the world that she was sexually molested twelve years before by the principal of her elementary school, a middle-aged, cauliflower-eared dolt, who categorically denies the accusation.

From *In Search of Melancholy Baby*

Closely akin to provincialism is the more endearing American trait of naiveté, which reaches even into Siberia, as human rights activist Natan Sharansky reported in his autobiography, *Fear No Evil*. "What will you do in America?" he asked a fellow inmate in the gulag, a swindler who hoped to emigrate to the United States.

"Some of my colleagues are there already," the man replied. "My friends who left write that it's easy to find work in Europe, and even easier in America. Although the Americans are business-minded, they're as naive as children. That's why I'm learning English."

Vignettes

Norwegian actress Liv Ullmann had a blind date with Secretary of State Henry Kissinger during one of her visits to America and wrote the following account:

I am expecting an important visitor.

Henry Kissinger is to escort me to a big ball.

He has inquired in Los Angeles who would be the most suitable date for him on this "event of the year" in Hollywood. Someone came up with me, and for a couple of days they have been calling me from the White House. Today he called himself.

It is the year of his glory, and everybody wants to meet him. Later it turns out to be two days before the whole Watergate story will begin to put an end to the President. This will be Nixon's last public appearance before the scandal is known by the whole world. . . .

Since Mr. Kissinger is the first blind date of my life, I was confused on the telephone and forgot to ask when he would fetch me. Consequently, I have been dressed for the last three hours.

From some official department in Norway has come a letter about oil. It is obvious they want me to inform Mr. Kissinger about something, but it's not clear to me what. (It turns out he didn't even know we had found oil.)

From Sweden I receive a note from the secretary of a certain politician asking me to deny some comments he has made about Kissinger. (A week later he repeats his comments at a press conference.)

. . . My suite has been searched—so whoever recommended me was not convincing enough: I might still be a secret agent or have bombs under my bed.

All this is very unusual for someone who never had a blind date, and I become so agitated that I change my dress, and choose one that is less pretty than the one I was wearing originally.

A Norwegian journalist sends up his card, asking if he may disguise himself as a butler. He has come all the way from Oslo hoping for this. We reply that the post is already filled. . . .

A knock at the door. . . . [Kissinger] is smiling and much smaller than I. I know I picked the wrong shoes.

We shake hands while he waves reassuringly to some grave-faced men in the corridor.

[My girlfriend] who is to pour wine lets most of it spill on his trousers. Feverishly all three of us try to remove the stain, and in the end one can hardly see it.

It is only in the elevator that I realize that the cleaner's tag is still attached to my second-best dress, and I tug and tug and tug, and tug off a little bit of dress as well. The strap has gone on my handbag.

[My girlfriend] remarks on my return that this was clearly visible on television.

I swish into a car with bulletproof windows, followed by men with little microphones into which they speak all the time.

I think that I am very far from Trondhejm.

Late at night I lie in the double bed with my girlfriend, who has stayed awake waiting for my report.

I have a thousand things to tell her—and then the telephone rings. It is the Norwegian journalist, talking from the lobby. His trip has cost hundreds of dollars, he has waited all night, he reminds me of a service he once did me. After a long discussion and a few threats, he works himself up to my bedside. Notebook in hand, he looks at me expectantly and asks me to tell him what I said to Kissinger and, more important, what Kissinger told me. I am silent, but my friend mutters something about a light she thought she saw around his head. In my heart I forgive her, because she has been up all evening waiting to express herself. Besides, she must be quite tired now.

The next day I am waltzing through the world press, saying:

"It is as though there is a halo over Henry Kissinger."

From *Changing*

★

Paul Theroux, an American author who has made London his home for many years, had the following encounter in 1979 with a college student on a train through New York:

Her name was Wendy. Her face was an oval of innocence, devoid of any expression of inquiry. Her prettiness was as remote from my idea of beauty as homeliness and consequently was not at all interesting. But I could not blame her for that: it is hard for anyone to be interesting at twenty. She was a student, she said, and on her way to Ohio. She wore an Indian skirt, and lumberjack boots, and the weight of her leather jacket made her appear round shouldered.

"What do you study, Wendy?"

"Eastern philosophy. I'm into Zen."

Oh Christ, I thought. But she was still talking. She had been learning about the Hole, or perhaps the Whole—it still made no sense to me. She hadn't read all that much, she said, and her teachers were lousy. But she thought that once she got to Japan or Burma she would find out a lot more. She would be in Ohio for a few more years. The thing about Buddhism, she said, was that it involved your whole life. Like everything you did—it was Buddhism. And everything that happened in the world—that was Buddhism, too.

"Not politics," I said. "That's not Buddhism. It's just crooked."

"That's what everyone says, but they're wrong. I've been reading Marx. Marx is a kind of Buddhist."

Was she pulling my leg? I said, "Marx was about as Buddhist as this beer can. But anyway, I thought we were talking about politics. It's the opposite of thought—it's selfish, it's narrow, it's dishonest. It's all half truths and short cuts. Maybe a few Buddhist politicians would change things, but in Burma, where . . ."

"Take this," she said, and motioned to her bags of nuts. "I'm a raw-foodist-nondairy vegetarian. You're probably right about politics being all wrong. I think people are doing things all wrong—I mean, completely. They eat junk. They *consume junk*. . . . They're just destroying themselves and they don't even know it. . . ."

"Nondairy," I said. "That means you don't drink milk."

"Right."

"What about cheese? Cheese is nice. And you've got to have calcium."

"I get my calcium in cashews," she said. Was this true? "Anyway, milk gives me mucus. Milk is the biggest mucus-producer there is."

"I didn't know that."

"I used to go through a box of Kleenex a day."

"A box. That's quite a lot."

"It was the milk. It made mucus," she said. "My nose used to run like you wouldn't believe."

"Is that why people's noses run? Because of the milk?"

"Yes!" she said.

I wondered if she had a point. Milk drinkers' noses run. Children are milk drinkers. Therefore, children's noses run. And children's noses do run. But it struck me as arguable. Everyone's nose runs— except hers, apparently.

"Dairy products give you headaches, too."

"You mean, they give *you* headaches."

"Right. Like the other night. My sister knows I'm a vegetarian. So she gives me eggplant parmyjan. She doesn't know I'm a nondairy raw foodist. I looked at it. As soon as I saw it was cooked and had cheese on it, I knew that I was going to feel awful. But she spent all day making it, so what else could I do? The funny thing is that I liked the taste of it. God, was I sick afterwards! And my nose started to run. . . ."

I asked her whether she ever got violently ill. She said absolutely not. Did she ever feel a little bit sick?

Her reply was extraordinary: "I don't believe in germs."

Amazing. I said, "You mean, you don't believe that germs exist? They're just an optical illusion under the microscope? Dust, little specks—that sort of thing?"

"I don't think germs cause sickness. Germs are living things— small living things that don't do any harm."

"Like cockroaches and fleas," I asked. "Friendly little critters, right?"

"Germs don't make you sick," she insisted. "Food does. If you eat bad food, it weakens your organs and you get sick. It's your organs that make you sick. Your heart, your bowels."

"But what makes your organs sick?"

"Bad food. It makes them weak. If you eat good food, like I do," she said, gesturing at her pumpkin seeds, "you don't get sick. Like I never get sick. If I get a runny nose and a sore throat, I don't call it a cold."

"You don't?"

"No, it's because I ate something bad. So I eat something good. . . . Sometimes I look at a piece of cheese. I know it tastes good. I know I'll like it. But I also know that I'm going to feel awful the next day if I eat it."

I said, "That's what I think when I see a magnum of champagne, a rabbit pie, and a bowl of cream puffs with hot chocolate sauce."

At the time, I did not think Wendy was crazy in any important sense. But afterward, when I remembered our conversation, she seemed to me profoundly loony. And profoundly incurious. I had mentioned to her that I had been to Upper Burma and Africa. I had described Leopold Bloom's love of "the faint tang of urine" in the kidneys he had for breakfast. I had shown a knowledge of Buddhism and the eating habits of Bushmen in the Kalahari and Gandhi's early married life. I was a fairly interesting person, was I not? But not once in the entire conversation had she asked me a single question. She never asked what I did, where I had come from, or where I was going. When it was not interrogation on my part, it was a monologue on hers. Uttering rosy generalities in her sweetly tremulous voice, and tugging her legs back into the lotus position when they slipped free, she was an example of total self-absorption and desperate self-advertisement. She had mistaken egotism for Buddhism. I still have a great affection for the candor of American college students, but she reminded me of how many I have known who were unteachable.

From *The Old Patagonian Express: By Train through the Americas*

Australian Clive James found himself among other Wendys when he interviewed several Playmates during a May 1984 visit to California:

The Playmates ... don't want you to think they are just pretty bodies. Called such names as Kelly Tough and Shannon Tweed, they have deep reasons for taking their clothes off. "I'm excited about the oppatoonity to be a Playmate. I think I've learned a lot about myself." She has learned, among other things, how to go big-game fishing in the nude. "I dew feel like I have an affinity for the ocean." Inevitably this affinity is best demonstrated by a lot of lying around on deck, alone with the sea and with nobody else in sight except the camera crew hanging from the mast-head.

"I have the *greatest* family," says Patti Farinetti. "My mother's behind me in everything I dew, and she's very proud of me. Wherever we go, she says, 'This is my daughter! The one who was in *Playboy!*'" All the girls have supportive mothers. ("Supportive" is an American word meaning "insane.") Some of them even have supportive boyfriends, such as Kim McArthur's fiancé Cal. "I think Kim has *grown* a great deal because of her involvement with *Playboy.*"

The emphasis on self-realization is universal. "Look where I am today" says Patti or Kelly or Kim Shannon. "It's really unbelievable." And it really is. Tough, for example, is out in the woods, lying around starkers next to a camp fire. "Noodity and camping go together as far as I'm concerned." Kelly seems undaunted by the possibility that a bear might eat her, or worse. "After you become a Playmate you learn confidence," she says gratefully, having interpreted the camera's unrelenting attempt to get between her legs as an offer of assistance in her quest for fulfillment.

Clearly, she is a nice girl. They are all nice girls. With the current clamp-down on hard-porn videos, soon these nice girls will be all that's left. It should be a comfort, but somehow they are far scarier than the hookers, perhaps because they find it all so natural. That's it: they have nothing to hide.

From *Snakecharmers in Texas: Essays, 1980–87*

★

In northern Arizona British author Adam Nicolson talked with a former security guard about how it feels to kill another man:

I had never met a man who had killed before today. K. J. Mackenzie—
that's how he introduced himself—laughed at the end of nearly every
sentence. "Yuhu," he said in the Winslow Tire Company this morning, looking at me through his one eye, "Ah killed him." He laughed
while looking at us all around the edges of the room. Mackenzie is a
tall man and big across the chest. He wore a sort of khaki safari suit,
hanging loosely about his body. He stood out from the rest of us in
our blue jeans as a vaguely military man who was so used to the idea
of uniform that even when in ordinary clothes he appeared to be
wearing one. . . . "Ah was Special Agent to the Atchison, Topeka and
Santa Fe Railway at the time," he said. "Tell them about it, K.J.," Mr.
Matlow, the owner of the garage and hunter of bison, said, before
sitting back with folded arms to hear the story once again. K.J. pulled
up his safari shirt. Tucked inside the waistband of his trousers,
between the trousers and his pants, was the gun that had done it,
just stuck in there, without any kind of elaborate holster, but with its
muzzle nestled into a leather pouch. He gave me the gun. It was a 44
revolver, a big, black bit of metal. He flipped open the fluted
cylinder, took out three of the bullets, and gave them to me. They
were fat and short, really like stunted slugs, with brass caps at the
tips. "Don't drop them," K.J. said, "those are explosive caps on
there." It took me a moment or two to realise what this meant. These
bullets were not intended to wound or to catch someone a glancing
blow. If K.J. hit his man, the bullet would explode. Mackenzie told
the story. It was simple enough. He began at the crisis, the climax. A
Mexican was coming at him in the stock yard in Winslow. He had a
knife in each hand, one eight inches long, the other six. "He was
coming at me, and he was saying that if I didn't kill him, he would
kill me, so I killed him. I shot him here," K.J. spread his hands in a
double web across his stomach, "and that killed him, always does,"
and then a long bout of rolling laughter. "He's a real character, K.J.,"
Matlow said. "What did it feel like?" I asked. "Oh, it didn't feel like
nothing," K.J. said.

From *Two Roads to Dodge City*

In 1988 the Colombian-born novelist Gabriel Garcia Márquez published
Love in the Time of Cholera, a novel about two people whose love,
thwarted in their youth, finally flourishes when they are close to eighty. In

an interview with Marlise Simons of the New York Times, *Márquez talked about the source of his story:*

Many years ago in Mexico I read a story in a newspaper about the death of two old Americans—a man and a woman—who would meet every year in Acapulco, always going to the same hotel, the same restaurants, following the same routine as they had done for 40 years. They were almost 80 years old and kept coming. Then one day they went out in a boat and, in order to rob them, the boatman murdered them with his oars. Through their death, the story of their secret romance became known. I was fascinated by them. They were each married to other people.

Russian writer Viktor Lishchenko spent a month in 1986 visiting farms in America and later reported on them for the Soviet Writers' Union weekly publication, Literaturnaya Gazeta, *of Moscow:*

In the U.S. I was the guest of my old friend John Crystal, an agrarian banker. We usually spent the night in his father's old farmhouse near Coon Rapids, Iowa. After supper we would sit on the front porch and talk.

One evening, as we were sitting there, a farmer drove by in his pickup truck. John told me the farmer was going dancing. I said, "He seems a little old for dancing. He could have asked a woman out to a restaurant."

"No, he couldn't," John replied. "That is too expensive. By going dancing, he can get by with a bottle of Coca-Cola." An American millionaire farmer is unable to ask a woman to dinner because his million is in machinery, livestock, land, fertilizers, and buildings. His wallet is empty. . . .

John introduced him to his brother Tom, a farmer who has a wife and son and one hired hand—sometimes two. Tom is not concerned about technology; he runs things with his eyes closed. He is most interested in marketing: How to sell the crop? To whom? When? These are agonizing questions. . . .

I often had breakfast with Tom at a roadside diner, where every morning farmers gather, eat their fried eggs, discuss the news and curse. They let Western European governments have it; we get cursed least of all. After all, we are customers, while the Western Europeans are competitors.

Europe has learned to produce huge grain harvests based on the most advanced American technology. The Common Market has outdone the Americans in financial assistance to farming, and its grain has become cheaper than the American product. So America is buying more and selling less. This is unprecedented in U.S. history. Agriculture was the last bulwark in which the U.S. had a favorable balance of trade.

As a result, the American farmer is vanishing. Where recently there were three or four farms, now a single one is standing. The owners go broke and leave. As we drove along, Tom would point and tell me, "There's an abandoned house; the owner went broke and committed suicide. And over there a house was burned down. Only the trees remain, to provide a decent appearance."

. . . One time I was sitting with John Crystal in front of his house, looking at the field. He recalled the days of his father, 60 years ago, when the land was not arable because of poor drainage. They put in drainage manually over these enormous expanses. It was extremely hard excavating work.

"When I was little," said John, "we had an Irish immigrant working for us, and he worked from morning till night five days a week to make enough money so he could settle on his own farm. I remember that he ate a lot, because he worked a lot, and we kids had to peel potatoes for him. We sure had to peel a lot."

I think that if we tell our Russian readers and TV viewers not only about America's high-tech food consumerism, but about that Irishman, about those potatoes and about the work-filled childhood of the now-prosperous banker John Crystal, then there is no reason to fear that we will misunderstand one another.

From *World Press Review*, February 1987

When Polish writer Malgorzata Niezabitowska traveled across America in 1986 on assignment for National Geographic *magazine she spent an afternoon engaged in a political discussion with David Duke, a former president of the Ku Klux Klan who in early 1989 was elected to the Louisiana state legislature. She found it a most unnerving experience:*

We saw them from a distance in the French Quarter in New Orleans during Mardi Gras in New Orleans. They were walking slowly down the street, holding hands, young and handsome. He was dressed in black; she was in red, costumed as a devil.

After Tomek photographed them, the man, pointing at his girlfriend, said, "Actually we should exchange costumes. Many people think I'm the devil."

"Are you?" I asked.

He laughed.

"I'm just famous."

"Better say infamous," the girl said.

"So, who are you?" I was curious now.

"My name is David Duke."

Seeing that that meant nothing to us, the girl added, "He is the former national president of the Knights of the Ku Klux Klan."

Three months later we visited David Duke at home. He lives alone in the suburbs of New Orleans in a big, modestly furnished house. The first thing you see when you enter is a large portrait of the Confederate general Nathan Bedford Forrest, founder and first leader of the Klan.

A few days earlier Duke had declared his candidacy for the Presidency of the United States, and I now ask him about his platform. David Duke talks, grows excited, opens up. What makes this easier for him, as he explained, is the immediate sympathy he felt toward us. In his eyes our blond, blue-eyed daughter is "a perfect representative of the white race." He reproaches us for not having more such children.

For the next three hours I listen to his views—views I knew existed but never believed could be uttered in all seriousness. Yet here they were being propounded not only seriously but with unwavering conviction, and, what is more, by someone who is obviously intelligent and well educated.

Duke's obsessive racism appalls me. But to hear that the Holocaust never happened is truly traumatic for someone like me, who was born and raised in a country that during World War II lost six million of its citizens, most of them to concentration and death camps and mass executions.

Let him talk, let him talk . . . , I calm myself.

"The white race is endangered," he warns. "In a few decades we will be a minority, even here in the U.S.A. We have to defend ourselves while there is still time."

When he left the Klan eight years ago, David Duke founded the National Association for the Advancement of White People and has been its leader ever since.

After our conversation David leads us to the basement, which serves as the national headquarters of his organization. It looks like a well-equipped office: computers, tape recorders, videos. The large set of book-lined shelves catches my eye. There are multiple copies of each title, obviously for sale or free distribution.

"This is absolutely off the record," Duke says. "Don't write anything down." He leads us away.

I close my notebook. But some of the titles I don't need to record in order to remember: *The Testament of Hitler, Hermann Goering: The Man and His Work*, Hitler's *Mein Kampf*.

"How do you see your chances of becoming President?" I ask Duke as we part.

"I have no doubt that I will become President. I'm only 37. I have time. Americans will wake up."

From "Discovering America," in *National Geographic*,
January 1988

★

R. H. Growald writes "Countywide," a thrice-weekly column for the San Diego Union. *In one he profiled Mark Likgalter, a recent immigrant from the Soviet Union, and his encounter with an American con man:*

Mark Likgalter is from the Soviet Union. He says he began learning more about America in June [1988] when a man from somewhere walked into his Lone Star Barbecue at 2321 Fifth Avenue.

"He said his name was Mike Hunt and that he was a Delta Force secret agent," Mark says.

"I believe Americans. I believed Mike Hunt," Mark says.

So began the conning of Mark Likgalter.

"Why shouldn't I have believed him? He wore squeaky black boots, checked jacket, white shirt, blue jeans, brown hair, and mustache and he looked like a shorter Clint Eastwood. And he liked very much the Georgian omelet that is our breakfast specialty."

. . . Mark, a Russian, was an editor in an art publishing house in Tbilisi, the capital of Soviet Georgia, when his family got permission to get out.

"In New York I found little opportunity for Dumbadze experts. I went to Texas, learned how to barbecue, and came to San Diego to find my streets of gold," he says.

Fifth Avenue is his street of gold. In 1985 he opened his first barbecue place. He sold it 18 months later. "I couldn't resist the offer of a Japanese tycoon who wanted to open a sushi parlor. So now I've opened the Lone Star Barbecue. Mike Hunt was one of the first to walk in," he says.

Mark says the shorter Clint Eastwood swallowed a Georgian omelet and leaned forward.

"He told me he was waiting for a money transfer from an organization he could not name. I was sure it was the CIA," Mark says.

Mark has seen movies of Arnold Schwarzenegger, Sylvester Stallone, and the taller Clint Eastwood undoing godless commie red rats for the CIA.

"I like them. I lived under the Soviet KGB. I love America," he says.

"I'm no fool. I asked Mike Hunt to prove he was a secret agent. 'OK,' Mike said. He opened his suitcase. In it was an Israeli submachine gun, a German Luger, and a machine pistol. I knew he was genuine," Mark says.

He says the fellow asked him to drive him to Harbor Island.

"Mike said his speedboat was coming in. He needed a slip to moor it. I drove him out there and watched while he gave a marina man a check for $3,150 to rent a slip.

"Back at the Lone Star, Mike ate a Hungry Man sampler plate— barbecue beef, pork, chicken, ham, ribs, and sausage—and told me to expect a visit from Doc," Mark says.

"Doc, he said, treats wounded members of Mike's Delta Force team. But for God's sake, he told me, don't mention this to Doc. It was all top secret.

"Later that day Mike brought in Doc. Doc began eating barbecue. Mike, too. I sidled up and said to Doc that Mike was a great man. Doc, busy eating, said sure, sure. I said what an honor it was for a man from Russia to meet a man like Mike. Sure, sure, said Doc, sampling the ribs," Mark says.

The next day, Mark says, the shorter Clint Eastwood began eating barbecue and beans. "He pulled out a tab from an automatic bank machine. Mike pointed to the place where the machine prints out how much money one has deposited. It read $164,000," Mark says.

Mark says too late he found out that the shorter Clint Eastwood had held the tab so that a finger covered the machine's notation that the money was "not available." It seems, says Mark, that the con man went to one bank, deposited a phony check for $164,000 for an account in a second bank, waited and then got the tab from the second bank's automatic teller.

On July 1, says Mark, "Mike came in, ate a plate of barbecued pork, he said he'd soon pay the $120 he owed me for meals and, oh yes, Mark, could I borrow your Mercury?"

Mark has two vehicles. One was a pickup he uses to haul meat, mesquite, and hickory. "The other was my gorgeous 1970 Mercury. My parents so loved being driven around in that great hunk of capitalism. But if the CIA needed my Mercury, who was I?" Mark says.

On July 2, the shorter Clint Eastwood drove off in the Mercury. He promised to be back July 3. He has not been seen since.

On July 5 Doc telephoned Mark.

"Doc, it turns out, is an eye doctor. He made five pair of glasses and two pairs of contact lens for Mike. Mike had paid him with a bad $750 check. I asked Doc why he call me. Doc said Mike had told him that he owned the Lone Star Barbecue," Mark says.

A nearby hotel manager called. Mike owed the hotel $700. "And, yes, Mike had told the manager that he owned the Lone Star," Mark says. . . .

Word spread.

"My friend Sasha telephoned, heard my voice, and asked to speak to 'The Sucker,'" Mark says. "My parents, told of the Mercury's loss, didn't speak to me for a week. My girlfriend calls me an idiot."

"I called the FBI and told them all," Mark says.

"The FBI laughed."

From the *San Diego Union*, August 15, 1988

★

British writer Geoffrey Wagner spent the 1971–1972 academic year teaching in the English department of a New York City university. Afterward he drove through the American West. In a remote part of Monument Valley, Arizona, a chance encounter with a state highway patrolman took an unexpected turn:

It is when pulling out of Navajo National that it happens.

I am tooling along one of those incredible Western roads that makes you feel someone mixed velvet in the asphalt. I certainly don't seem to be speeding. I'm dawdling.

Not only isn't there a car around, there is not so much as a constipated Indian burro in sight for the—oh!—five or six hundred square miles of this or that state I can see spanning out about me. I feel just great, the vibes right. Everything blue and pure, with the mesa a nice rich red.

Until this monkey hits my tail and starts playing pinball lights behind me. The Porsche is in third. It resents being treated like some dodgem car and I feel it surge disdainfully forward, under my instep. . . .

He comes out towards me—*at me* would be the better expression—looking like Warner Baxter as the Cisco Kid, only with a better press in his khaki pants and his face a dull glow that might have come off the mesa, but undoubtedly didn't.

"I been on yuh tail for three whole miles, son."

I hop out, close the door with a blue-chip click, and start the usual burbling.

"Was I exceeding the limit, officer?" Etc.

I haven't the foggiest what it is but . . . I have a sort of recollection of the needle gliding reproachfully down from eighty. As I say, I wasn't speeding. The Porsche, I repeat, was in three. Out of five forward.

"I didn't see a marker," I try.

"Is that right?"

The big man has by now extracted ticket and pencil and is industriously licking the latter.

"Sixty-five all the way, son."

"I had no idea," I pursue more and more hopelessly. "Why, I'd just been studying the . . . mammals of Navajoland. It's my first visit to this colorful part."

"Is that right?" He listens gravely, as if it were merely a painful process, and then he asks to see my license. I hand it over. Laboriously, he begins writing down my name, frowning into the sun. . . .

"What's your company, son?"

"I don't have a company. I'm a writer."

He squeezes his eyes tight shut. There exists a blank, and he has to fill it.

"Who you work for is what I mean."

I reluctantly surrender the name of my university.

"Teacher, huh?"

"Kind of. When the place is in session."

"Whaddya teach?"

"English."

"That figures."

He folds his pudgy arms and rests them on the white of his wagon a moment. He stares eastward, the direction all true Navajo dwellings face, and his chinablue eyes go smoky in memory. Under a wisp of cirrus a slim Indian girl in dark velvet dress winking with silver ornaments glides her sheep with a bent stick. Beside this immemorial image my mentor looks most modern, some extra searching vainly for the costume department of *Stagecoach*. Old actors never die they simply turn into John Wayne.

Suddenly I start. Have I heard aright?

"Did you know that E. M. Forster has passed away, son?" the man asks gently, still staring ahead.

"I did not," I reply. "When was that?"

"Two three days ago. You ain't bin keeping up with your home-work, son." His eyes are full of distances now. "Tell me, you really think the way he finished *Howards End* come out right? I mean, all that sword stuff, and business? And I mean like cupboards falling on people."

Still startled I say: "It isn't one of my favourite novels of his. But I try to understand what he was doing."

"So do I, son, so do I."

Together we gaze ahead, side by side, cop and coped, into the eroded sandstone wastes. A light breeze tugs at our faces. The girl and her flock are a little farther off. I'm thinking: Morgan gone. The world a somewhat smaller place without him.

"Frankly," and I hear myself say it with a kind of embarrassment, "I far prefer *A Passage to India*."

"So do I, son, so do I." The man beside me chuckles. "Boom-boom. All them caves, and engines. What were they called?"

"Marabar."

"Yeah, yeah. I tellya, the key to early Forster is in that little short story . . . know the one I mean . . . this, uh, old English lady, and, and . . . how do you say it . . . 'abroad'?"

"The Eternal Moment," I supply. "I take that up in class, too. When anyone listens. Forster isn't considered very 'relevant' in today's curriculum."

"Still say he was better than Ford."

Which one? I wonder wildly. Henry or Ford Madox?

"The Good Soldier was pretty fine. I include that in my course, too."

My interlocutor shakes his head. "Novelist's novel." (He has got this from somewhere, surely.) "Rest of the crap he wrote. That fake Eton bit. Forster's talent, uh, far firmer, son."

I say nothing. Our voices are lower. I realize that now we are speaking of Morgan in the past tense. No longer will he be *Mr.* Forster in the TLS—he will be Forster, for ever.

"What's that course you teach, son?" He turns his almost purple, punched-beef face on mine.

"The modern novel." I name some names.

Again, the heavy head shakes heavily. "You ought to have some Gide in there, son."

"Sometimes do."

"Forster should have read more Gide. The trouble with all them Bloomsbury . . . you realize, son, Conrad did everything Virginia Woolf required of the novel long before she, uh . . . hell, I'm forgetting everything . . ."

"You're doing better than some of my students."

"That, that piece she wrote on Walpole. Almost at the end of her life, wasn't it?"

"The Humane Art."

It is an improbable conversation. Enough so for me to want to conclude it. Trooper and teacher, side by side in the sun in the middle of Nowhere, Arizona, discussing E. M. Forster. . . .

"Hell," says the Arizona [cop], "you durn ought to get some Gide in there."

"What would you recommend?"

"Les Nourritures Terrestres." He pronounced the first word as if it were an abbreviation for Lesley, but I don't mind. I really don't mind at all, since he has picked up the ticket and is slowly shredding it to pieces. "Kind of makes it invalid, I guess," he is saying to the enormous air. "Stoopid mistake like that, I mean. Ain't any sich beast as a VW Porsche, you say. Well, now, that invalidates the summons,

careless error of that kind. Why, I'd have to write you out another by rights, wouldn't I?"

"By rights," I agreed.

His slap on the back almost sends me sprawling.

"Drive real careful, son." At the door to his pearly motor he turns—" 'Nother thing, Doc. 'Nother book you might use in that there course of yours. Can't quite 'member the name, but period's durn the same." He chuckles as he stands. "Cholera an' . . . an' a cute kid . . ."

"*Death in Venice*," I say at the door to mine.

Strange meeting, in Navajoland.

From *Another America: In Search of Canyons*

And finally the Russian novelist Vassily Aksyonov remembers a singular breakfast chat in Sweetwater, Texas:

We crossed the Texas border at night, stopped at a Howard Johnson, and went down to breakfast the next morning not suspecting where we were. Trained as we are to avoid cliches like the plague, we forget they often have a basis in reality. That morning we were surrounded by faces from the westerns that had made my youth: there sat John Wayne, Gregory Peck, Gene Autry. I had seen them too many times to be mistaken. And although I can only suppose that most if not all of them were truck drivers, they dressed in the same hats, vests, and boots as their cowboy antecedents.

The waitress brought us juice, eggs, two stacks of bacon, toast, griddle cakes, butter, syrup, and jam. "I was wondering, folks," she drawled as she unloaded her tray, "what language that is you're talking."

"What do you think?" I asked.

"Sounds mighty like German."

"No. Russian."

"Just what I thought," she said. "Russian or German."

"They're actually quite different; they don't sound at all alike."

"Really?" She was sincerely surprised. "You mean you're Russians from Germany."

"No, we're from Russia."

"Germans from Russia?"

In the mind of this middle-aged Texas woman, Russians and Germans were inextricably intertwined. . . . Shaking her head in confusion, she went over to a group of "cowboys" and, pretending to clear their table, told them about the weirdos at table four: they say they come from Russia, but they're not German. The men turned to have a look at us, but the moment our eyes met they averted theirs, pretending to study the weather outside.

When the waitress came up to us again, she looked worried. "The fellows, they say the papers print a lot about Russia. A lot of nasty stuff. Are the papers lying?"

"Afraid not."

"The fellows say that Russia has the type of government that doesn't permit you to write the books you want. Is that so?"

I was astounded. What a question to be asked in Sweetwater, Texas!

"Yes, ma'am, that unfortunately is also true. You see, I'm a writer and the government kicked me out for writing books it didn't like. That's why we're here."

Suddenly the waitress threw open her arms and said with a warmth I count among the greatest of American charms, "Welcome to America!"

The cowboys smiled reservedly.

From *In Search of Melancholy Baby*

3 ★ AMERICAN ★ CULTURE

"THE *Yanks have colonized our subconscious," complains one of the movie-mad Germans in Wim Wenders's films,* Kings of the Road.

Karl Marx was wrong. American culture, not religion, has become the opiate of the masses worldwide. American movies, magazines, television programs, and music reach not only into Canada, Mexico, and Western Europe but also into most of the Third World.

Clearly for hundreds of thousands of people abroad, America is less a state of society than a state of mind, the home of the most emulated culture in history. If we are as bad as our critics insist, then why does the rest of the world—from college students in Moscow's Arabat Square to business executives in Tokyo—want to copy our culture? A Gallic version of "Wheel of Fortune" is the most popular show on French television, while in Belgrade, Yugoslavia, the first McDonald's in a communist country serves over six thousand Big Macs a day to eager diners. The American who travels through the Third World and wants to fit in with the natives had better pack his suitcase full of Dallas Cowboys T-shirts and Levis. In 1984 the American writer and editor William Broyles returned to Vietnam, where he had once served as a combat soldier. This time the locals jived along to "Born in the U.S.A.," Bruce Springsteen's anthem for the disenfranchised Vietnam vet, and greeted him with cries of

"America Number One." As Broyles observed later, "America is going to be much more difficult to defeat in this battle than we were in the others. Our clothes, our language, our movies, and our music—our way of life—are far more powerful than our bombs."

Few Americans comprehend the extent to which our culture has pervaded even the most remote reaches of the world. "Such cultural presence not only contributes to the global awareness of the United States and of American mass culture and its material products, it also offends the upholders of indigenous tradition and culture and the bearers of elite cultural values everywhere," observes Paul Hollander, a professor of sociology who has made the subject of anti-Americanism his specialty. "While the worldwide popularity of these American cultural offerings is undeniable, this very popularity generates further condemnation of the perniciousness of American mass culture by local intellectuals, opinion leaders, and guardians of indigenous traditions."

In 1969 the celebrated British traveler Wilfred Thesiger predicted that the world was moving toward a uniform, mechanized, stereotyped culture, a mass culture that struck him as a form of mass suicide. He anticipated with dread a coming era of American "cultural imperialism." As he recalled in his autobiography:

In July 1969 I happened to be in Kenya, on the shore of Lake Rudolf, when I heard with incredulity from a naked Turkana fisherman that the "Wazungu"—as he called Europeans, including Americans—had landed on the moon. He had heard the news at a distant mission station. To him this achievement, being incomprehensible, was without significance; it filled me, however, with a sense of desecration, and of despair at the deadly technical ingenuity of modern man. Even as a boy I recognized that motor transport and aeroplanes must increasingly shrink the world and irrevocably destroy its fascinating diversity. My forebodings have been amply fulfilled. Package tours now invade the privacy of the remotest villages; the transistor, blaring popular music, has usurped the place of the tribal bard.

From *The Life of My Choice*

★

But not even Thesiger at his most pessimistic could have imagined the speed and extent to which an American-generated mass culture would soon engulf the entire world. Pico Iyer, a writer for Time, *who defines himself as "a British subject, an American resident, and an Indian citizen," in 1985 and 1986 spent seven months crisscrossing Asia. His goal was "to find out how America's pop-cultural imperialism [had] spread through the world's most ancient civilizations." He discovered in his travels that the most popular and respected American in the Far East was—no, not Ronald Reagan—but John Rambo, the larger-than-life comic book warrior Sylvester Stallone had portrayed in three films. Rambo-mania had infected all Asia:*

Rambo had conquered Asia. In China, a million people raced to see *First Blood* within ten days of its Beijing opening, and black marketeers were hawking tickets at seven times the official price. In India, five separate remakes of the American hit went instantly into production, one of them recasting the macho superman as a sari-clad woman. In Thailand, fifteen-foot cutouts of the avenging demon towered over the lobbies of some of the ten Bangkok cinemas in which the movie was playing, training their machine guns on all who passed. And in Indonesia, the Rambo Amusement Arcade was going great guns, while vendors along the streets offered posters of no one but the nation's three leading deities: President Suharto, Siva, and Stallone.

As I crisscrossed Asia in the fall of 1985, every cinema that I visited for ten straight weeks featured a Stallone extravaganza. In Chengdu, I heard John Rambo mumble his *First Blood* truisms in sullen, machine-gun Mandarin and saw the audience break into tut-tuts of headshaking admiration as our hero kerpowed seven cops in a single scene. In Jogjakarta, I went to *Rambo* on the same night as the *Ramayana* (though the modern divinity was watched by hosts of young couples, stately ladies in sarongs and bright-eyed little scamps, many of whom had paid the equivalent of two months' salary for their seats, while, on the other side of town, the replaying of the ancient myth remained virtually unvisited). Just five days later, I took an overnight bus across Java, and, soon enough, the video screen next to the driver crackled into life and there—who else? —was the Italian Stallion, reasserting his Dionysian beliefs against Apollo Creed. As the final credits began to roll, my neighbor, a soldier just returned from putting down rebels in the jungles of East Timor, sat back with a satisfied sigh. "That," he pronounced aptly, "was very fantastic."

Silencing soldiers, toppling systems, conquering millions and making money hand over fist across the continent, Rambo was unrivaled as the most powerful force in Asia that autumn. "No man, no law, no woman can stop him," gasped the ads in the Bangkok papers. "Everyone is Applauding Screen's Most Invincible Hero," agreed one of the three ads on a single page of India's respected *Statesmen*. "The Second Greatest U.S. Box Office Hit in History," roared the marquee in faraway Sabah. "I think he's very beautiful," cooed a twenty-three-year-old Chinese girl to a foreign reporter. "So vigorous and so graceful. Is he married?"

Rambo had also, I knew, shattered box-office records everywhere from Beirut to San Salvador. But there seemed a particular justice in his capturing of Asian hearts and minds. For Rambo's great mission, after all, was to reverse the course of history and, single-fisted, to redress America's military losses in the theaters of Asia. And in a way, of course, the movie's revisionism had done exactly that, succeeding where the American Army had failed, and winning over an entire continent. Some of the appeal of the blockhead-buster lay, no doubt, in its presentation of a kung fu spectacular more professional than the local efforts and more polished than the competing displays of Norris and Bronson. Some might just have reflected the aftertremors of its earthshaking reception in the States. But whatever the cause of the drama's success, the effect was undeniable: millions of Asians were taking as their role model an All-American mercenary.

From *Video Night in Kathmandu*

Pierre Billard detailed the extent of American cultural penetration of Western Europe in an article in the Paris magazine Le Point:

The inscription on the Acropolis reads, I CONSECRATE YOUR INSTITUTION FOR TIME ETERNAL—AESCHYLUS. This monument, "the most beautiful poem written in stone on the face of the Earth," as Alphonse Lamartine described it, now lies in near-ruins.

At one of several concerts in Europe by the American rock sensation Bruce Springsteen, 30,000 enraptured youths wear jeans and T-shirts bearing the names of American universities, states, and products. At their feet are thousands of empty Coca-Cola bottles.

Springsteen addresses the crowd in English and sings—to roaring applause—his hit, "Born in the U.S.A."

These portraits, however much they are caricatures, pose a question: Is European culture in danger, and is American culture supplanting it?

Another development casts an even darker shadow. Hovering high above Europe, a satellite transmits programs made in the U.S. Each hour of broadcasting carries six advertising slots. Four are reserved for the firms that financed the program, and two for Europeans. Consequently, Europe is blanketed in American images, culture, and products.

The U.S. earns 50 per cent of worldwide film profits, 35 per cent of the French market, 50 per cent of the Italian, Dutch, and Danish markets, 60 per cent of the German market, and 80 per cent of the British market.

The U.S. is responsible for 75 per cent of all important television programs. . . . Series such as *Starsky and Hutch, Dallas,* and *Dynasty* draw the greatest number of viewers.

In the recording industry U.S. firms supply 50 per cent of the global market. It is not by chance that Spaniard Julio Iglesias, an international star, has his headquarters in Miami.

In journalism the U.S. leads the world with two agencies—the Associated Press and United Press International. In advertising it leads with three companies—Young and Rubicam, J. Walter Thompson, and McCann-Erickson.

Mickey Mouse and his Disney pals are familiar to Europe's children; the exploits of Superman are well known, as are those of the reprehenible J.R. and Sylvester Stallone's Rambo. The disco beat reverberates through European apartment buildings. Americans are everywhere.

From *Le Point,* July 22, 1985; reprinted in
World Press Review, October 1985

British writer John Ralston Saul warned in The Spectator *that the decision to build a European Disneyland at the gates of Paris in Marne-la-Vallée may lead to a takeover of French culture:*

Disneyland is one of the great symbols of modern America. People who have seen the dream cities which already exist in Florida and

California understand this without a word of explanation. Anyone who has grown up in North America with Walt Disney's weekly television hour is an accomplice. The French government has decided to implant the heart of American mythology within Metro distance of Paris. . . . Whatever their polls are telling them, it is difficult to believe that the government has actually understood how the American way works. It is preceded not by the law, but by communications. The Marshall Plan, for example, included a proviso for the distribution of American films. Or, again, the first item on the American list for their free trade talks with Canada is free access for all American cultural systems. The American myth always rides ahead to raise expectations. The hard goods come behind.

Disney is one of the seven major Hollywood studios; it has expanded into video; created both prime time television series and animated television series, quite apart from their traditional hour-long programme and cartoons. The Disneyland they build will be an advance post disseminating all of these things; pre½paring the way from their Lourdes-like dream city at Marne-la-Vallée. The modern politicians seem helpless before this force. . . .

From "Disneyland Sur Marne," in *The Spectator*, March 1, 1986

A distressed Ivar Smith-Nilsen wrote a letter to the Oslo paper Aftenposten *to protest the erosion of Norwegian culture under the avalanche of American culture:*

A new shopping center in Oslo has opened, with stores such as the Tie Rack, Stop & Shop, Cosmetic World, Cookie Man, Hot Gossip, etc. This is Oslo's tourist image. It seems that the only differences between us and Americans are that we speak poorer English and have fewer cars.

Quoted in *World Press Review*, February 1989

In the view of many polemicists, the leading American cultural menace is Coca-Cola, Europe's most popular soft drink. Some younger Europeans define themselves in part through their loyalty to Coke:

I am of neither Dutch nor European culture. I am of the Coca-Cola culture.

A university student from Amsterdam, to the author

Even in faraway South Africa, writer Mark Jacobson found that in a real sense he had "come home," so effectively had American culture supplanted the local culture:

It could not have been an easy task, purging Africa from South Africa, but the state, if it hasn't totally exorcised indigenous culture from white South Africa, has absolutely managed to marginalize it, drive it underground. This isn't to say that black culture doesn't maintain itself in the townships, but I'm talking about what you see. . . .

For an American, however, almost as disturbing is how familiar it all is. It's brain-fissuring to pull your Avis car off the blacktop into a roadhouse outside Krugersdorp, hear Lacy J. Dalton blaring from the jukebox, have a paste-faced Indian run out from among the half-dozen pickup trucks to affix a tray containing a pineapple burger to your rolled-down window, and hand you a card on which is scrawled: NO ROLLER SKATE WAITER TODAY—RAIN AND HAIL. It keeps happening. They search you for limpet bombs outside a Checkers or OK Hypermarket, but once you're inside it's all Safeway, except with more brands and brighter lights. And it's more than simply being surrounded by brand names. There is an American texture to the place. The sprawl of the freeways, the endless open fields, the red clay of the Eastern Cape, it's all so heartland, you can just about hear the torpid chords of John Cougar Mellencamp hanging limply over the majestic Drakensberg. It was awful, being this comfortable, in a place like South Africa. I wanted South Africa to be hideous, alien. And it was nothing except home.

From "Greetings from South Africa," in *Trips*, Spring 1988

Rod Nordlund, a deputy foreign editor for Newsweek, *had a vivid demonstration of the power of the American dollar while on a trip to Poland:*

I once paid a taxi driver in Warsaw to get me from the domestic to the international airport in under ten minutes, which seemed clearly impossible to do, given the traffic jam we were in. So I offered him twenty U.S. dollars, which was an enormous amount of money on the black market, equivalent to two or three hundred dollars at the time. To accomplish this he drove on the wrong side of the street, ran buses off the highway, terrified me to the point where I was lying on the floor of the back seat, certain I would be killed, drove over a curb and across a grassy field, broke every law, and got me to the airport on time. This was the last plane I could get to Rome and be there in time for the installation of the Pope, which I had to cover. At the time, I didn't have an appreciation for how valuable twenty dollars was.

From *Trips,* Spring 1988

★

The paninari, *a popular Italian youth movement which sprang up in Milan in the eighties, reflects an addiction to American culture, as the writer William Murray discovered while there on assignment:*

"In Milan these days everyone's interested only in success and material well-being," the manager of my hotel informed me over a glass of wine one afternoon. "Who cares how you got it or what you did before? The important thing is to have it."

That point of view is also reflected in the activities of the young, few of whom belong to social or political movements or take any interest in politics in general. They are much more likely to join gangs, and all over town there are sizable contingents of skinheads, punks, "rockabillies," and other groups identifying themselves mainly with pop music trends. By far the largest and hottest new wave, however, consists of the *paninari* (the term doesn't translate literally). These are mainly young teenagers, but the fad has now begun to include children of elementary-school age. . . .

The *paninari* are united exclusively by their clothes. Their wardrobes must consist entirely of jackets, shirts, pants, socks, and shoes that look American and have been made by one of perhaps a dozen approved designers and companies. They are expensive, with shirts and sweaters priced from a hundred dollars and shoes as high as two hundred dollars. Money-saving imitations will not pass; immediate ostracism is the fate of any would-be *paninari* who tries to sneak a counterfeit article past the watchful eyes of his contemporaries. "To dress well means to dress with things that cost," a sixteen-year-old named Maurizio Gelati recently told a reporter. When asked if wealth was so important to him, the boy answered, "It's almost everything."

From "Muscular Milan," in *Condé Nast Traveler,* June 1988

★

Writer Charlie Haas found that American culture had sparked a similar sort of rebelliousness in the far-off Kingdom of Tonga in the South Pacific. He talked with a Western expatriate in the city of Nuku'alofa who told him the following:

"The older generation still respects the system, but from twenty-four down to adolescence, there's this very restless group who rejects it. You go in the villages, or in the street in Nuku'alofa and you can feel that tension coming from them—an *explosive* generation. . . . Where the kids want to go is this image of America that they get from videos. I tell them that some people starve in America and they don't believe it, because here nobody starves. You grow your own food, and if you're hungry, you go to your neighbors' house and they share with you.

"When I came here just a few years ago there were maybe two video stores on the island. Now every village has one. Houses in the country that don't have furniture, they have a TV and VCR. And it's changing everything because they think all that stuff is *real.* Except for the handful of well-educated guys, who have a knowledge of English and so on, the idea of actors playing parts and making believe hasn't penetrated. Since they don't know English, they tend to like action things, such as *Rambo,* and they think *Rambo* really happened. They think that, since you can't take a picture of someone unless the person is really there, you can't make a video of something unless it really happens—including violent horror stuff, *kung fu,* special effects, everything. It's only when they see the same actor get killed over and over and keep coming back that they wonder—although they have some interesting beliefs about that."

From "The King and, Well, I," in *Trips,* Spring 1988

Located some 2,500 miles off the coast of South America, Easter Island enjoys the dubious distinction of being the world's most secluded piece of inhabited land. No other people in human history have endured such extreme cultural isolation as this community. In 1980 the Chilean government, which owns the island, introduced color television. An official who had lived on Easter Island for over two decades fretted about the impact of the local culture:

I was worried about the effect of a steady diet of "Streets of San Francisco," "Kojak," and other crime drama series on the island's people. So we requested that our superiors in Santiago send over some cultural programs. Within a few weeks the airplane brought video tapes of concerts, opera, ballet, and other cultural presentations, which we proceeded to air over the island's one television transmitter. I happened to be in a native home one evening when a tape of a Leonard Bernstein concert—he was conducting Brahms, as I recall—aired. The half dozen men in the room suddenly collapsed into hysterical laughter. I looked at the screen. There was nothing there but a picture of Bernstein vigorously conducting the orchestra. The men continued to laugh. "What is so funny?" I finally asked. "Ho, ho, ho," they roared. "We have never seen so many people play just so *one* man can dance!"

Anecdote told to the author, March 18, 1981

★

Monopoly is the world's most popular board game. A version exists in virtually every major language around the globe. Recently one went on sale in the Soviet Union. Adi Ignatius reported for the Wall Street Journal *on the game's enormous popularity in communist Shanghai:*

Chinese officials proudly reported last week that a 40-year-old worker has bought the first apartment ever sold on Shanghai's open market.

Big deal. Tang Chi, 11, has been buying and selling property, houses, and hotels here since he was eight. Of course, the play money makes it easy. Tang Chi is a devotee of Shanghai's latest fad—Monopoly, Parker Brothers' viciously capitalistic board game.

"I love Monopoly. And I never lose," chirps the elfin youngster in fluent English. "Sometimes, I even play little tricks. For example, when no one's looking, I steal money from the bank."

Tang Chi, who wears a New York Mets T-shirt and likes to be called Tony, seems to have caught on to the spirit of a game that couldn't have less in common with socialism. In Monopoly the winner gets rich, often by squeezing opponents until they go bankrupt. For the Chinese, this is a fairly radical concept. Nonetheless, the game has taken the city by storm. . . .

Unbeknownst to [Parker Brothers], a Shanghai factory has been churning out an unauthorized, Chinese-language knock-off of Monopoly for the last three years. After a slow start, sales have taken off. This year alone the Shanghai Lishen Toy Factory has sold 200,000 copies of the game, which has won praise from some of this city's reform-minded economists.

"Everyone in China should be raised playing Monopoly," says Yao Weiqun, deputy secretary general of the Shanghai Association of World Economy. "That way everyone can understand how a market economy is supposed to work."

. . . Shanghai's Monopoly isn't exactly like the original. The board is a direct copy of the original, albeit with Chinese-language names. But, in an apparent nod to China's still-undeveloped status, all of the tokens are wheelbarrows; there are no sports cars or dandy top hats. And the Chinese version doesn't permit players the option of paying a fine to win release from jail.

"We don't want children to learn the Western system in which people can simply buy their freedom," says Lin Zhihui, vice director of Lishen Toy Factory and the one responsible for introducing Monopoly to Shanghai. "That would just encourage lawlessness."

. . . Ms. Lin also wrote a disclaimer, which accompanies the rules. "This game is a microcosm of Western society," it explained. "We hope it can help children understand the West."

From the *Wall Street Journal*, October 4, 1988

Time magazine writer Pico Iyer visited his native India and investigated the readiness of that country's film industry to make over popular American movies:

The Indian movie industry is the biggest, most popular, the closest to the heartland of any in the world. But the American is still regarded as the best. Hollywood, not Bombay, is the capital of glamour, the nerve center of show biz, the source of every trend. And so, quite sensibly, Bombay takes its cues from Hollywood; what goes down well in America goes up quickly on the screens of India. . . .

Often [the Indians] pilfer an entire movie. The heist was managed easily enough, an editor of a movie mag explained. By hook or crook, through contacts in the West or relatives in the Gulf, each of the Bombay movie moguls got hold of a video of the latest Western hit. Often, they were in possession of such tapes within two months of the movie's U.S. release and before it had even been shown in Britain. No sooner had the last credit rolled across their screens than they furiously set about cranking out frame-by-frame remakes. Thus, for example, five separate replicas of *Death Wish* assaulted the screens of India almost simultaneously. . . .

The process of turning an American movie into an Indian one was not very difficult, [the editor] explained, but it did require a few changes. "The Americans like a straightforward story line," he explained, "something uncomplicated. An Indian audience likes everything complicated, a twist and turn every three reels." In addition, he continued, the Indian hero had to be domesticated, supplied with a father, a mother and a clutch of family complications. "Take *Rambo*, for example. Rambo must be given a sister who was raped. He must be made more human, more emotional. His plight must be individualized—not just an obscure vendetta against the system." Also, of course, there had to be extra flourishes. "The average U.S. movie is only ninety minutes long; the average Hindi picture lasts a hundred and forty minutes. So we must add singing, dancing, more details." And since even kissing, not to mention nudity, had long been banned in India, explicitness and expletives had to be toned down, while suggestiveness had to be turned up. . . . The Indian adaptation would, in effect, be faithful to its model, but bigger, broader, louder. In the Indian cinema, nothing succeeds like excess.

From *Video Night in Kathmandu*

Hana Roditi, director of a Tel Aviv school, is optimistic about the impact of American culture in her country:

Of course, American culture has conquered our country, the wonderful things and the terrible things. Jews came to Israel from Europe and from the Arab countries with two different cultures that were very far apart. I think American culture has become a bridge between them because everyone likes it and both sides have copied it.

Quoted in the *Dallas Morning News*, July 6, 1986

However, the internationally renowned composer Sándor Balasse fears the destructive impact of American culture on his native Hungary and the rest of the world:

Let me select from among the infinitely many faces of America the one that has become unavoidably attached to my life and has become the unwished-for reality. Living in a small, remote country, Hungary, I have since my childhood been aware of the influence and radiation of the giant overseas power. It appeared in the guise of the Land of Dreams, in a glittering gown, always holding out promises, always alluring. It made us believe that our own life was bleak and poor—but there, beyond the sea, everything might come true. Freedom, wealth, and happiness were awaiting us. That mendacious dream is still enticing us. Its influence is, in fact, stronger today than ever before.

That influence has forced itself into my life like a shadow and has spurred me to protect myself. Now I am able to do so because my emotions and ideas are based on a unified world outlook. Simple people, however, have not got a chance. The foreign code sticks to them like a thistle, changes the working of their minds and deforms them.

They have become distant slaves of a new "Roman Empire." However, that empire is not ruled by caesars and the people but by money and Mickey Mouse. The cultural kitsch emanating from your country has colonized the youth of mine. The generation of the 12–22 year olds, brought up on cartoons and dum dum music, have relinquished their own culture and individuality. Their thinking and conduct are like those of metropolitan mobs in the United States.

That manipulated, shallow rabble is incapable of taking its destiny in its hands. They can, however, be motivated to regard consumption and entertainment as the goals of their lives.

The USA-made style encouraging one towards easier solutions is a symbol, an idol, the object of unreserved admiration. In being the exclusive power capable of moving the young to action it wrenches them from their European and national cultural traditions. They have become a faceless mass with no country, no principles. They cannot consciously assume responsibility for the human state. They are unable to recognize their individual or common historic heritage. [They have become] a sad flock of lotus-eaters, totally oblivious of their lot.

American society, based as it is on self-interest and profit, educates selfish and individualist people. But the world needs cultivated, public-spirited men if we are to survive the catastrophe brought on us by greed, stupidity, and irresponsibility. Money as a measure of value, giant motorisation, a life-style that destroys Nature—all of that make it inconceivable for me to want to live there. The big cities especially are a nightmare for me. America wants an import of oxygen.

If the American life-style spreads throughout the world, we shall suffocate.

From a letter to the author, dated August 1, 1988

What united the Ayatollah Khomeini, the Shi'ite mullahs, and the true believers of Islamic Jihad is a sense that for 150 years the West has totally overwhelmed the Islamic world culturally and, in the process, made its traditional institutions and values seem second-rate. Because Islam represents a wedding of religion and politics, the sense of religious betrayal always leads in time to political action to restore the purity of an Islam thought to have been corrupted. The Indian-born British novelist Salman Rushdie learned this, to his distress, in early 1989 when the publication of The Satanic Verses *provoked rioting, demonstrations, book burnings, bomb threats, and the rupture of international diplomatic relations throughout the Muslim world. The underlying nature of the conflict can perhaps be more clearly understood in the story of an Iranian youth who came to San Diego, California, in 1976 at the age of fifteen to study and found himself cut adrift by the Iranian revolution of 1979 and then the Iran-Iraq*

war. As the years passed without his return to Teheran, he gradually became more Americanized and eventually found himself engaged to an American woman. His family, conservative practicing Muslims, feared their son had lost his roots and turned away from his culture. His mother wrote her son's fiancée a letter, published in the San Diego Union, *to argue against the proposed marriage and ended it with this anguished plea:*

You might ask me then, why does my son not follow these Islamic rules? If he had not left his country and family, he would have applied these edicts. But what can we do? The way of life and outlook in your country robs our youth of their beliefs and culture. The low moral attitudes and corrupt society in your country is now well known in the world.

The global flood of slick Hollywood special effects has also had other, unexpected consequences. Among many Third World peoples it has under- cut the credibility of America's supreme technological achievement, the landing of men on the moon in the summer of 1969. Michael Ledeen, a fellow at the American Enterprise Institute, noted the profound worldwide skepticism toward the event.

Even those of us who pride ourselves on our international sophistica- tion sometimes get a useful dose of shock therapy, reminding us that the world as viewed by others is very different from the way we see it. In the past few years I have had four cultural shocks, each time dealing with the American mission to the moon. I am slowly coming to the conclusion that many people outside the U.S. and Western Europe do not believe that it ever happened.

The first time I ran across this phenomenon came during my negotiations with the Iranians in 1985. Talking with a top official of the Khomeini regime, I was surprised to hear him say, "We know how tricky you Americans can be. That story about landing on the moon, for example. We know that never happened, that it was all propaganda . . ." I asked him if there were others in Iran who shared his view, and he replied that most everyone in Iran knew it was a fake, and that Hashemi Rafsanjani himself often referred to this as an example of American cleverness.

I wrote it off as yet another example of Iranian lunacy—there was no shortage of such examples—and filed it away under "amusing stories to tell grandchildren." But then a few weeks ago I was talking to a friend in Soweto, South Africa, and he came up with the same reaction.

"Tell me the truth," he said, "there were never any Americans on the moon, were there?"

"Why do you say that?" I asked.

"The folks in Soweto don't believe it," he replied. "We think it was all propaganda. Hollywood."

Now, there is a world of difference between Sowetans and Iranians. Sowetans are remarkably literate, for example (almost all of them speak a minimum of four languages: Zulu, Causa, Afrikaans, and English), and they are intensely interested in international affairs. Yet my friend was undoubtedly right.

Next, over Thanksgiving weekend, I was at dinner with Gen. Ivan Yershov, the Soviet officer who commanded the invasion of Czechoslovakia twenty-one years ago. He was in Washington for a couple of months to visit his children and grandchild, and had recently been to the Air and Space Museum, where he had looked with fascination and disbelief at the moon rocks.

"So it was true all along," he said to me in a tone of amazement.

"What did you believe?" I asked.

"We thought the Americans had probably touched down briefly on the moon and then left right afterwards. But no one believed that you actually spent twenty-two hours on the moon's surface."

He clearly had not believed it until he went into the Air and Space Museum and looked closely at the moon rock display. I do not know why he thought the Americans capable of staging a deception on national television and not in the museum, but his conviction and surprise were palpable.

My final cultural shock came when I started to share my great discovery with some friends in Washington, whereupon I found that I had, as the Italians say, discovered the umbrella. It's actually old news. Back in the early seventies someone or other did a poll on this subject, and discovered that the vast majority of the planet believed that the moon landing was staged in some Hollywood studio. It seems there was even a movie about it, starring O.J. Simpson.

One might have hoped that in the age of the global village reality had made a significant impact on the past twenty years. Not so. We're still in the era best described by an eighteenth-century wit commenting on dogmatic philosophy: "For, he argued razor-witted, that can't be which is not permitted."

Iranians and Africans don't believe that we landed at all, while Russians—including the people at the very top—don't believe that Americans walked on the lunar surface, mined moon rocks, and generally cavorted on the moon for nearly a full day. In the Iranian and African cases, they don't believe it because it conflicts with their most fundamental convictions about the nature of things. Mr. Rafsanjani knows that man can't set foot on the moon, so it didn't happen. So it is with most of the world. In the Russian case, it is somewhat different; they know it's possible, but they just don't want to believe it.

One is tempted to draw some other conclusions as well—for example, that most of the world is deeply skeptical of the stuff that appears on American television. Or that religion, and traditional culture generally, are more convincing to most people than science. But however you slice it, it's a useful reminder of the diversity of mankind, and how far we are from that global village that mass communications were supposed to create.

From the *Wall Street Journal*, January 23, 1990

The View from Moscow

For over a decade the Soviets, like the Chinese, imported Marlboro cigarettes, paying for them with Western hard currency gained by selling tobacco grown in Soviet Georgia. Marlboros soon became more popular than Soviet brands, from the filtered Kosmos to the unfiltered Cossack, the latter jokingly called "instant cancer" by some Russians.

Marlboro cigarettes were but one aspect of a Russian fascination with all things American. In his book In Search of Melancholy Baby *the Russian novelist Vassily Aksyonov recalled the enormous underground popularity of American culture during his youth, when he attended parties where American music, clothing, dances, and slang were all the rage. "Those who are today in their twenties and thirties," one Russian intellectual confided to a reporter for the* New York Times, *"passed their whole adolescence in the belief that to have something American was the highest chic—American jeans, American rock, American chewing gum."*

Video recorders, which made their entry on the Soviet scene in the late 1970s as novelties that only the elite could afford, have started to become a mass phenomenon. A growing number of Russians are staying at home to watch movies the American way, on a VCR. And most of the films they watch are American. The action films of Clint Eastwood and Sylvester Stallone are as popular in Moscow as in Houston. Virtually all the films are officially banned. But the Soviet government has learned a hard fact of modern ideological warfare. The Voice of America radio broadcasts can be jammed, but stopping the latest weapons of cultural warfare has proven virtually impossible. American videocassettes, with their enormous potential for subversion, are small enough to be smuggled through border checkpoints on whim with little chance of detection. And throughout the Third World, Sylvester Stallone's films continue to shape the public's perception of Soviet actions beyond the wildest fantasies of state propagandists. In a series of press conferences in 1986, Soviet deputy ministers of culture denounced such popular films as Rambo *for allegedly crude, harmful, and officially inspired anti-Soviet themes. The* New York Times *reported on one such press conference:*

A group of Soviet cultural officials and artists today denounced the movies *Rocky IV* and *Rambo: First Blood, Part II* as part of a deliberate propaganda campaign to portray the Russians as cruel and treacherous enemies.

Sitting behind the same table in the Foreign Ministry press center where Soviet spokesmen usually condemn United States government policies, the group—including the poet Yevgeny Yevtushenko—singled out the two popular movies starring Sylvester Stallone as representative of what they called a rash of anti-Soviet propaganda in American movies and on television.

In *Rambo: First Blood, Part II,* Mr. Stallone plays an anti-Communist Vietnam veteran who returns to Southeast Asia to try to rescue American prisoners, killing more than a dozen Russians in the process. In *Rocky IV,* as prizefighter Rocky Balboa, he battles a villainous Soviet boxer.

Georgi A. Ivanov, a Deputy Minister of Culture, told a news conference that American films are "pushing onto the screen a new type of hero, a killer with ideological convictions." This new hero, he went on, "kills 'Reds' and Russians not for money but with a kind of perverse relish." Such fare, he said, was part of "an anti-Soviet campaign mounted in the United States."

The announced subject of the news conference was the resumption of American-Soviet cultural exchanges, but the panel devoted much of the 90-minute briefing to criticizing American films.

Mr. Yevtushenko, who created a stir at a congress of Soviet writers recently when he called for an end to censorship in Soviet literature, described movies like Mr. Stallone's as a form of pornography.

"I call them war-nography," Mr. Yevtushenko said.

Genrikh Borovik, a secretary of the Soviet Writers' Union, said Hollywood was "using art to sell hatred and fear."

From the New York Times, January 4, 1986

Critic Al Naloev of Sovietskaya Kultura (Soviet Culture) *in 1984 attacked American pop star Michael Jackson, whose music circulates in illicit cassettes and records in the Soviet Union:*

However, not even to one mercenary-minded person does this [Michael Jackson's] way of life look great. Its bearers are people of exceptional moral quality. Let's say Michael is a believer, a vegetarian on top of it, doesn't smoke or take drugs. He is sentimental, loves children, and enjoys the movies. Why wouldn't this be an example to follow? And so what if such an idol is totally apolitical? That's a plus, not a minus: only poor blacks and "reds" ever riot. Well-mannered "people of color," recognizing their "primordial masters," serve them with faith. It wasn't an accident that Jackson had plastic surgery, so much did he want to look 100 percent white, not like a troublemaker, so much did he want to become a full-fledged member of "consumer society," and even more, he wanted to show by his career that the Negroes, with their desires and abilities, can be "equal."

That's the rub—why Michael rewards the white establishment. . . .

Many black performers, seduced by the emissaries of show business, went for the remaking of their musical culture. But only one succeeded—Michael Jackson—and even though his producer Quincy Jones talked about the return to "African roots," in reality he stood up for a total "leveling" of Michael Jackson's art.

I wanted to know if that was indeed the case. I listened carefully to all nine of his compositions. I remember four: "Billy Jean," "The Girl Is Mine," "Beat It," and the song "Thriller," which doesn't go beyond the boundaries of the already-canonized "New Wave." What amazed me was the . . . composer's complete unoriginality . . . characteristic of that ill-famed American lifestyle which the U.S.A. is trying to foist on the rest of the world.

Translated and quoted in Robert English and Jonathan J. Halperin,
The Other Side: How Soviets and Americans Perceive Each Other

G. Gochevarov, a Soviet citizen, protested in a letter to Izvestia after Phil Donahue in 1987 cohosted with his counterpart Vladimir Posner a series of live shows with Russian audiences:

The American Phil Donahue has earned a reputation as a political provocateur and an ideological saboteur among Soviet television viewers, and he arouses burning hatred in all Soviet patriots.

Soviet party boss Mikhail Gorbachev wants to introduce incentives to spur workers to produce more and revive the nation's stagnant economy. But some workers aren't so sure. Tanya, a 35-year-old single mother, cuts and weighs meat in a canning plant. She's grateful for a freedom Soviet society provides in abundance: the freedom to loaf. "I don't want to work like an American," she insists. "The Soviet Union is a good place because if you don't want to work hard, you don't have to." (Quoted in Reason, October 1987.)

New York Times *Moscow correspondent Serge Schmemann informally surveyed Soviet citizens about their images of America and found that among the intelligentsia books have played an important role in Soviet perceptions of the United States:*

The first images of America to gain wide dissemination in the Soviet Union—ones that survive to this day—were created by Soviet poets and writers who traveled to the United States. [Their writings] supplied the pioneering pictures of soaring skyscrapers, industrious workers and throbbing factories, millionaires and beggars. They became a source of indelible images against which all subsequent perceptions have been tested. . . .

Rare is the Russian who was not reared on *The Deerslayer* and *The Adventures of Tom Sawyer,* who is not familiar with *The Catcher in the Rye,* Ernest Hemingway, William Faulkner, and John Steinbeck. Classics and contemporary American literature are a mainstay of the Soviet reading diet, either through dog-eared copies or through translations in the enormously popular monthly journal *Foreign Literature.* . . .

[According to one Russian,] "It would not be an exaggeration to say that in childhood we all were reared on American adventure literature—James Fenimore Cooper, Jack London, Edgar Allan Poe, Mark Twain, O. Henry—a whole constellation of names. All subsequent attitudes toward Americans are bent through this prism—not consciously, of course. Every person looks at the world in his own way, but we all played at cowboys and Indians in our childhood."

From "The View from Russia," in the *New York Times Magazine,*
November 10, 1985

American Culture from the Inside

For those foreign visitors to the United States with both the time and inclination, American culture can exert as great a fascination as, say, our landscape. Often aspects of our culture will strike them as being as exotic, bizarre, comic, or unfathomable as the cultural practices of a tribe in the New Guinea highlands may appear to an American observer.

Few foreign visitors experience a more extreme sense of culture shock upon arriving in the United States than the first-time visitor from the Soviet Union. Alexandra Costa was the wife of the First Secretary of the Russian Embassy in Washington, D.C., when she defected in 1978. In her autobiography she recalled the shocks she experienced during her first day in America:

The men left. I cleaned up the apartment and tried to get familiar with the things in it. I figured out fairly quickly what a few containers on the kitchen counter were for. Most appliances were familiar. The stove did not look at all that different from the one we had had in Moscow, although I would have to get used to the fact that we did not need matches to light it—Soviet stoves do not have pilot lights. The toaster on the counter was similar to the one I used in Moscow. Earlier, Gennady had shown me how to use a coffeemaker.

As I started to do the dishes, I remembered that nothing on the counter seemed to be a dishwashing liquid. Perhaps the apartment owners had run out of it before they left. I took soap from the bathroom and used it on the dishes. It also seemed strange that there was no rack or some other place to put clean dishes to dry. I started looking in the cabinets, and discovered that one of them had several rows of drying racks. Some still had glasses and plates on them. I put the dishes in and called my new acquaintance next door, a woman named Valentina, to tell her I was ready to go shopping. She came over and we started making a shopping list. I mentioned dishwashing liquid. "But you have a whole box of detergent, right here," she said, and pointed to one of the boxes that I thought to be a clothes detergent. "You should not use liquid in the dishwasher." Seeing incomprehension in my eyes, she laughed. "Of course, I forgot," she said. "You know, after you spend several years here, you begin to forget all the things that do not exist back home." She opened what I thought was a cabinet with the racks. "This is a dishwasher. Here you don't have to do dishes by hand." And she showed me how to use the machine.

My first reaction was embarrassment. The rest of my feelings were more difficult to sort out. What else was in store for me on my first day in this strange country? Here I was a worldly woman by Moscow standards. Lev and I were very well off back home. Our apartment was well equipped, or so I had thought up till now; we had access to special stores and many things that were out of reach for most of my countrymen. I had traveled to several foreign countries as a tourist, and Lev had visited many countries, including the United States, as a member of scientific delegations. He had often told me of his travels and of the different things he had seen. And yet I could not figure out some of the obviously everyday things in this rather modest apartment. What next?

"Next" turned out to be the supermarket where Valentina took me after we had finished the list. The shopping trip turned into a guided tour. At least half the items simply did not exist in the Soviet Union. The produce and household goods aisles were most confusing. I did not even know that so many varieties of fruits and vegetables existed on earth, let alone on supermarket shelves. The household goods took at least half an hour to go through while Valentina patiently explained the merits of such things as plastic wrap, various detergents, "quickie" floor mops, and the myriad of other items. I had already been introduced to the wonder of disposable diapers the night before, but the selection of baby food and instant baby cereals stopped me dead. In Moscow, having a baby meant hours of labor every day: washing diapers, cooking, cereals, grating and mashing fruits and vegetables by hand. All of a sudden it occurred to me that having a baby here did not mean being tied up in the kitchen for half a day. What a wonderful surprise! I remembered my American friends who had visited us in Moscow. When they mentioned that they had six children, it sounded unbelievable to me that a charming woman such as my American acquaintance would want to spend her life between the kitchen counter and the clothesline. Now I realized that in this country you could have more than one child and still have time and energy for other things in life.

Another incredible thing was that I could buy everything in one place, have it packed in bags, loaded into the car, and be home in an hour! In Moscow I often had to go to several different stores to do my grocery shopping: the bakery, produce store, general grocery store, and on and on. Without a car I had to make several trips to complete my shopping because I could only carry so much in two bags. Even in larger stores that had produce and bakery departments, each department had its own counter and, naturally, its own line. I decided that someday I would calculate how many years of my life I had spent standing in lines and doing household chores. Even without exact calculations, I knew that this country was already giving me the greatest gift I could dream of—my time.

But the most amazing thing was the profusion of color. Color, color everywhere. Things *looked* pretty. Soviet life is essentially colorless. The consumer products are generic and often scarce. An item may be produced by hundreds of factories through the Soviet Union and will look the same everywhere. A bar of low-grade household soap is invariably brown; a better hand-soap is always pink. A typical grocery shelf in the Soviet Union looks like a generic brand section in the supermarket—plain paper with dark lettering on everything. There is no need to make things attractive. . . .

The lack of color partially explains the fascination Russians have with foreign goods. Not only is the product better, but it also looks pretty and brightens up your apartment. It is not unusual to keep empty containers from foreign-made hairspray in the bathroom, or a dishwashing liquid in the kitchen, long after the contents are used up, just for decoration. When I was a student of foreign languages, I often worked as an interpreter with foreigners and received a lot of small gifts, especially cosmetics, and my friends always asked me to give them the empty containers.

By the time we got home from the supermarket, my head was spinning from all the new information I was trying to absorb.

From *Stepping Down from the Stars*

★

It is not just the Russian visitor who is overwhelmed by the choice offered everywhere in the American culture. Britisher John Blundell, who now works as the executive vice-president of the Institute for Human Studies at George Mason University, was just as impressed:

So what is it like to be a "Brit" in America?

A few weeks after I first landed on a limited visa in the spring of '82, I met an old college chum in Greenwich Village. He took me to a pub-style bar for lunch. Within seconds a waitress was hovering. What did I want? inquired my friend. Cheese sandwich and a beer, I replied. A barrage of questions followed. There were 10 different cheeses, 8 different breads, innumerable "fixings"—whatever *they* were—and on the beer front, imported or domestic, draft or bottled, and light or dark to choose from before we narrowed it down to a manageable list.

I felt I'd been pulled right along a complex decision tree! And, had it not been for our accents, I doubt the waitress would have been so understanding.

Choice and service impress the Alien enormously. A year ago I was showing the well-known British economist Arthur Seldon around northern Virginia, where I now live after several years in California. We stopped off at the posh Fair Oaks Shopping Mall, just west of Fairfax. "This is clear evidence of the failure of capitalism," he announced ironically, drawing blank looks from shoppers as he waved his arms around at the vast, two-level, indoor, air-conditioned collection of 100-plus stores. "Any of my fellow countrymen thinking of joining the Labour Party should spend a day here first," he concluded.

From "What About All Those Drug Stores?"
in *Reason*, January 1988

When does the immigrant suddenly start thinking of himself as a real American? When he finally masters perfect English? When he automatically adds cream to his coffee? When he stops dreaming at night of Italy, Greece, or Poland? Klára is a woman from Hungary who has lived for nine years in Los Angeles. She remembers both the long lines and shortages of basic consumer goods that characterized life in her native country, and that day when she knew she had become irrevocably an American:

I can recall the exact moment when I suddenly knew I had become an American. We had been living for four years here. Then one day I sent my son to a nearby market for several items, and he returned with a package of green toilet paper. "Freddy," I said impatiently, "you march right back to the store and exchange this green toilet paper for the pink. You know it doesn't match the tile color of our bathroom!!!!"

From a conversation with the author, August 11, 1988

★

M. Daud Nassery is a medical doctor from Kabul, Afghanistan, who settled in Eastham, Massachusetts. He first came to the United States as a high school exchange student. Years later he recalled what impressed him the most on that first visit:

In August 1969 I was sent to Eastham, Massachusetts, a small working-class town on Cape Cod. It's very American, settled in the 1600s by the Pilgrims. The local people are very friendly.

Edward and Bernice Brown treated me like one of their own children. I still call them Mom and Dad. The youngest of their three sons, Peter, was in the same class as me. We played soccer on the same team. . . .

One of the first differences I noticed in America is the size of the families. In Afghanistan even the smallest family has five or six kids. And extended-family members are very close-knit: brothers- and sisters-in-law, aunts and uncles, and grandparents all live together or nearby.

Only the father works and takes responsibility to provide for the family. Even if he doesn't make a large amount of money, he shares whatever he earns with the extended family. Even in households where people are hungry most of the time, everybody shares what little food they have.

I saw in America that everyone in the family works to pay for his or her life. Even teenage children like my American brother worked part-time in the summer to pay for college and contribute some rent to his parents. Mom and Dad were teaching the children responsibility. From an American point of view, that's good. But from my cultural point of view, it was shocking and strange.

In Kabul I knew families who had stores. Nephews and nieces worked for them, but none of them got paid. They believed that it was their duty to help the family business.

The first weeks that I lived with the Browns, while everyone in the family went out to their jobs, I stayed alone at home and felt kind of bored. One morning while we were having breakfast, I asked my American mother if I could work at their grocery store.

What I meant by "work" was that I wanted to help them. I didn't know that there is a difference between "work" and "help" in this country. If you say "help," it means you don't expect to get paid. I said, "Mom, I'd like to work with my brothers in your store." She said, "I'm sorry, how much money do you want?"

My face got red. I was kind of embarrassed. I said, "Why is money being mentioned? I don't want money. I just want to help you because I am a member of the family."

Quoted by Al Santoli in *New Americans: An Oral History*

On the other hand, Kathryn Court, an editor with Viking Penguin publishers in New York City, found life in the United States made for an effortless transition from her native England when she moved here:

Living in New York didn't feel like being in a strange place. This country and England share so much history and tradition. Other ethnic groups may tend to cluster closer together because of cultural and language differences. But from the time I arrived, I've felt quite at home. And there were things in English society I was happy to get away from— the kind of snobbishness, the English are very class-conscious.

One of the things that amazed me when I was job hunting here was that nobody asked about my university degree. And when the subject came up, no employers emphasized, "*Where* did you get your degree?" In this people's main concern is "Can this person do the job? And do it very well? If they can't, we'll fire them."

In England there are very strict rules about how an employer can or cannot fire people. A very complicated process of verbal warnings and written warnings. Then six months must go by before re-evaluating the employee. So America is better for most people because they are given the chance to prove themselves. People can accomplish an awful lot when their employer has confidence in them. In a purely working environment people here have a better shot to be what they *think* they want to be. It's a great country for confidence building.

Quoted by Al Santoli in *New Americans: An Oral History*

The American Love Affair with the Car

Our national passion for automobiles is really more of a passion for the personal freedom that comes with ownership of a car that can take anyone anywhere anytime. The car has become the all-purpose solution to physical and social mobility, and an expression of individuality. Britisher Adam Nicolson fell in love with the enormous American automobiles from a different era:

I've spent two days trying to buy a car. The rental I picked up at the airport was a mean un-American thing. (Only an un-American can say that without sounding racist.) So I decided to get rid of it and buy myself a car, a real American car. David, a friend who is a car enthusiast, understood my delight and fascination for something as American as a real American car and my impatience with compact, economy, and all the rest of it. "What you need," he said, "is a Pontiac Catalina convertible." Of course, I had no idea of what he was talking about. He found me one for $900. This was a coup. It's vast, about thirty feet long and ten feet wide, what David calls "a real boat, a land yacht, a cream puff." But it's not really a cream puff, it's more like a wide flat sliver cut from a side of salmon, all horizontal, not bright and perky like European cars, but slit-eyed, low and lazy.

It's a crook's car and I love it. You don't need to do anything by hand; the gears are, of course, automatic, the windows electric, the lowering and raising of the roof at the push of a button. Even the adjusting of the position of the seats is done by electric motor.

The aerial for the radio extends and contracts automatically when you turn it on and off. But better than all this is the ride. The engine accelerates like a millionaire growing angry, the suspension slides it around bends as if there's a rudder at the back, the power-steering means that one finger can swing the whole cruiser on a corner, the sheer length of it rounds off bumps in the road into no more than a mild swell. Of course, it's wildly out of date and guzzles gas, but I don't care!

Do you know that song by Dionne Warwick "LA is just one big freeway/ Put a hundred down and buy a car . . ."? That was on the radio this morning, so I did. The man selling it was an architect named Dave Miller. . . . I said to him after a short test spin around the block that it was like sitting on a sofa while trying to drive a tennis court. "Oh no," Miller said slowly. "She's a beaut. Looks good, goes great. There's 4,000 pounds of car there." That made it slightly under 25¢ a pound. "You couldn't get anything else at that price," Miller said smiling, and that clinched it.

I am now in possession of my own bit of mobile real estate. I lie back on the seat like a redneck, watching the world slide past the windscreen like a long-running TV show.

From *Two Roads to Dodge City*

When he was twelve, Walter Polovchak emigrated with his family from the Soviet Union to the United States. But a few months later, his parents decided to leave Chicago and return to the Ukraine. Walter then made a momentous decision: No matter what his parents did, he would remain in the States. Thus began an international struggle which lasted several years and eventually involved the courts, the KGB, the American Civil Liberties Union, and the Soviet and American governments. In time, Walter was permitted to remain without his parents. In his memoirs he remembers his first impressions of America as they drove to their new home from the airport:

We piled into cars and headed for the city. Before I knew it, we were stopping at a booth of some sort. I thought, damn! I need a passport! That's where I got my first lesson in what America was all about.

It was a toll booth for the parking lot. No passports needed. Just money! Somebody paid the toll and off we went. I thought, You can go anywhere you want here, nobody cares.

Driving into the city, there were solid streams of cars and trucks whizzing all around us, thousands of streetlights everywhere. . . . I was just freaked out, asking my cousin, "Who in hell owns all those cars?" You go down the street and it's cars all over, traffic everywhere, without a break even. Even at night cars whiz all over the place. This was like another planet.

"Where the heck do people get all this money? Are those government cars?"

"No, people buy their own," he said, "and sometimes they have two or three cars."

I was like . . . wow. America was an amazing place. Everything was so spectacular. It's like, oh, Lord . . . there's action and stuff going on everywhere, different things to see, different places to go. I was only twelve then, and I didn't know one car from the other, but they all fascinated me.

From *Freedom's Child*

Speaking American

Londoner Jane Walmsley reminds her readers that the common language shared by Americans and Brits masks a set of vastly different attitudes toward everything from death to interior decoration:

George Bernard Shaw said it best, though many have said it badly ever since. America and Britain are two nations divided by a common language. Between us is a Great Philosophical and Cultural Divide, which is obscured by the familiar lingo. Our respective heads of government may burble on about "common bonds" and "special relationships"—but the truth is that, in the eighties, Brit-think and Ameri-think are lightyears apart. We cherish widely different values and aspirations, and have developed separate habits of mind. Only the names remain the same . . . and there's some doubt about those. In some ways, a camel and a porpoise have more in common.

From *Brit-think, Ameri-think*

★

Brits visiting the States have to remember that over here "chips" are french fries, a "lorry" is a truck, a "fag" is a cigarette, and a "biscuit" is a cookie. And they must always remember in polite society that "rubbers" can get them into trouble. Ian is a middle-aged exporter from Capetown,

*South Africa, who spends four months of every year in Southern Califor-
nia on business and can still be tripped up by the "common" language:*

As often as I am in America, you'd think that the language would
never be a problem. Still, I find myself baffled on occasion by
American English. One time I entered a stationery shop in La
Jolla and asked them for pencil erasers. Only in South Africa
we called them "rubbers." I approached an elderly woman behind
the counter. "Madam," I asked, "do you have any rubbers?" She
just stood there with a strange look on her face, not saying anything. And so thinking she may be a little hard of hearing, I
raised my voice. "MADAM, DO YOU STOCK RUBBERS?" Suddenly,
everyone else in the shop stopped what they were doing and
gave me these shocked looks. Finally, a young female clerk came
over and said quietly, "Sir, you will find those in the drugstore
down the street."

From an interview with the author, September 15, 1988

*The Russian comedian Yakov Smirnoff voiced the complaint of numerous
immigrants when he insisted that learning to speak English is easy, but
that learning to speak English like an American is the hard part. He
offered up the following common American expressions and what they
"really" mean:*

1. *"The check is in the mail!"* means, depending on the spelling, either
that someone hasn't sent out your money yet, or a gay guy from
Czechoslovakia got lucky on a date.
2. *"Think of it as an investment"* means "Think of it as overpriced."
3. *"Of course, it's tax deductible"* means "Welcome to prison."
4. *"The shit hit the fan"* means "Uh-oh."
5. *"You can earn up to a thousand dollars a day"* means "Forget it! It's
either illegal or it's Herbalife."

From *America on Six Rubles a Day*

American Obsessions

Nick Davies covers the American scene for the Illustrated London News.
In one column he examined our eating habits:

The Queen of Sweden visited Texas earlier this year, and she was being shown around a hospital there when she asked the question that sooner or later comes to the lips of most visitors to the United States. "We have seen so many people who are very fat," she observed. "Why is that?"

The answer she got from her guide, Dr. Michael DeBakey, was simple and unequivocal. "They eat too much," he said. And yet the honest doctor was only nibbling at the truth of the matter.

First, let us be clear: the Queen was right. These are fascinating fat people—one out of every three of them are overweight, according to the National Research Council, and one out of four dangerously so.

The sight of Texans at the trough is particularly memorable. I watched them feeding recently in a hotel near Houston. First, a mature female sniffed out the buffet and then beckoned to her mate, an amiable hippo in Bermuda shorts, who waddled to her side. Soon they were filling their plates: half a dozen rashers of bacon, a couple of fried eggs, a handful of sausages, a few waffles, cheese sauce over the eggs, maple syrup over the bacon, and some buttered toast on the side. They were still loading up as other couples arrived, and soon the whole buffet was a wobbling wall of flesh. "Pass the cream . . . Try the pizza . . . Is there any more of that cheesecake?" This was only breakfast.

But the mere fact that Americans are greedy does not in itself explain why they have to indulge themselves in such a fattening fashion. The answer here, it seems to me, is that the diet is, in many ways, dangerously similar to the rest of their culture. Everything is for sale. Therefore, everything is designed for the mass market, which means instant gratification, the minimum of subtlety and the maximum of overstatement: it's Jimmy Swaggart instead of the Archbishop of Canterbury; its *Dallas* instead of Dennis Potter; it's loud clothes, mawkish movies, and crass politicians.

Americans sneer in disbelief at people who eat Rich Tea biscuits, for example, when they could be filling their faces with blueberry and cheese muffins. And why put salt on your peanuts when you could be roasting them in honey? And why cook steak unless you are going to flavour it with hickory-wood smoke? Everything must be instant and over-stated, a fact which is horribly exemplified by the work of Mr. McDonald, the junk-food king. . . .

The Queen of Sweden politely suggested that her hosts should take more exercise. I prefer the approach of Robert Malone, aged 33, of New York City, who was arrested after a sequence of more than 50 armed robberies. Mr. Malone turned out to be no ordinary heist-merchant. It transpired that every one of his victims was a confectioner, and he was a kind of Robin Hood, stealing from the fat to fill out the thin. "The cookies are garbage, and you have to pay too much for them," he shouted as they led him away in handcuffs.

From "Brandywine Street," in the *Illustrated London News*,
August 1988

★

Gautam Adhikari, an associate editor of The Times *of India, also spent considerable time in America, as a resident fellow at the Center on the Press, Politics, and Public Policy at Harvard University. He offers up these thoughts on his days of low-cal dementia:*

Ten years ago if you were told in India that an American was coming to visit you and you didn't know what he looked like, you would probably conjure up an image of a large man—"beefy" is the word—who wore a baseball cap and ate most of the time. When he was not eating hamburgers, he was chewing sugar-coated gum. But then the Great American Dietary Revolution came along. . . .

A couple of years ago when I came to this country a few times on short visits, the food habits struck me as noteworthy. On the one hand, fast-food outlets tried to entice you at every corner, and you could in the major cities find the widest variety of international cuisine available anywhere in the world. Restaurants overflowed. . . . On the other hand, whenever I actually went to a restaurant with friends, I would be made to feel vaguely guilty all the time about my archaic eating and drinking preferences. Not that my companions were openly disparaging; they would simply ask for food that was less fatty, less sugary, less fried, less everything than I would. Their ordering always sounded more informed and less indulgent than mine.

For example, when I went to Mel Krupin's restaurant in Washington, D.C., with friends from the networks, I found myself ordering a dry martini to everyone's embarrassed laughter. They had ordered Perrier or seltzer water, and one had asked for a glass of white wine when I hit them with my demand for the real stuff. "Ah, a martini," exclaimed someone. "What a great idea!" Clearly, it wasn't a good idea. But I stuck it out, adding defiantly, "And make it extra dry."

Therefore, when I came to live in this country a couple of months ago, I came prepared. To begin with, I gave up smoking; lighting up a cigarette is less of a health hazard than it is a social hazard here. In France and in England, they puff away as merrily as ever, but in America you have to be brave to smoke in public. People make you feel like someone in need of psychiatric help, and there are more and more office buildings and airplanes where you cannot smoke at all.

More significantly, I began to plan my lunch and dinner menus carefully. So much red meat and eggs and no more; plenty of lettuce, carrots, and cabbage; very little alcohol and virtually no sweets, especially no more of my beloved chocolates.

As a result, I rapidly lost a lot of weight and a bit of my sanity. . . . Soon, however, I noticed strange things. Most people around me were reaching into chocolate bins and popping handfuls into shopping carts. Ice cream shops were always crowded. Was I one of the few loonies who had taken this business of a healthy diet at its face value?

Now the *New York Times* has exposed it all. In a survey in "The Living Section" the writer Marian Burros declares: "Most Americans, regardless of age, have not responded in a significant fashion to calls for decreasing fat in the diet, reducing sodium, taking in fewer calories or otherwise eating more healthfully."

The article went on: "They still like french fries more than baked potatoes, red meat more than chicken or fish, and soft drinks more than fruit juice. Snacking is a national pastime."

Exactly what I had always suspected.

I am happy to announce that I have begun to regain a few lost pounds and a lot of that general sense of well-being that you have when you eat chocolates regularly.

> From "A Dry Martini and Double-Nut Mocha,"
> in the *New York Times,* January 15, 1988

Chinese editor Liu Zongren was amused at the American inconsistencies over exercise:

Americans will spend an hour jogging, but will usually drive to work over a distance they could cover in twenty minutes by walking.

> From *Two Years in the Melting Pot*

The rapid pace of American life, especially in the bigger cities, has often drawn the attention of foreign visitors. A German proverb insists:

In America an hour is forty minutes.

The American obsession with cosmetic surgery brought forth these comments by Londoner Jane Walmsley:

"If I've only one life to live," breathes a beauty in a famous American TV commercial, "let me live it as a blond!" As has been noted, it goes against the Ameri-grain to concede that "we pass this way but once." Just in case, however, true Yanks are determined to make the most of it. Appearance is vital. Suggest that beauty is only skin-deep, or that character counts most, and natural skepticism overwhelms them. It's all very well to have a fabulous personality; but—if you want to reach for the stars (and every American does)—you'll also need straight teeth.

They're equally pragmatic about nature and its wondrousness. "If nature's blown it, we'll fix it" is the national *cri de coeur* that's launched a million cosmetic operations. It's clear that the quality of your life—and your enjoyment of it—are largely dependent on the way you look. There's little doubt that appearance affects popularity, and financial success. "Just as God Made Me" is not always good enough. Look what He did with earwigs.

Ironically, Yanks—with most of life's basic necessities under wraps—are the world's greatest malcontents. They seek perfection, and cannot rest until they've made the best of a bad job. *Every* bad job. When it comes to themselves and their personal prospects, no effort is too great, no correction or refinement too insignificant, no orthodontist too expensive. Americans invest in themselves happily, guilt-lessly. After all—when life is so precious, why waste a single day feeling bad about your nose?

This is the blessing and the curse of American affluence. If everything's possible, and no real obstructions stand in your way, you've no excuses. Failure is your fault. So is unhappiness.

From *Brit-think, Ameri-think*

The British novelist Nancy Mitford voiced a common complaint of foreign observers when she insisted that Americans are obsessed with money:

Americans relate all effort, all work, and all of life itself to the dollar. Their talk is of nothing but dollars. The English seldom sit happily chatting for hours on end about pounds. In England, public business is its own reward; nobody would go into Parliament in order to become rich; neither do riches bring public appointments.

From *Noblesse Oblige*

The French architect Le Corbusier, however, strongly disagreed, pointing to the difference between his home city of Paris, which sold off the greatest part of its parkland in 1910 for development, and New York City, which kept Central Park in the middle of Manhattan:

You like to accuse Americans of being concerned only with making money? I am struck with admiration for the strength of character of the municipal authorities of New York who have preserved granite rocks and trees in the center of Manhattan, a park more than four and a half million square yards in area.

The park is surrounded by fine buildings—apartment houses in tall blocks or in the form of skyscrapers—all with windows opening on this unexpected space, a fairylike situation unique in the city without trees. If the precious ground of Central Park is valued at from two thousand to four thousand dollars per square yard, the commercial value of these granite rocks amounts to anywhere from ten billion to eighteen billion dollars. To keep this immense treasure untouchable in the very center of Manhattan, I think shows a high civic attitude, an extraordinary attitude. It is the sign of a strong society.

From *When the Cathedrals Were White*

Russian novelist Vassily Aksyonov rails against the American obsessions with sex and statistics:

Imagine what a recent émigré thinks when he first comes across gay pride parades and the gay press. Of course, America has come a long way from its original level of sexual hypocrisy, and hypocrisy here must have been worse than in Russia if even today certain states maintain laws against oral sex. Like other forms of liberalization in America, however, sexual liberalization has gone a bit too far. It has ballooned into an obsession, a craze, a mass orgy; it has bad taste written all over it.

During my first trip to the States I heard a TV preacher berating his fellow citizens for indulging in mass sodomy. "There are twenty million homosexuals in this country," he thundered. "Where are we going?"

"Twenty million?" I remember thinking then. "Impossible." Now I realize it was just another American obsession. The statistics obsession or, rather, the obsession with *terrifying* statistics. . . .

Every morning the newscasters astound us with figures. Eight hundred thousand Americans had partial hearing lost in the left ear last year; six million saw doctors for flat feet. One day I heard that there were two million kidnapped children in America. How many children are there altogether? Fifty, sixty million? If one in every thirty children is gone, disappeared, then why are we sitting at home watching television? Why aren't we out there looking for them? When I looked into it, I found a lengthy FBI report admitting that the number is actually . . . well, rather exaggerated. It's not two million; it's thirty thousand. And half of them are runaways. And two thirds of the rest were taken by a divorced parent. A zero here, a zero there . . . Somebody seems to have been trying too hard.

From *In Search of Melancholy Baby*

Jane Walmsley agrees on the issue of sexual obsession. She writes:

Yanks Treat Sex Seriously (as they do all other areas of personal development). They approach it with the earnestness and single-minded determination you'd expect from a marathon runner in training. They mean to win, to experience the Ultimate Orgasm. And they like to do things scientifically.

From *Brit-think, Ameri-think*

German-born film star Marlene Dietrich makes the same observation:

In America sex is an obsession; in other parts of the world it is a fact.

Quoted in *Morrow's International Dictionary of*
Contemporary Quotations

Armenian Lucy Koouyoumdjian emigrated from the Soviet Union to Cambridge, Massachusetts, in 1987. She deplores the American preoccupation with sex:

What I want to talk about is the morality of the people. Americans have a really low morality, especially the females and teenagers. I don't have any data in this area but I believe that what I'm saying is true. The Armenian women have been famous through the ages for their high morality. They are conservative about having sex without marriage. Here, starting from the teens the boys and girls play at love which ends by having sex at an early age and which brings a lot of trouble at the end. The TV, newspapers, and magazines print articles and pictures about sex which make teenagers much more interested in sex. In Armenia the person who wants to marry must be an adult who understands his duty in making a young family. I wish I could help the American teenagers understand that [sex carries] very serious responsibilities.

From a letter to the author, dated May 25, 1988

On the other hand, rock singer Terence Trent D'Arby, who expatriated himself to London seven years ago, finds America much too conservative about sex and other things:

[In the U.S.] I obviously wouldn't say on nationwide TV that I thought America was racist, sexist, homophobic, and violent if they asked me why I left. I would just say America wasn't a culture I felt comfortable in. But anybody with a brain would understand what I'm trying to say.

Quoted in *People,* May 9, 1988

★

Saeki Shoichi teaches American literature at Chuo University in Japan. In 1987 he spent a semester teaching at the University of California's campus in Berkeley. He too is distressed at the changes in American society he has observed over the past four decades:

America has changed to an astonishing degree since the latter half of the 1960s, and it can never return to what it was. What happened to America during that period? While China was in the throes of the cultural revolution, America was undergoing a cultural revolution of its own. Certainly the Vietnam War acted as a powerful catalyst for change. Yet a foreign war that had no appreciable impact on domestic living conditions cannot fully account for such an extraordinary overhaul of morals and values.

It was only half a century ago that Americans imposed on themselves the Prohibition Amendment, which remained in effect for a dozen years. As late as 1950, most universities had strict rules against selling alcoholic beverages on campus; on arriving at the University of Wisconsin in 1950, I was amazed to hear that it was the only college in the entire country that allowed beer to be drunk in the student dining halls. However, in the wake of the marijuana boom of the 1960s, the nation swung to the opposite pole. All manner of drugs permeated society, creating a major social problem. Sexual mores, likewise, shifted from an almost absurd insistence on forbearance to a complete removal of taboos and restraints.

I would venture the opinion that this upheaval in American morals was basically a matter of religion. That is, it reflected the weakening of the society's Christian underpinnings. . . . There is no escaping the impression that a vast chasm yawns within the soul of the American people, a gnawing hunger that, to the outsider, is almost grotesque. Certainly the fitness fever that made its first appearance at the beginning of the 1970s suggests the antics of a people desperate to fill some void. Might it not be in fact the random redirecting of a religious, moralistic impulse that suddenly finds itself without an object? The fervor of the recent anti-smoking movement, similarly, can be taken as an indication that the American proclivity for moralizing is alive and well.

From "Rediscovering America's Dynamic Society,"
in *Japan Echo,* Spring 1988

American Festivities

British observer Alistair Cooke was struck by the American readiness to set a day, a week, or even a month aside as an anniversary:

America, as you know, is a great place for anniversaries and there is hardly a week in the year that some mayor or governor doesn't dedicate to a worthy cause or a cause that would like to be thought worthy. So we have National Dog Week, National Shoe Week, National Friendship Week, National Tea Week. Almost nobody but dog-lovers, shoe salesmen, and tea-drinkers ever know when these things are going on or what they are about. (Friendship Week has me beaten completely.) Like Mother's Day, no man would dare say a word against them in public or a good word for them in private. They are tolerated as necessary nuisances, since they do somebody— the florists' associations and the telegraph companies usually—a lot of good. Even children, if they are well brought up, get to take these things with the proper cynicism. The pity is that many good anniversaries pass by unhonored because it's assumed that some local chamber of commerce thought them up.

From *One Man's America*

In September of 1979 British author Jonathan Raban set about realizing a childhood dream, a voyage by a small boat down the entire length of the Mississippi River. His adventure began with an evening at an old-fashioned Midwestern state fair on the outskirts of Minneapolis:

Then, suddenly, I was part of the crowd. The street had merged into an expressway, and the expressway was jammed solid. We were elbow to elbow in the crush, a grumbling herd of dusty pickup trucks, all windows down, all radios turned full up. I spoke to my nearest neighbor, a colossal jellyfish in a plaid shirt.

"Where's everybody going?"

"*You* goin' to the Fair, man. . . ."

Everyone in our crowd was wearing a plastic cap with a long shovel-brim. The caps gave the cavalcade a vaguely military air, as if we were off to sack a city. The fronts of the hats were decorated with insignia and slogans. OH BOY! OH BEEF! advertised a kind of cake that cows ate. Others peddled farm machinery, Holsum

Bread, chemical fertilizers, pesticides, corn oil, cement, and root beer. Under these corporation colors, the owners of the caps looked queerly like feudal retainers riding around wearing the arms of their barons. A few self-conscious individualists wore personalized caps announcing I'M FROM THE BOONDOCKS and YOU CAN KISS MY . . . followed by a picture of an ass in a straw bonnet. [My companion's] cap said JOHN DEERE; I took this for his own name, and only gradually noticed that several hundred men at the fair were also called John Deere, which turned out to be a famous brand of agricultural tractor.

The state fair sprawled across a hillside and a valley, and at first glance it did indeed look like a city under occupation by an army of rampaging Goths. I'd never seen so many enormous people assembled in one place. These farming families from Minnesota and Wisconsin were the descendants of hungry immigrants from Germany and Scandinavia. Their ancestors must have been lean and anxious men with the famines of Europe bitten into their faces. Generation by generation, their families had eaten themselves into Americans. Now they all had the same figure: same broad bottom, same Buddha belly, same neckless join between turkey-wattle chin and sperm-whale torso. The women had poured themselves into pink stretch-knit pant suits; the men swelled against every seam and button of their plaid shirts and Dacron slacks. Under the brims of their caps, their food projected from their mouths. Foot-long hot dogs. Bratwurst sausages, dripping with hot grease. Hamburgers. Pizzas. Scoops of psychedelic ice cream. Wieners-dun-in-buns.

Stumbling, half-suffocated, through this abundance of food and flesh, I felt like a brittle matchstick man. Every time I tried to turn my head I found someone else's hot dog, bloody with ketchup, sticking into my mouth.

On either side of us, the voices of the freakshow barkers quacked through tinny loudspeakers.

"Ronny and Donny. The only living Siamese twins on exhibit in the world today. Now grown men, Ronny and Donny are joined at the breastbone and the abdomen, facing each other for every second of their lives. . . . You will remember your visit with the Siamese twins for the rest of your life—"

Crushed between the bust of the woman behind and the immense behind of the man in front, I did not find it hard to imagine what it might be like to be Ronny or Donny. There was no chance of visiting with them, though. As the sluggish current of the crowd passed them by, I was carried with it, deep into the heart of the state fair.

I was going down fast. The air I was breathing wasn't air; it was a compound of smells, of meat, sweat, popcorn, cooking fat and passed gas. Wriggling and butting my way out of the crowd, I found myself in the sudden blessed cool of a vaulted cathedral full of cows. They stood silently in their stalls with the resigned eyes of long-term patients. The straw with which the stadium was carpeted gave the whole place a ceremonious quiet. Grave men, whom I took for bulk buyers from the hamburger industry, padded from stall to stall. The cattle stared back at them with profound incuriosity. I wondered what they made of the smell of charred beef. Soon they'd be minced, ground up with cereal and soybeans, and turned into Whoppers and Kingburgers. For now though, the animals had a lugubrious dignity that put the people at the fair to shame. They were the real heroes of the day. . . .

I'd never been much good at being one of the crowd. Now, feeding myself back into the flow, I tried to settle in, to feel part of the blood being pumped through the fair. Be a corpuscle. Let go. We oozed down a long sticky tunnel of cotton candy, came up against some invisible obstruction, and were channeled into a mass of separate thread veins and arteries. The going was hot and smelly, the pace jerky, as if the whole coronary system was clogged and subject to frequent breakdown. All nerve ends and elbows, I kept on getting stuck.

I was shown a selection of snow blowers. A lady dog handler demonstrated the latest psychological technique for dissuading Ajax and Hercules from leaving piles of poopie on the rug. I found her frank, instructive, but a bit too academic for me. I nearly bought some vitamin pills. I looked at a display of swimming pools, custom-designed to suit my yard; I did my best to covet a threshing machine; I moved fairly swiftly through the extensive exhibit of chemicals that promised to enhance the nutrient values of my poor soil. I did pause, in mute assent, in front of a placard which asked me: DO YOU SUFFER FROM THE LITTLE PAINS USUALLY ASSOCIATED WITH ARTHRITIS? . . .

As each sticky, claustrophobic minute went by, I felt less real, less human, less alive. I thought how curious it was, this crowd. No nation in the world ever put quite such a high value on privacy and space as the United States, and nowhere in the country did people live so far apart, in houses islanded in acres of sequestered green, as here in the Midwest. When Minnesotans got together on Labor Day, they did so with the fervor of people for whom being part of a crowd is a rare holiday luxury. The playgoers were like children playing sardines.

From *Old Glory: An American Voyage*

Alistair Cooke reminds us of the importance of Labor Day in the American calendar:

The real end of the American year is not the thirty-first of December but the old festival of Labor Day. It is the day when the summer is put away, the swimming-trunks squeezed for the last time, the ash-trays in country cottages filled with mouse-seed and rat-paste, the storm-doors hammered into place, the lock turned for the last time on your private world of sun and sand and picnics and the pride of growing children. Labor Day brings you back to the world of schools and offices and radio commentators, to dark nights and the dark horizon of politics.

From *One Man's America*

★

For Russian comic Yakov Smirnoff, that very American celebration of Thanksgiving is the most special day of them all:

Thanksgiving is my favorite American holiday. I really like parades without missiles. (I'll take Bullwinkle over a tank any day!)

Now, when Thanksgiving in America was first explained to me, I said, "Wait, it doesn't make sense. I mean, for every freedom and all the opportunities you have here, the only thing you've got to say is 'thanks'?" It just didn't seem like it was enough.

My parents and I had our first Thanksgiving dinner in a little apartment in New York, and we joined hands and my father said a prayer for good food and our health, and then something happened. Instead of releasing our hands, we couldn't let go. We kept holding on to each other tighter and tighter, as we realized we were together and we were free. Here we were, three grown people looking for a way we could possibly show our appreciation, and we couldn't.

Now I know what it is. It's "thanks."

America. What a country!

From *America on Six Rubles a Day*

4 ★ ★ ★ ★ THE AMERICAN LANDSCAPE

"THE *first thing a foreigner has to take in about America—and it is not something automatically grasped even by all the natives—is the simple size of the place and the often warring variety of life that goes on inside it," Alistair Cooke once observed.*

America is big, eighty times larger than Britain, if you include Alaska. Everything seems bigger in America—and it usually is. The cars, the houses, the vistas. Coke seems to come in three sizes—large, larger, and bucket.

Americans often take for granted the stupendous beauty of the Tetons, the deserts, and Yosemite, which leave many foreigners, especially Europeans, feeling they have come face to face with their maker. In America geography takes the place of history. For Russian novelist Vassily Aksyonov, a drive across America is always an adventure for the mind as well as the senses:

Among the indisputable and unsurpassed fascinations America has to offer is natural beauty. Its variety and state of preservation never cease to amaze us. The hills of Virginia, Kentucky, and Tennessee in their autumn splendor; the Florida shoreline with its businesslike pelicans and mysteriously mincing herons; the green slopes of Vermont and their affinity to the Caucasus and the Carpathians; the monumental ridges of the Rockies; the stately California sequoias and never-ending California beaches; the mirage-like horizons of Arizona; yes, and the Kansas flatlands—the impression is always one of plenty, of superabundance.

We have driven across country twice now, and both times we moved into the heartlands we thought of the pioneers for whom the same journey was tantamount to discovering a new planet. Strange as it may seem, the "new planet" sensation has not yet died out. It is amazing how sparsely populated much of the continent remains, even in the east. Northern Pennsylvania, where for fifty miles at a stretch you will not see a single house, reminded us of parts of Siberia. I would venture to say that America is less densely populated and a good deal less polluted than the Soviet Union, at least than European Russia, the Caucasus, Central Asia, and southern Siberia. Northern Siberia is, of course, almost entirely unpopulated, but the Ukraine (I once drove across it from the southeastern to the north-western tip) has been polluted by chemical plants and heavy industry in a way that exceeds the worst nightmares of Michigan and Massa-chusetts environmentalists.

Closely related to our fascination with America's landscape is a fascination with her open borders. Although I'm afraid Americans will have trouble appreciating the connection, a Soviet gazing at the horizon cannot help feeling how wonderful it is that the spaces are really open and how unusual that no one is watching and he can go in any or all directions, as far as he pleases.

From *In Search of Melancholy Baby*

Britisher John Blundell now works in the States but never ceases to be impressed by the vastness of America:

When I think of America, its sheer size overwhelms me. It takes as long to fly the North Atlantic as it does the USA. Coming from a minuscule country off (not "off of") the European mainland, I strug-gle to make Americans realize the different scale. Australians catch on faster.

From "What About All Those Drug Stores?," in *Reason*, January 1988

And Polish author Leopold Tyrmand observed:

The vastness of this continent makes me think with excessive sympa-thy of the nice, cosy, secure claustrophobia of Europe.

From *Notebooks of a Dilettante*

For Englishman Stephen Pern, who spent six months trekking 2,500 miles along the Continental Divide from Mexico to Canada, the absence of history in the American landscape at times caused him some distress:

Coming off the ridge on May 30th I lost fifteen hundred feet in altitude and was back into the sage brush once more. By midday I'd reached route #66, striking the highway at a straggle of motels and gas stations actually called Continental Divide. The place looked like a gauntlet of hitchhikers, each with some gimmick in winking neon to persuade the traffic to stop; electric punctuation on a landscape which itself was wordless.

There were times, here in the New World, when I felt despairingly European. I needed the comforts of history, the muddled adaptations of ancient landscapes. I wearied of relentless utility. For a moment, crossing the motorway bridge, I became a Celt on a hill top. I understood why, when the Romans left Britain, their wonderful roads were ignored. Roman roads were simply objects, vehicles in themselves. But tribal paths aren't like that. They don't have fixed widths, they allow you to stray, they evolve with the people who use them. And this disconcerted me about America: religions, diets, whatever you like—people were forever jumping into vehicles and driving off at high speed. Life here was first established, then lived. Back home it was the other way around.

From *The Great Divide*

Britisher Alistair Cooke finds in the rugged New England countryside one of America's most unhospitable landscapes:

There is a British delusion that you have to go South or West in America to see anything resembling a beautiful landscape. The North-east and the Midwest, these travelers say, are a dull and poverty-stricken thing. This is not a prejudice, for it is an observation made on the spot. But the reason it is so often made must be that most Englishmen who contrive to come here at all—on something called "business"—do so usually in winter. And it must be said that there is surely no landscape known to temperate man that is so shorn and blighted by the coming on of winter.

Most of New England is glacial country and is, geologically speaking, a rocky shambles made by an ice-sheet that ground its massive way eastwards, ripped off the tops of hills and scattered a hailstorm of stones and boulders in all the lowlands. It also smeared some places with layers of good soil. But the only crop you can absolutely depend on anywhere through New England and along the North Atlantic coastal plain is a crop of stones. So, although New England is God's garden to a native (unless he happens to be a farmer), to an Englishman it is pretty rough ground. I remember one Briton who lived here moodily for years until he found the source of his homesickness: "There isn't a field you can lie down in," he said. This may sound very fussy but when you consider that the grass-pack of the pasture regions of Iowa and Minnesota is the pride of the United States, and that it is still only about one third as tight and luscious as the grass-pack of southern England, it is easy to see why southern Englishmen can seem so snooty when real-estate men confront them with a "rural paradise" in Connecticut.

The North Atlantic coastal plain suffers in the same way from having had its face ground down by that old continental ice-sheet. Then it has been bruised by industry. This all sounds very forlorn. But there is enough forest still to smother and glorify the land from spring through the autumn. Then we run into our regular blight—a winter keen and cold that blasts the land and withers it. And it is from mid-November on through March that we can appreciate, if we weren't born here, the remarks of a Californian who said that if the United States had been settled from the Pacific Coast eastwards, New England would still be undiscovered.

From *One Man's America*

★

When Alexander Chancellor visited Chesapeake Bay on assignment for the British magazine The Spectator, *he found himself particularly fascinated by the crabbing there:*

The Potomac River flows from Washington out into Chesapeake Bay, a huge stretch of water, 140 miles long, which is rich in oysters and crabs. Most of the people living on its shores supplement their incomes by catching the creatures. I was there last weekend and learnt a rather disgusting fact. The most popular bait used for catching crabs is bulls' lips. The bulls' lips are exported to Maryland from the slaughter-houses of Texas, a by-product of the meat industry. The crabs think them irresistible and, because of their rubbery texture, find them easy to cling on to. But how anybody ever had the idea that they would make good bait is a mystery to which I could not find an answer.

From *The Spectator*, May 23, 1987

In the nineteenth century, when the wonders of the West were not readily accessible, Niagara Falls was the supreme natural wonder that was required viewing for foreign visitors to America. Nigel Nicolson, on his 1986 visit, found the sight still impressive:

The first surprise is that the Falls should be there at all. One expects cascades in rugged, desolate country where millions of gallons of water suddenly erupt down a sheer mountain side. Ontario and New York in this region are dead flat, heavily populated and loaded with factories, convention-halls, and generating stations. Down the centre of all this flatness is a gorge, and at the top of the gorge are the Falls. Of course, they haven't been there very long on the geological scale of time, about ten thousand years, and won't be there much longer, since all cascades, as you know, self-destruct. The rate of erosion is two feet a year. Eventually Lake Erie will slide uninterestingly into Lake Ontario.

Still, while it lasts, it is a phenomenon well worth seeing, if only because Niagara is America's Stratford—you have to go there at least once in a lifetime, preferably on your honeymoon. We had a honeymoon couple in our group of twelve, who walked about nervously hand-in-handas if they expected to drown and preferred to drown linked together. Our guide, Tony, an elderly man slightly hard of hearing but never short of speech, reeled off the statistics, for this is a very statistical place, but I'll give you one of my own calculations. The two Sissinghurst lakes containing a million gallons would disappear over Niagara in 0.75 of a second.

From *Two Roads to Dodge City*

★

In 1979 the British author Jonathan Raban made a trip in a sixteen-foot boat down the Mississippi River from Minneapolis to New Orleans. Since his boyhood reading of Huckleberry Finn, *the Mississippi for him had belonged more to myth than geography:*

It is as big and depthless as the sky itself. You can see the curve of the earth on its surface as it stretches away for miles to the far shore. Sunset has turned the water to the color of unripe peaches. There's no wind. Sandbars and wooded islands stand on their exact reflections. The only signs of movement on the water are the lightly scratched lines which run in parallel across it like the scores of a diamond on a windowpane. In the middle distance, the river smokes with toppling pillars of mist which soften the light so that one can almost reach out and take in handfuls of that thickened air. . . .

It is called the Mississippi, but it is more an imaginary river than a real one. I had first read *Huckleberry Finn* when I was seven. The picture on its cover, crudely drawn and colored, supplied me with the raw material for an exquisite and recurrent daydream. It showed a boy alone, his face prematurely wizened with experience. (The artist hadn't risked his hand with the difficulties of bringing off a lifelike Nigger Jim.) The sheet of water on which he drifted was immense, an enameled pool of lapis lazuli. Smoke from a half-hidden steamboat hung over an island of Gothic conifers. Cut loose from the world, chewing on his corncob pipe, the boy was blissfully lost in this stillwater paradise.

For days I lay stretched out on the floor of my attic room, trying to bring the river to life from its code of print. It was tough going. Often I found Huck's American dialect as impenetrable as Latin, but even in the most difficult bits I was kept at it by the persistent wink and glimmer of the river. I was living inside the book. . . .

I found the Mississippi in the family atlas. It was a great ink-stained Victorian book, almost as big as I was. . . . I looked at the Mississippi, wriggling down the middle of the page, and liked the funny names of the places it passed through. Just the sounds of Minneapolis . . . Dubuque . . . Hannibal . . . St. Louis . . . Cairo . . . Memphis . . . Natchez . . . Baton Rouge . . . struck a legendary and heroic note to my ear. . . .

The Mississippi was my best invention; a dream that was always there, like a big friendly room with an open door into which I could wander at will. Once inside it, I was at home. I let the river grow around me until the world consisted of nothing except me and that great comforting gulf of water where catfish rootled and wild fruit hung from the trees on the towhead islands. The river was completely still as the distant shore went inching by. I felt my skin burn in the sun. I smelled sawn timber and blackberries and persimmons. I didn't dare move a muscle for fear of waking from the dream.

From *Old Glory: An American Voyage*

Now a professor of American literature at a big Midwestern university, Egyptian-born Ihab Hassan arrived in America on a Liberty ship, steaming up the Mississippi River to New Orleans through a landscape of mythic proportions.

At last one morning the ship rounded Key West. A long night after, it began to glide through the Mississippi Delta. As a schoolchild, I had learned that the Nile was the longest, stateliest river, the great artery of history. . . . The Mississippi ranked only third in length. Yet sliding through the bayou in that strange dawn, the air thick, the horizon still clotted with darkness, I sensed hidden luxuriance and menace. Everywhere a nameless vegetation threatened to clog the channels and ensnare the ship which slipped through like a huge sea snail. The air was humid as I had never known it in Egypt, the sky low. I had not sailed farther up the Nile than Abu Simbel, and so never felt the wild pulse of Africa. Yet knowing Conrad, I now imagined myself, like Marlowe, pushing into the heart of darkness. Blacks began to appear in curious skiffs around [our ship]. And how odd! These blacks spoke English, a kind of English, wore European trousers, shirts, hats.

I had entered America, it seemed, from its secret, gloomy underside, not like Columbus or "stout Cortez." Yes, I had read the boys' books, *Deerslayer, Tom Sawyer,* but had never really believed that modern America could be anything but a romance of Europe, El Dorado civilized. I felt now, exhilaration contending with dread, that I had come to a land more extravagant than any of my recent dreams. A country younger than Egypt but also older, claiming the precedence of a primeval jungle over the most archaic temple. Here I was on my own at last. But what awaited me at the end of this swampy river? Liberty—or some immane power, without bounds or name?

From *Out of Egypt*

★

Liu Zongren is a Chinese editor of an English-language magazine who spent two years in the early eighties as a student in Chicago. He took one vacation on a farm in Missouri. To get there, he rode a bus through the Midwestern heartland and was impressed by the sharp contrast between the American farm culture and that of his native China:

What struck me most during the many hours that followed was the vastness of this land. China has a population five times that of the United States, while the United States has five times the amount of China's arable land. Eighty percent of the Chinese people live in the countryside, struggling to produce enough food to satisfy a billion people. Less than four percent of the American people live on farms. All the way from Chicago to Marshall, across the states of Illinois and Missouri, I saw no one actually working in the fields. This was the month of August, the time when one would see Chinese peasants working their hardest in the fields, hoeing corn and weeding rice.

In the heartland of America, farmers have replaced manual labor with machines, crop rotation, fertilizers, herbicides, and pesticides. I did see an airplane in the sky spraying bean fields with some kind of pesticide. I also saw isolated farmhouses dozens of miles from one another sitting in the middle of huge lawns. On the northern China plains, one never sees isolated farmhouses; villages of several dozen families are the rule. The Chinese government, of course, encourages peasants to produce as much food as possible on every foot of available land. The U.S. government, on the other hand, pays the American farmer not to grow crops in order to maintain higher market prices. I saw large stretches of land that were left fallow, growing only wild grass. The abundant natural resources give people wealth and spare them a lot of worry. "The United States is God's country," as Americans like to say.

From *Two Years in the Melting Pot*

★

Polish writer Malgorzata Niezabitowska traveled across America with her husband and eight-year-old daughter in the summer of 1986, on assignment for National Geographic *magazine. She too was impressed with the American breadbasket and spent several days on a farm in Iowa:*

We came upon a farm set among the rolling hills of Iowa, which reminded us of our favorite vacation spot, a rural homestead in eastern Poland. And Curtis Petersen, the farm's owner, told us what we had often heard from Polish peasants: "Work, work, work. Seven days a week, all year round."

The similarities ended there. On his 320-acre farm Curtis has more tractors and agricultural equipment than several Polish villages put together. But when showing them to us, he said, "What we have here seems small to many farmers."

On the farm there are also several riding horses and ponies used solely for riding. In Poland, where over two million horses work on private farms, no one uses horses for recreation. Polish farmers consider horseback riding an aristocratic pastime.

Fresh cow's milk and the cheese and butter produced from it are the symbols of the Polish countryside. But the Petersens buy their dairy products at the supermarket. They raise only beef cattle, and even if they had dairy cows they wouldn't drink the milk because "it's not pasteurized." But what surprised us even more was Curtis's statement, "The government pays us not to raise a crop." He spent the next several hours trying to explain to Poles, accustomed to food shortages and ever rising prices, the problems of over-production and low prices. . . .

Curtis cannot imagine giving up this land, where he was born 43 years ago. What is even worse, he worries that none of his sons will be able to take over the farm, as he took it over from his father.

The Petersens have three sons: Trent, four; Justin, six; and Aaron, twelve. All three help out on the farm. Aaron had been listening to our conversation. At one point he suddenly walked up to his father and gravely said, "I'll stay here, Dad. I'm not going to leave. I promise you."

From *National Geographic,* January 1988

Trevor Fishlock, the New York correspondent for The Times *of London, journeyed across the vast distances of Texas on assignment and began his report with these observations:*

When Alaska achieved statehood Texas did not for a moment surrender its historic place in the grammar of American language and braggadocio: big, bigger, biggest, Texan. Texans argue that while Alaska is twice as large in terms of crude bulk it is Texas that remains, in more significant ways, powerful, grand and pre-eminent, the basic American metaphor for size, grossness, power, wealth, ambition, high-rolling, and boasting: in a word, Texanic.

Texas is a great geographic, geological and human confluence. Its configuration, roughly that of a horn of plenty, is celebrated in Texas-shaped bathmats, fruitcakes, ice cubes, keyrings, buckles, spectacle frames, stationery, jewelry, and soap. It is the dominant state of the main body of the United States. Covering 267,338 square miles, it is larger than France, larger than Spain, more than twice the area of Italy, nearly three times larger than Britain. The 800-mile length of Texas is the same distance as that between London and the Faeroes, and between Paris and Naples. The state is almost as broad as it is long and the people talk of being on Texas Standard time.

Texans believe themselves to be both the distillers and guardians of the holy American stuff, the mystical, original raw spirit they fear has vanished in other sucked-out parts of the country—a keen devotion to the rumbustious, vigorous and unhindered pursuit of wealth. Isn't this, they ask, what America is for? Does not freewheeling capitalism constitute freedom's fortress? Isn't this what American democracy and ideas of liberty are predicated on?

From *The State of America*

Englishman Adam Nicolson visited the Navajo and Hopi Indian reservations in northern Arizona and ended up at the ancient village of Walpi, perhaps the oldest continuously inhabited site in America:

We drove through the incredible country of the Navajo Reservation. This must be one of the most beautiful places on earth. The mesas stand out on the horizon, sharp-edged or whale-backed. The colours are all smoked, the grassy plateau lifts and drops in billows. Now and then there is an Indian hogan, usually surrounded by the wrecks of a couple of cars, one of them helplessly upside down like a beetle. I tried to persuade Olivia that this sort of undividedness, with all its invitations to the horizon, was the best landscape there was. She didn't agree. She liked fields, organisation, interruptedness, detail. . . .

We drove up on to the first mesa in the Hopi Reservation. After the Pueblo Revolt in 1680, the Hopi took their villages up on to the defensible mesas and there they are today. Notices warned visitors not to behave badly. Our guidebook told us not to go into people's houses without knocking and not to pick at the jewellery that the Hopi might be wearing nor to ask how much they would sell it for, as this would be rude. God knows what white people must have done here in the past. The village of Walpi is built on the end of a finger of rock, cliffed on either side and with long, protective views to north and south across the grasslands. It has a stronger sense of place and permanence than any white settlement in America. It is the only village I have seen where the houses touch each other. They are packed together like boxes in a warehouse, with a dusty lane leading in and out between them. The twin tree-poles of ladders stuck out through the roofs of the hidden kivas. Olivia said she hated doing this to a place, hated looking in on somewhere that had its arms tightly bound around its chest in a sense of privacy and difference that is almost absent in white America.

From *Two Roads to Dodge City*

For Englishman Geoffrey Wagner, the highlight of this trip west was a visit to Monument Valley on the Navajo Reservation, probably the setting for more Western films than any other locale:

Monument Valley has been described as a sort of Indian Stonehenge. As a giant's chessboard of eroded red and yellow pieces. Not bad, yet not quite. The miracle of the place is the way in which it moves around you, envelops you. The jeep chugs fifteen miles into the savagely scarlet plateau with the only habitation in sight being the occasional hogan, the squat circular Navajo mud house or sand igloo that blends almost imperceptibly into the surrounding terrain. There are a few gnarled trees, remnants of firs clinging to the more sheltered buttes and arches, but the sight that dwarfs any Dali lies in a series of natural stone ramparts, varying from finger spires a thousand feet high to slabby mesas resembling medieval castles. Within these fortress-like lines lie weird stone bridges, such as Spiderweb Arch (under which three Indians picturesquely pose themselves as we pass), totem poles of towering stone, skyscraper structures at whose feet the ruins of prehistoric dwellings cluster. It is all too much.

From *Another America: In Search of Canyons*

The foreign travelers who journeyed through the Rocky Mountains 150 years ago found an American West that subverted their comfortable assumptions about man and his place in the world. When Stephen Pern hiked the entire length of the Continental Divide from Mexico to Canada, he found the mountains to be a profound and sometimes unnerving experience:

It was snowing next morning and took three hours of heavy effort to reach the saddle of Bonito Pass. From there I bailed out, cutting off the next six miles of the Divide by describing another wide curve through the rest of a long afternoon. But by noon the next day—the third from Platoro—I was back above 12,000 feet again, on a summit called Table Mountain.

Strange to say, I began to cry; sometimes the sheer scale of America overwhelmed me.

I sniffed, frowned, and wiped a sleeve across my cheek. I suppose that an American coming to England would do the complete opposite and burst out laughing. I wouldn't blame him—our diddy little fields and tinky-winky hills must look like a model. Scotland is grander, but even there a valley twelve miles long is impressive. Here valleys twelve miles long were sideshows. It wasn't just the size of things continental that hit you, but their extent. You saw whole geographical features from up here—complete mountain ranges, entire drainage systems. You began to see how massive the scale of things really is. You saw weather sweeping in, cloud shadows racing over sage miles below, dappling whole forests, sweeping unhindered across snowbound tundra, the clouds themselves torn on the jagged peaks. And you saw all this in a single glance. No craning your neck or driving on to the next lay-by. All you had to do was stand there and look.

From *The Great Divide*

★

Ever since Teddy Roosevelt declared in 1903 that the Grand Canyon is "the one great sight every American must see," it has been the premiere American natural attraction for foreign visitors as well. Each year millions of tourists arrive at the small village of Grand Canyon to stare off into the awesome gorge below with its monumental buttes and erosion-scarred slopes. One who made the trip was Alistair Cooke:

We walked out onto a terrace, and there it was: the biggest hole on earth, thirteen miles from rim to rim, two miles deep, down a hellish immensity to a trickling river. And a silence as absolute as death. The Grand Canyon of Arizona.

Travel writers usually announce that something is indescribable and then proceed to writhe through inadequate descriptions. I won't be caught in this trap. No matter how many home movies you've seen of it, or colored centerfolds, the thing itself is beyond human experience. . . . If we'd been there the morning Christ was born, it would have looked much the same. We marched a mile or two along the rim and watched the sun go over, and the mile-long shadows shifting across layer after layer of red and purple and yellow mesas the size of cities. And we peered into the immensity and spotted a hawk gliding down there as tiny as a housefly. But no other movement.

In the end it becomes unbearably beautiful, or preposterous, or unreal. And you have to turn away and seek the company of your own kind in an enclosed space—in the restaurant—because otherwise you'd doubt that human beings had yet been created. Maybe the Grand Canyon—along with the exquisite, incomparable Bryce Canyon—was God's main purpose, and once they were done, it was a piddling afterthought to make Adam and Eve and the billions of scattering ants we now call "the human family." Look at the Grand Canyon long enough and you are in danger not so much of total misanthropy as of a fixed, stony indifference to our world and its inhabitants. It simply doesn't matter whether the Chinese or the Russians or the Arabs come out on top. When all the empires are dust, it will be there, with the little hawks and the big buzzards wheeling and gliding to the end of time.

From *The Americans*

5．THE AMERICAN CITYSCAPE

"I SEE *that every city within America is a world within a world," observed Yunona Gogia, a teacher of Russian literature and grammar to seventh- and eighth-graders in the Soviet republic of Georgia, during a 1987 tour of the United States.*

The most pervasive feature of the contemporary American landscape is the city and its attendant structures, the suburbs and the interstate highway system. They offer foreign visitors a complex set of unique experiences and a host of ambiguous details. Does that construction crane looming in the skyline suggest growth or destruction? Americans have abandoned or destroyed so much of what we have built that the processes of growth and destruction appear almost synonymous. Will the City of Tomorrow become the American Junkyard?

For foreign visitors the major concern is often the violence that plagues many of this country's larger cities. The Traveller's Handbook, a British guidebook, offered this advice for independent travelers:

Most people equate America with violence, and it is certainly an aspect of that country that must be lived with, as over 200 million Americans do. The chance of your falling victim to motiveless violence is very small and there's nothing you can do about it anyway. But you can take precautions against robbery; if you want to, or have to, visit ghettos or wander around late at night, carry money and valuables in a money belt but keep enough in your pocket to pacify your attacker. Always lock your hotel room and keep your valuables in the hotel safe. Lock your room when you are in it; you should really ask to see identification before you let anyone into the room, although many people would prefer to take a risk than bring paranoia to these lengths. In fact, it's really much more enjoyable to trust people. Let your European naivete carry you through, as so many of your predecessors have. Don't be afraid to hitchhike or walk through Central Park or talk with strangers, and bear in mind the story I heard recently of a British couple visiting Chicago. As they stepped from their car near the hotel, three armed men approached and demanded money. "Don't be ridiculous, we're British!" said the wife. The men put away their guns and walked away.

New York: It's a Helluva Town

"The galling fact is that New York demands tribute in some form," a writer in the British paper, Daily Telegraph, *observed. "It is the yardstick, the essential unkind testing ground for talent, acumen, power, the place to which people stream to invent and prove themselves."*

What emerges from travelers' accounts and observations is a portrait of brashness and energy, a city that ought not to work but somehow and exuberantly does. More than any other American city, New York lends itself to visceral images and metaphors as shortcuts to coming to grips with its reality, as the following suggests:

New York—the nation's thyroid gland.

> Christopher Morley, British author, quoted
> in the *New York Times*, March 2, 1970

New York, home of the vivisectors of the mind, and of the mentally vivisected still to be reassembled, of those who live intact, habitually wondering about their states of sanity, and home of those whose minds have been dead, bearing the scars of resurrection. . . .

> British novelist Muriel Stark, in *The Hothouse by the East River*

★

A hundred times have I thought: New York a catastrophe, and fifty times: it is a beautiful catastrophe.

Le Corbusier, French architect, in *When the Cathedrals Were White*

★

"New York is like a snazzy broad who fusses with her hair but forgets to wipe her ass." Such was the view of the Russian musician who showed us the city during our first week in America. "And, unfortunately, we émigrés inhabit her nether regions."

"Surely a bit of art-for-art's-sake overstatement on your part, eh, Vova?"

"More like art-for-art's-sake understatement, I'm afraid. Feast your eyes on the skyline—fantastic, isn't it? Now look down at the street. All the bumps, pits, and puddles. Add a couple of pigs and you've got a village as rude as Gogol's Ukrainian backwater. And you don't need to look far for pigs, either. Take that gentleman over there. A model swine, don't you think?"

One of the strongest impressions in that first week. Scene: Madison Avenue, a place where svelte, six-foot models alighting from limousines are as common as long queues of squat old crones armed with net shopping bags in Moscow. A pasty-faced gentleman steps up to a large cracked pot with a withered flower in it, undoes his fly, hauls out his equipment, does his business, tucks his equipment back in, and totters merrily on his way.

"Hm. See what you mean, Vova. . . ."

"And doesn't a taxi ride down Seventh bring back the mud paths of Ryazan you wrote about in *Surplussed Barrelware?* Though in Ryazan you didn't have to put up with noxious fumes. And those steam clouds of unknown provenance rising up from the cracks in the asphalt a few feet from Tiffany's jewels. And the filth! Not even Fifth Avenue can be hosed down to decency, and you don't see anybody taking a scrub brush to it."

"Then why do you live here, Vova? You've been all over since you emigrated—Paris, Jerusalem, London, Berlin, Rome. Why here?"

"Because New York's the only place you *can* live," said our fastidious friend. "Why do you think I went to all those other places? To

make sure I'd come to the right one. Now I know: New York is it."
He paused a second and added: "New York or Moscow."

And then, after another pause: "Though there's no going back. . . ."

Russian novelist Vassily Aksyonov, from
In Search of Melancholy Baby

★

*"We did not come to the USA to look for measure, but to look for conviction
and enthusiasm," Le Corbusier declared. "Our European wearinesses require
a tonic." The celebrated French architect found it in the Brooklyn Bridge,
which symbolized for him much of what he admired about American culture:*

One fresh November morning—Indian summer prolongs the fine,
sunny days up to the threshold of the new year—I had myself driven
to the far end of the Brooklyn Bridge, on the left bank of the East
River, and I returned to Manhattan on foot, over the bridge. It is a
long distance on the foot walk and you are surrounded and dominated by the lanes for elevateds and cars. The sky before you bristles
with the skyscrapers of Wall Street; they are rose-colored, gay, in the
maritime sky. They are shaggy, crowned with gold or debatable
architectural ornament. A violent feeling takes hold of you; the feeling
of unanimity. There should be sensations of contriteness, of troubled
judgment and taste, reservations, doubt, cacophony. But no! There is
a dominating force: unity; a subjugating element: magnitude. . . .

Brooklyn Bridge, which is old (elevateds, cars, trucks, pedestrians all
have special lanes), is as strong and rugged as a gladiator. . . . In this
case the two large Gothic towers of stone are very handsome because
they are *American* and not "Beaux-Arts." They are full of native sap and
hey are not graceful, but strong. The vertical cables are black and not
silver, but in perspective their vertical fall fixes a spidery veil. It is an
imposing architectural sensation; vertical, slender, immense, yes, I come
back to the immense and like a barbarian I enjoy it, or better, as a man
animated by a constructive spirit, active but wearied by the depressing
atmosphere of cowardice and abdication in Paris, crushed, often dishon-
ored, treated as a madman and Utopian, consigned to the Greek calends,
etc. . . . here I find reality. And it brings me a profound satisfaction.

Reality, that is the lesson of America. It gives our boldest specula-
tion the certainty of imminent birth.

From *When the Cathedrals Were White*

The British novelist T. H. White visited New York a few months before his death in 1964 and recorded the following observations in his journal:

The two things that appealed most to me about New York were the Queensborough Bridge and the comicality of the skyscrapers. The bridge, with its traffic as ceaseless as hell, was the sort of Colossus which Gustave Doré might have imagined—London Bridge in a way, but with elephantiasis, an enormity of grandeur, of sheer size that could not fail to be impressive. You expected to see King Kong swinging about among the girders.

The skyscrapers . . . were more than huge building blocks to overhang and terrify you. They had taken pains to be cheerful or individual or artistic and, what is more, their owners had been willing to spend money on the decoration. The only part of a skyscraper that can afford to be different from its neighbors is its top. The rest has to be utilitarian. So the tops have a gaiety of their own. I can't help thinking that it is a good thing when even businessmen are ready to acknowledge beauty, whatever their idea of it may be, by ornamenting their structures with gargoyles that must weigh hundreds of tons and cost thousands of dollars. "Look at me," said one sky-scraper, "pretending to be something to do with Santa Sofia." "Or me," says another, "I am Gothic, as you can see by my perpendicular arches." In a way it is a funny charade, like a lot of huge square ladies trying on Paris hats. My favorite one—and you do get to have favorites—had an airy gilt crown . . . which she illuminated at night, coquettishly.

From *America at Last*

Russian comedian Yakov Smirnoff came to America in 1977 and settled in New York. Later he penned this account of his search for an apartment:

When my parents and I came to New York, getting a nice, large apartment was a big priority. Now, if any of you reading this are also trying to get settled in the Big Apple, let me give you some advice. If you don't speak the language, save yourself some time and take along an interpreter. The problem I ran into was that I couldn't speak any English, and to make matters worse, I didn't realize that most of the apartment managers in New York City speak only Spanish. There I was, trying to ask if there were any apartments available, and all they kept answering was, *"No comprende! No comprende!"* Finally, I figured out that *no comprende* must be the English words for "no apartment." So at the next building I went to I said, *"Comprende?"* and the manager said, "We don't rent to Puerto Ricans."

From *America on Six Rubles a Day*

Polish dramatist Janusz Glowacki set his 1987 play Hunting Cockroaches *in a Lower East Side Manhattan apartment. The lead characters are Anka and Jan, both recently arrived from Poland, who have this exchange in the first act:*

JAN: I told you, always close the windows before you go out.
ANKA: I came back and there was this pigeon sitting on this table pecking at a potato. I went over to it, the pigeon looked directly at me, spread its wings, opened its beak and hissed.
JAN: Hissed? You mean, cooed?
ANKA: Not cooed, hissed. Then he raised one of its legs with claws on it. . . .
JAN: Claws?
ANKA: Claws. It tried to peck my eyes out.
JAN: *(In despair, without the will to resist.)* Oh, my God.
ANKA: I got scared. And then the pigeon stopped picking at the potato and slowly hopped over to the window. But you know, I understand that pigeon. It has to be like that. It wouldn't survive otherwise. And I wanted to tell you that everybody's got to behave like that pigeon. Scientists have proved that New York babies are born with thicker eardrums, smaller lungs, and more hair in their noses than the average Colorado baby. So as to muffle the sound and inhale less air. You see, they naturally acquire an anti-pollution defense system. They grow more hair in their noses, the windpipe through which the hair goes to their lungs get shorter, their skin becomes thicker and their nails harder. That's what the latest research has shown.

★

For Trevor Fishlock, the New York correspondent for The Times *of London, former mayor Edward Koch symbolizes much of the essence of modern New York:*

The mayor is a metaphor for New York, abrasive, fast-talking and ornery. He is Jewish, like two million—more than a quarter—of the city's people, and his life has been a classic American dream progress. Born in the Bronx, the son of Polish Jewish immigrants, he knew hard times in the Depression, worked in a shop to pay his way through law school, entered politics, became a congressman and, in 1977, won the top job in American municipal government. He was elected to a third four-year term in 1985 and said he wanted to be mayor forever. He once remarked that God had a hand in getting him the job and a rabbi rebuked him for such presumption. . . .

Americans like a boss figure, a modern wagon train leader, to run their towns. They want to feel led, to have a focus, and they prefer to deal with and grumble about a person rather than an anonymous council; and many American mayors have wide powers and responsibilities. Mayor Koch's assertiveness, candour, chutzpah, and big mouth often rub the wrong way, but New Yorkers on the whole approve of these qualities. They would not want a mouse for mayor. He is the sort of person many New Yorkers think they are, or what they think they ought to be: abrasive, street-smart, confrontationist and . . . quick on the draw with a stinging retort. New Yorkers love repartee. A friend of mine was sitting in a bar when a glamorous model walked in. "Hey," he nudged his companion, "that's Christie Brinkley." "So what?" said the man, refusing to turn his head. "She ain't gonna screw any of us."

From *The State of America*

★

After ten years as a journalist with the Manchester Guardian, *Britisher Geoffrey Moorhouse struck out on his own and wrote a dozen books. His travel books, in particular, have won him international acclaim. The* Imperial City, *his book on New York, appeared in 1988 to rave reviews. At the end he summed up the city in the following terms:*

[New York] is a city of powerful urges, such frantic endeavors, such enormous determination, such insatiable appetites, that it dominates any natural rivalry more than is perhaps healthy for anyone; but that has always been the way of the world, as an Englishman should know as well as anyone, and better than most. London, the old imperial capital, appears to be suffering from pernicious anemia now, to anyone who commutes between the two. All human life is here these days, not there or anywhere else in the Western world: which means that New York can be disgusting, frightening, maddening, cruel. It also means that New York can be uplifting, exciting, enchanting, warm.

It is most noticeably, perhaps, a city of boundless energy, and in this too it is without rivals in the West. New Yorkers can be as indolent as anyone when working for someone else unless the whip is cracked. But whatever they are doing on their own account, they give it everything they've got. It is as though they understand a great and universal truth more clearly than the rest of us and have conditioned themselves to abide by it. The truth can be expressed in many ways, but the neatest, the most New Yorkish way of putting it, has lately been visible in a shop window on Fifth Avenue, corner of 42nd Street. The shop specializes in T-shirts bearing slogans across the chest, which are meant to catch the eye and give people a laugh, more often than not. One, however, is nothing less than a serious reminder of mortality and a call to renewed vigor while the opportunity is still there.

"Life," it says, "is not a dress rehearsal."

The Suburbs

Visitors from Russia and Eastern Europe often have been fascinated by the large suburbs on the outskirts of the big cities of the East Coast. Russian novelist Vassily Aksyonov and Polish author Leopold Tyrmand are two in particular who observed closely life in the suburbs. First, Aksyonov:

Once we went up to Sarah Lawrence College in Bronxville, just outside of New York, for a concert of Russian chamber music. The half-hour ride from Grand Central Station deserves a few lines.

After rumbling through endless tunnels, the train surfaced amid the ruins of Stalingrad, also known as the South Bronx. Picture gaping windows of burned-out—or was it bombed-out?—buildings, deserted streets overrun with weeds, an alleycat crossing a dump (I shudder to think of the life it leads), here and there a decrepit hole in the wall with a crooked COLD BEER sign hanging over the door, and a bunch of multiracial down-and-outers hanging out in front—perfect illustrations for the most vehement anti-American propaganda sheet. Picture a Soviet who has never believed a word of that propaganda set down by some miracle in the middle of the South Bronx and told, "Welcome to America!" The first thing he would do is cover his eyes and moan, "So *they* weren't lying. It really is the way *they* say it is."

Don't worry. *They* were lying. Stay on the train a few more minutes and you'll come to Bronxville, the real America of neat little towns, well-stocked gas stations and supermarkets, spacious shopping centers, and white clapboard houses. America's prosperity becomes apparent the moment you leave her large cities. In Russia the opposite is the case. What remains after the military has drained off most of the resources goes toward maintaining a minimal level of decency in the cities; the countryside and villages are left to rot.

From *In Search of Melancholy Baby*

To escape the noise and lack of privacy of a big-city dwelling, American genius created suburbia—which became but one more proof that the incapability of escaping is inherent in the human condition. A single lawn mower has the noise power of ten neighborhood cocktail parties.

Leopold Tyrmand, from *Notebooks of a Dilettante*

Boston

For almost 150 years Boston has been a favorite with British travelers, who have appreciated its culture, history, and intellectual distinctions. Iain Finlayson covered the Fourth of July festivities of 1988 while in Boston on assignment for the Illustrated London News:

The Fourth of July, if you happen to be a Brit in Boston on that date, is a profoundly embarrassing anniversary. It felt like a nice day for a lynching as we were mustered like a gang of reprobates under the balcony of the State House. The Declaration of Independence was being read out in a ceremonial voice to a crowd of attentive New England patriots, the historic grievances declaimed a mite too vividly for perfect Brit composure. To hear the litany of complaint (much of it perfectly justified) was unnerving—yet another country, one felt, where the British are not much loved. Maybe, finally, we have been forgiven but, once a year at least, our sins are not forgotten. . . .

But I feel at home in Boston anyway. It is my soul-city. I love it, I think, because it appears to combine a history of austere, aristocratic, neo-Athenian intellectual grandeur with an underside of frankly opportunistic, blunt, bare-knuckled brio. It is a place that combines the gilt artifice and cynicism of Edinburgh with the pugnacious verve of Glasgow. Boston is a city of commerce and the arts, finance and philanthropy, high-tech industry and deeply held traditions.

It is a sophisticated, prosperous, picturesque, glamorous city, less hard-edged (but more hard-headed) than New York and less laid back than San Francisco. It easily embraces a diversity of ethnic communities—from the Italians in pretty North End where they celebrate come-one-come-all Saints' Days in the streets, to the blacks, the Vietnamese, the Chinese, and the Irish. The founding families of Boston are still ensconced in the elegant Georgian town houses of Beacon Hill, still fighting ruthless battles to preserve their cobbled streets and window panes of violet glass. The aspiring liberal middle class inhabit elegant apartments in Back Bay, which is buttressed by Brooks Brothers and Bendels for consumer security. The younger yuppies are discovering South End and a constant pounding of hammers sounds out the inexorable [advance] of gentrification.

The chic centre is Faneuil Hall and Quincy Market, a glamorous open-air market bursting with sportswear shops, restaurants, wine bars, flower shops and food stores. It is almost exactly the equivalent of—and was the inspiration for—London's Covent Garden development.

From Quincy, it is a short step to the waterfront where palatial new hotels, expensive condominiums and pedestrian precincts spring up like asparagus in May. Boston, increasingly, has all the hard, glittery elegance of the very rich. To its credit, beautiful 19th-century facades are often incorporated into the modern architecture that springs up around it.

Boston and New England are conscious of tradition and heritage to a degree perhaps not found elsewhere in the States. The general feeling is that New England symbolises Origins and that it is the curator of a national heritage that should be preserved. England is not like Florida or California—roots here go deep, and there are fewer incomers than in the south or west.

From "New England Roots," in the *Illustrated London News,*
September 1988

Cincinnati

In 1832 British author Frances Trollope published her Domestic Manners of the Americans, *perhaps the most controversial travel book on this country ever to appear. It recounted in graphic detail her stay of twenty-five months in Cincinnati, then the largest city in the northwestern American frontier. Mrs. Trollope proved to be a shrewd, if prejudiced, observer with a style laced throughout with an acid wit. "I do not like Americans," she confessed. "I do not like their principles. I do not like their manners. I do not like their opinions."*

In 1986 Nigel Nicolson paid a visit to Cincinnati, which because of the Trollope book, has continued to enjoy a certain notoriety among the British people even to this day. He found himself pleasantly surprised:

Cincinnati ought to have a beautiful riverfront, but hasn't. The Ohio is historically more important than the Mississippi, for it was downstream from Pittsburgh to Cincinnati and Louisville that the great tide of pioneers flowed until the railways were built, and it is lovelier. Jefferson described the Ohio as "the most beautiful river on earth." (That he never set eyes on it did not diminish his enthusiasm.) ... But Cincinnati turns its back on the river, and its five bridges are in different ways ugly. Its beauty lies within it. This was the place where Frances Trollope spent many unhappy months and wrote of it insultingly. But today no other American city is so civic nor so civil. There is no great pressure of traffic in the centre, for the expressways divert it. There are open spaces like Fountain Square where you can stroll and sit; and, best of all, pedestrian ways on several levels from building to building and by bridges across intervening streets. I've never seen anything like it. It's as if you could walk the length of Bond Street without ever emerging into the open air, passing through office lobbies, department stores and restaurants in an unbroken chain. The shops are luxurious, the cafes set out like those in the great piazza of Venice, but indoors.

From *Two Roads to Dodge City*

Chicago

Polish author Leopold Tyrmand found this major Midwestern metropolis to be one of his favorite American cities:

New York is opulence, decadence, and culture. The southwest is grandeur, space, and future. California is wealth, epicureanism, and luxuriance. Chicago is strength. Dark strength and real power. Here in Illinois I first understood exactly why the Confederacy was doomed to lose the Civil War. The reasons are still visible and perceptible a hundred years later.

This is America as Europeans of my generation imagined it to be. A genuine American urban landscape, an immense wilderness of fire escapes, engraved deeply in our memories during the Twenties. Tough, filthy, and great. One can imagine the merciless and heroic struggles when this city was the prize. It must be the only place where all that happened here in the Twenties *could* have happened. . . . Chicagoans do not like any mention of the Twenties; they consider this period shameful. They are wrong. What actually counts is the impact of a legend; its moral background or implications are secondary. No matter if Chicagoans wish it or not, their city remains a symbol of the bloody facts of the Twenties. And it would be better to turn that legend into a cultural value, taking care not to slip into the opposite extreme of pride. Such pride would be more shameful than today's ambiguous discretion; shops would stock Al Capone skull-ashtrays.

From *Notebooks of a Dilettante*

Liu Zongren, editor of an English-language magazine published in Beijing, China, spent two years on a fellowship at a university in Chicago. Several of his most vivid experiences involved encounters with street crime:

Shortly after I moved, I learned my first lesson about what it means to live in the city with the third highest crime rate in the United States. At four o'clock one afternoon, Zhao took a bag of garbage out the back door. No sooner had he dropped the bag in the trash bin than a black youth of about fifteen years of age came up and grabbed him, demanding money. Zhao was scared. He had heard others talking about people being stopped on the street for money, but he had never had a problem himself and never thought anything would happen in daytime. Zhao took out his wallet, thinking two or three dollars might pacify the young man. But the youth snatched the whole wallet and ran off.

Zhao, pausing in astonishment, ran after him, shouting, "You have the money. Give me back my I.D. cards." Perhaps his English was not clear enough, for the black youth turned and threatened, "One step more and I'll kill you." Zhao stopped short. He understood the young man clearly, even though he could not make out every word. The youth vanished around a corner.

After that incident, two friends visiting us had bags and sweaters snatched at the same spot. We obviously had not learned how to cope with street crime. People advised us not to go to court to identify the criminals because they could get off easily and would then come after any witnesses. So we did not report the incidents to the police. Zhao applied for new I.D. cards.

There was one more crime that we finally had to report. The victim was a Chinese woman who had been in Chicago only two months and was staying in our home temporarily. One afternoon, two of my roommates went with her to the post office, several blocks away. On their way back, two young black men approached them from behind and grabbed the purse the woman was carrying. In her purse were seventy dollars and her passport. She screamed. My two roommates turned around and ran after the youths, shouting, "Stop, thief!" The two purse snatchers disappeared into a housing project.

The day was clear and warm and people were coming and going, but nobody bothered to help. Children playing nearby just watched. My roommates felt indignant and silly at the same time. It was as if they were staging a comedy for an American audience. They now hesitated about whether or not they should go into the project after the thieves. They approached an elderly black man at the entrance to a building and told him what had happened.

"I saw all this," the old man said with sympathy. "You can't find them yourselves. Go and call the police." From his tone of voice, my roommates sensed that he knew who these young blacks were and that the police probably did also. They followed his advice.

Two policemen arrived in a squad car, and after taking a lot of notes, asked my roommates if they could identify the two black youths in court. My friends gave them a definite "no." One policeman smiled knowingly at the other and said to my friends curtly, "We'll do our best. If we find out anything, we'll get in touch with you." They never contacted us. The Chinese woman got a new passport a year later.

In China the government would never permit the mugger of a foreigner to get away so easily. The public security department, from the top down, would make every effort until the culprit was caught and punished. Perhaps the problem in Chicago is that there are so many crimes the police have become indifferent.

From *Two Years in the Melting Pot*

Milwaukee

Ihab Hassan, an Egyptian-born professor of American literature, settled happily in the northern Midwest:

I like this spacious Midwestern city of Milwaukee, except in the reluctant spring. I like its candid cityscape, spare population, fitful lake, forever changing colors from tan to blue-green through a spectrum of fluid shades. I like even its cold climate—let others seek the Sun Belt.

From *Out of Egypt: Scenes and Arguments of an Autobiography*

Miami

Taking up the television message of "Come on down," Trevor Fishlock, the New York correspondent for The Times *of London, visited Miami and began his report with the following observations:*

Searching for words to epitomise the character of his city, the Miamian gazed out of his window at the clamorous and sticky metropolis broiling under the afternoon sun. "Miami . . ." he murmured, drawing on a cigar large enough to have been wielded in self-defense. "Miami . . ." The way he breathed the word through the blue smoke evoked an image of a sultry and slightly dangerous woman. Below us lay the vivid and violent Miamian tumescence, an uncoagulated society of whites, blacks, and Latins, elbowing and tussling on a hot Florida strand between the mangrove swamps and the sea; a city suffused with energy and unashamedly on the make, in the tradition of its thin history. "No place for wimps!" the Miamian exclaimed with a short laugh and a spurt of smoke. "No place for wimps!" And his teeth crunched down over the cigar, like an alligator's over a leg.

Regarding alligators, I was surprised that this descendant of dinosaurs does not appear on the great seal of Florida. Rather than an alligator the seal bears a portrait of a gentle Indian maiden, a representative of the Seminole people slaughtered enthusiastically by settlers and soldiers in the extermination drives of the 1830s and 1840s. But the alligator surely deserves a place. He is not only the chief state beast, but also represents the opportunistic spirit of many of the people who have helped make Florida what it is today: pirates and pimps, land developers and hucksters, drug runners, sly bankers and other lurky saurians who have prospered here by force and wit. The continuing vitality of the commercial spirit was demonstrated in 1985 by a dying Floridian who advertised his willingness to deliver messages to the dead, at $20 [each]. He received many responses.

From *The State of America*

New Orleans

British reporter Zenga Longmore, who happens to be black, visited New Orleans and filed this report for The Spectator:

On a recent visit to New Orleans, I was tickled to see Scarlett O'Haras in full regalia, showing American tourists around plantation mansions, speaking in accents that would shame the most inexperienced RADA student. While tourists gaped at the genuineness of it all, girls wearing long red wigs drawled in nasal tones about the glory of the South. Never mentioning slavery, they referred to the ramshackle slave cabins as the "servants' quarters."

Even the jazz musicians "Oh Lawdied" to the tourists. Sitting in on one of the many jazz clubs in Bourbon Street, listening to thrilling music, my pleasure would be marred by the trombone player stopping in mid-flow to tell the audience: "Dis is how we black folks play down here in li'l ol' N'Orleans. Dis is *genuine* jazz, y'all. Yowza yowza!" The audience of American tourists would feel reassured, glad to be told that the jazz they were listening to was jazz after all.

And yet, withal, the Tennessee Williams romance still thrives in the haze that hangs above the city. The charm of the French Quarter beggars description. Exquisite wrought-iron railings, originally crafted by slaves to buy their freedom, ornament every gate and balcony.

Most houses have courtyards, with illuminated fountains and religious statues. The streets are lined with tropical palms, keeping
company with the roses and ferns which spill over the balconies.
Little mules, decorated with brilliant flowers, gauze and ribbons, pull
dainty carts along the cobbles. The shops are full of jewels, glittering
clothes, and souvenirs. The plush restaurants sell a dazzling display
of crawfish, crabs, jambalayas, gumbos, and Cajun delicacies.

Bourbon Street, the French Quarter's main road, is the most
electrifying place on earth. Music pours out from every club, bar,
strip club, and brothel. Black bands play jazz and down-home blues,
and the white bands, who invariably perform in the posher bars, play
in the grand old Kenny Ball tradition. If you can avoid the hustlers
who drag you into their clubs, it is possible to go jazz window-
shopping. The doors are all wide open, revealing the musicians,
along with the decadence of the bordellos. Waiters dance manically
in the streets to attract customers, twirling trays on balancing
fingers. . . .

The black people were suitably impressed, but the whites viewed
me with suspicion. What was a black woman doing with an English
accent? Was this some kind of villainous trick? There again, I have to
admit the suspicion was mutual. What were *they* doing being so fat? I
hate to sound sizist, but many of the white Southerners were so
obese as to be positively globular. Not that I took offence. What I did
object to was their shouting racial abuse at me. Walking around with
the Englishman I had come to meet, I was constantly accosted by
white men, who demanded, "Whadda ya doin' with white ass? Can't
ya find yourself a black dude?" My reply would be an indignant raise
of the eyebrows.

The clubs were mainly owned by white men, who treated the
musicians like dirt, often shouting vile abuse at them while they
sweated blood to entertain the tourists. I once saw a manager swing
into a table and knock over some customers' drinks. He instantly
turned on the waiter, yelling, "God damn, man, why d'ya leave that
***ing table there! Get the people more drinks, *** you!" The
waiter, a shrivelled black man, padded away obligingly. Maybe slavery is never mentioned because no one realises it has been abolished.

From "All That Jazz," in *The Spectator*, January 31, 1987

Denver

Geoffrey Wagner, a British author spending a year in America teaching courses on the modern novel at a New York City university, traveled to Denver, the gateway to the West:

Denver disappoints. Apart from a small section around the Colorado State Capitol (another of those damn gold-leaf domes), it seems an anonymous city with the usual boringly rectilinear street system common to nearly all American towns. There is no sense of what the French call *quartier* and certainly, in the striking sun, one longs for what the French planted in every second-rate *place*, namely big leafy plane or eucalyptus trees. You don't feel you want to walk about in Denver. But where do you in an American city, outside Boston, San Francisco, and bits of New Orleans? The average [American] city is indeed rigidly anti-pedestrian.

From *Another America: In Search of Canyons*

San Francisco

No American city has so charmed foreign visitors as San Francisco. Polish author Leopold Tyrmand first fell in love with the city during his youthful reading of Jack London:

I have wanted to know this city since my early childhood. San Francisco has the most widespread legend of any American city; its landscape, gold rush, the famous harbor and its pleasures, and Jack London. The last is perhaps the most powerful element of San Francisco's fame. London may be considered a second-rate writer here, yet he did more for America—and contributed more to the timeless American propaganda—than all American nineteenth (with the possible exception of Fenimore Cooper) and twentieth century writers combined. The force with which he ingrained his own dreams and desires in the minds and hearts of several generations has no comparison in American literature; it is an unusual literary achievement to make the names of Golden Gate, Sausalito, Oakland, the property of fourteen-year-old boys around the world. After my arrival, I went to Fisherman's Wharf; there are old ships lying there as museum pieces. My God, what magic Jack London had! It was the recapitulation of my most intimate boyhood. San Francisco Bay, the deck of *Wapama*, an old schooner named *L.A. Thayer*—who strangely a child's dreams fit reality here! It all came back to me at once, the simple combination of words, landscape, and the smell of seafood. . . . How deep Jack London is in all of us with his uncomplicated words of simple emotions and simple glory.

From *Notebooks of a Dilettante*

★

A highlight of British writer Adam Nicolson's 1986 visit to San Francisco was a lesbian basketball game, an event typical of this American city:

I went to a lesbian basketball match last night. . . . The match was between San Francisco and Los Angeles, and the idea was to raise money for the Gay Games to be held here in August. . . . I turned up at the stadium in the Haight district of the city. It was 8 at night and I put on my tweed jacket to look straight. Strictly the observer. Two thousand lesbians were queuing to get in. "Everything is extremely negotiable," I heard across the waiting crowd, but lost the rest of the message in the hubbub. "He's a snotty little yuppy at the moment, but you wait, he's working up to be a pissy queen. . . ." "They have some quite *terrible* diseases over there. . . ." "Did you see that in the papers? Sixty-eight people in the city died of AIDS in March?" And the answer: "Some people just don't know how to behave properly, do they?" I checked this figure this morning: 68 deaths in March, 75 new cases. Almost ten thousand people have died of AIDS in the U.S., over a thousand of them in San Francisco. But that wasn't the tone here at all. No sense of the gay community battening down. This was explosive. "What's the matter, Baby?" a nun with a beard and sparkle all over his eyelids said to me. "Got no date?" "I'm fine, thanks," I said like Lord Hailsham and he walked off, holding his habit out on either side like a spinnaker and saying, "Oooooh, I see." There was something strange in a gathering of two thousand people simply on the basis of their sexual proclivities, but if I hadn't known that was the reason they were there, I couldn't have guessed it. A complete spectrum surrounded me, all the way from snotty yuppy to pissy queen, moving through austere, superior New Yorker nose-lookers, chummy vegetarians, and muscle-bound sports fanatics, bypassing all too ordinary ordinaries like me on the way.

The heart of the evening was the basketball [game] but that was by no means everything. Our hosts were Patrick Toner, Mr. International Leather (distinguished by a sculptured black codpiece), and Sister Boom Boom, who, the rumour went, had recently got married. Toner was overshadowed by Boom Boom. She/he was carried in shoulder-high by four near-naked men. Surrounding her on the platform were several small palm trees to go with the leopardskin coif (is that the word?). "I knew this was a big game," she said, "and so I thought I'd wear my big-game outfit." Cheers from the crowd. Then the Pre-Game Entertainment. The San Francisco Gay Freedom Day Marching Band—nice uniforms, pretty tunes. Then the crowning of the Homecoming Queen, Sister Chanel 2001, in scarlet silk with an oversize crucifix in her hair. Then thanks to the organisers, the Sisters of Perpetual Indulgence, particularly Sister Sadie Sadie the Rabbi Lady, Sister Loganberry Frost, Sister Hysterectoria, Sister Nocturnal Submission, and Sister Krishna Kosher, who had done the lighting. Sister Amazing Grace Cathedral and Sister Salvation Armée then ran up and down the court with brooms, preparing it for the game. More applause and then the National Anthem by the San Francisco Gay Lesbian Chorus. They had already featured quite heavily in the crowning of Sister Chanel 2001. They too were in scarlet silk. . . . The "Star-Spangled Banner" began and to my amazement everybody stood up. *There* is the strength in this country. Even this incredibly marginal and wild crowd stands up and looks serious for the National Anthem, as if they were delegates to a bankers' convention in Kansas City. No wonder rebels feel frustrated here. Then we sat down and Sister Vicious Power Hungry Bitch announced the names of the players.

The game was a steal, as the saying goes. Los Angeles walked it, 106–78. . . . Whenever San Francisco managed to pop one in, the band played a snatch of "Ain't Misbehavin'." At half-time we had a thrilling display of karate by a woman who looked like a colonel in the Green Berets. Everyone sat in awed silence while she destroyed invisible enemies.

From *Two Roads to Dodge City*

Berkeley

Leopold Tyrmand tried without success to penetrate the leftist rigidity of the ideologues who had taken up residence in Berkeley:

Berkeley is full of (in Eastern European eyes) comical Marxist fans or Communist *aficionados* who form a strange school of dialectical idealism, probably under the pressure of the name of the place. One of these guitar-playing hippie First Church disciples said to me, "Communism is a wonderful, noble idea; it is pure and most human in concept. Last of all it can be reduced to the simplest and most beautiful demand that all men should be brothers."

"Maybe that is the trouble with it," I said. "Maybe it would have been wiser to call men to be cousins, at least for the first few years after every revolution. Brothers are more informal with each other and find it easier to kill one another."

From *Notebooks of a Dilettante*

Los Angeles

Generations of foreign visitors have discovered in Southern California a pagan world where science is wedded to superstition, an agreeably temporary paradise, bright, clean, bland, and permissive. For others its impermanence and anonymity, sprawl and sluggishness, and infatuation with cinematic illusions have made the region a kind of hell to be escaped as quickly as possible. Los Angeles is a city that blunts satire because its realities are often stranger than any fiction, as Evelyn Waugh discovered in The Loved One. *British scholar Peter Conrad insightfully summed up the unique attractions of Southern California:*

The psychological history of California is of paradise found, lost, chimerically regained. California caters to the dreams of successive generations of immigrants—gold diggers, chivalric squatters like Robert Louis Stevenson, the impoverished Okies Auden mentions, hippies, surfers, Zen-trained motorcycle-maintenance men. Its business is not only the satisfaction but the manufacture of dreams: Hollywood does the world's dreaming for it. But California is at the same time, as Isherwood says, "a tragic country—like Palestine, like every promised land," because it is strewn with the disappointments of those whose dreams have not come true. Perhaps it successes are even sadder than its failures. Those who do find El Dorado are liable to find that it doesn't content them. Like Watteau's Cythereans, they are sentenced to the misery of surfeit.

From *Imagining America*

133

British author Tom Bethell settled in America, where he writes political commentary for The American Spectator *and other magazines. Of Los Angeles he has observed:*

A persistent myth about America is the belief that its wealth can be attributed to "abundant natural resources." In fact, there is no natural wealth—only elements. Los Angeles illustrates the point. It is reclaimed desert. It was desert until the 19th century, and it would almost certainly still be desert today if it were not part of the United States. Natural resources didn't build Los Angeles, mental resources did: energy and effort, pride and envy, faith and hope. The city is a triumph of mind over matter.

From *The Electric Windmill*

★

"Anne" is a 39-year-old, middle-level Dutch executive from Amsterdam who spent a year in Los Angeles on assignment for her company. She has lived most of her adult life abroad, but finds Los Angeles her favorite American city:

Southern California is so open. Nobody is uptight here. Everyone says "hi." I've had people in wheelchairs, total strangers, start up conversations with me. *They* don't even have complexes! Anything goes here! I've had such marvelous experiences since I came here. Los Angeles is the most wonderfully nutty place I've ever lived. I visited a bra museum—can you believe that?—in Frederick's of Hollywood. I've been to Chippendale's, where men do striptease for women. I attended an opening of a chic disco where even some street derelicts had been invited! I met an author with several bestsellers to his name who was writing a book about breathing, which lots of people will probably buy even though they know it's a bit of a hoax. One of the first places I visited was Forest Lawn Cemetery. I just had to go there. Evelyn Waugh's *The Loved One* is one of my favorite novels. I met there a young man, an apprentice embalmer, straight out of his novel. "What do you like best about your work?" I asked him. "The children," he told me solemnly. "I like the children best of all." God, but we are so hopelessly conservative and constipated in Europe!

My European friends had warned me, "You will find Americans very nice but superficial." But they're not superficial. They really come through. I had a friend from England visiting me recently. He was stuck at my apartment without a car while I was at work. Then he met a man at a party one night. "Do you have a car?" he asked. "No," my friend replied. "Well, I have an extra car," the man insisted. "Borrow mine." And so my friend used his car for the rest of his visit here. That's fantastic! All the time it has been like that. Americans are such civilized people.

Los Angeles is just fabulous. I think one should always come back to Southern California to replenish oneself and see what humanity should be like. This is a different world!

From an interview with the author, June 13, 1988

Spanish director Pedro Almodovar visited Los Angeles after the popular success of his film, Women on the Verge of a Nervous Breakdown, *and later observed at a press conference:*

I knew that even in America life is different from the movies, yet though I was formed by the pop culture in the sixties, I wasn't aware of how it had installed itself in life here. Yes, Los Angeles is littered with bad taste, but I'm not afraid of bad taste. I am excited by it!

Quoted in the *San Diego Union*, January 8, 1989

From British author Adam Nicolson the sheer pleasure of Los Angeles's freeway system was a major discovery during his visit to the city:

"This is the city that is relaxciting," it said on my car radio yesterday. I spent almost the whole of it driving around, feeling marvelously relaxcited. It's the one adjective that bridges that place. I don't quite understand how somewhere can be so sedate and frenetic at the same time, but Los Angeles manages it. The traffic slides along at 35, the eye in the sky on the radio announces snarl-ups on the San Diego Freeway southbound between Rosecrans and Artesia or clogging on Ventura where three large bits of metal are blocking lanes five and six. Everybody slides along undisturbed, enjoying the freedom of their cars. It's famous that Los Angeles is the city designed around the car, but no one says what fun that makes it. Everything fits when you're driving here, everything works. There's no sense of the car being a large unwanted intruder. Traffic is the blood in the veins of this city, endlessly flowing, pumping between the parts. From the plane when I arrived the other day, Los Angeles looked like a hard white rash on the edge of America, with only the clean cut of the Pacific shore and lines of the freeways, snaking between the hills, giving it any shape at all. This is why it's relaxciting here, because everything goes, everything is fluid and easy and you never bump up against a sharp corner. Traffic on rubber wheels—that's the ideal picture of life in southern California, all neuroses ironed out, all awkwardness removed, leaving you with nothing but a seamless fluency of movement, gliding round the clover leaves, an existence made up of one long liquid slide.

From *Two Roads to Dodge City*

Leopold Tyrmand, on the other hand, found Los Angeles's distances intimidating:

How is it possible to conquer a city where even decent sight-seeing is impossible? Just leaving my hotel I feel lost—the distance to the nearest drugstore is the same as between two villages in France. One's helplessness in such vastness is paralyzing. In a car with an attractive girl, I said: "Let's go somewhere out of town," having in mind eventual kissing. "But where?" she asked. "Oh, no matter where . . . ," I smiled, trying to hide my intentions, "where the city ends." "Los Angeles never ends," she said firmly.

From *Notebooks of a Dilettante*

Film celebrities may work in Los Angeles. And they may live there. But many do not love L.A. They complain that it's shallow, snobby, and smoggy; that its temperatures are too high and its culture too low. Worst of all, they start the Academy Awards ceremony before dark. British actor Bob Hoskins (Who Framed Roger Rabbit?) finds himself in exile when having to work in Los Angeles:

The biggest attraction in L.A. is to sit around the swimming pool. I can't stand that. You sit there covered in oil. You try to read but you can't because the pages stick together and when you dive into the pool there's this slick on the water because all the lotion's washed off. I don't have to worry about that in London because no one has a tan.

Quoted in *M*, February 1989

★

Russian comedian Yakov Smirnoff observed:

Russians don't surf. In the Soviet Union "Hang Ten" has a completely different meaning.

From *America on Six Rubles a Day*

★

English author T. H. White was one of those rare individuals who did not enjoy Disneyland:

The enormity of Disney's fantasy, which he has realized, must, cannot but, compel respect. The whole tone is individual unmistakable (you could not mistake Disneyland for anybody else's land) and a solitary homunculus has created it, with all its billions of dollars.

Yet there is something wrong with Disney.

We tried on the way home in the car to put a fair name on it. Why those awful mermaids encountered on the submarine trip? Why were they so saccharine, insipid, dishonest, unworthy, coy? Why was the sea serpent a babyhood dream, not grand or terrible or beautiful or even reptilian? Why was everything just wrong, the galleon unsailable, the whale provided with toy teeth? Why was everything a toy, in fact? Why was everything a *pet?* It seems that to Disney women, animals, children, knights, dragons, and elephants are all pets. Even the mermaids were pet mermaids, dolls to play with.

Disney is a world of dolls and dollhouses.

Chaucer believed that animals must be true to themselves. He praised a horse for being "right horsely." Disney's horses are not, his mermaids are not mermaidly nor his sea serpents serpentine—nor are his humans human. For one thing, they are all completely sexless— which, so far as I can see, cuts out about 80 percent of human life.

From *America at Last*

Swedish actress Liv Ullmann attended a party at the Playboy mansion during a stay in Los Angeles in late 1972. She recorded the following impressions in her memoirs:

I am invited to dinner at Hugh Hefner's, publisher of *Playboy*. Upon our arrival we have to pass through several electric gates with built-in television cameras. Pictures of all who pass through are flashed onto a screen in the guardhouse, scrutinized by three private detectives with loaded revolvers in their belts. There have been several attempted burglaries and crimes of violence. Only a few weeks previously in this same neighborhood bestial murders were committed without any other purpose or motive than the murderer's delight in killing those who, in his eyes, were too rich and successful.

The Playboy king is wearing terry-cloth pajamas. Some girls walk around with long furry rabbits' ears fastened to their heads and little round tails on their bottoms.

We look at films: A dog makes love to a girl. . . .

Afterward we sit in small groups, not knowing what to talk about because our host is asleep on the sofa and the rest of us don't know each other that well. The rabbit girls show some of the guests around the house.

I walk through the grounds. An artificial mountain in the garden. Inside it a subterranean grotto with swirling warmed waves. Two people are doing things in the water under red and blue spotlights.

From *Changing*

Hooray for Hollywood

A Chinese youth in a small farming village near Changzhou asked a visiting American where she lived. "Los Angeles," she answered. "Los Angeles?" he replied, puzzled. "Is that anywhere near Hollywood?"

Hollywood has endured for much of this century as the film capital of the world and a symbol of glamour and hope to millions of people from Baltimore to Bombay. A measure of its continual attraction can be sensed at Universal Studios, where the half-day tour, second only to Disneyland as the West Coast's most popular paid tourist attraction, weaves its magic on as many as thirty-one thousand visitors a day or over four million a year. But those from abroad who have lived and worked here often find themselves quickly jarred loose from their dreams. Polish author Leopold Tyrmand found it a place of magic and legend:

Hollywood. This word can be placed next to names like Olympus, Arcadia, Sodom, Rome, Paris. It symbolizes a place where, in certain epochs, everyone wanted to be. Now Hollywood has the charm of the past, perhaps its first real charm. There floats around here a nostalgic memory of one of mankind's most charming dreams, that gives to Hollywood a solid, secure position in the hagiography of our century.

From *Notebooks of a Dilettante*

Other foreign visitors, however, have not been so kind:

Hollywood is an extraordinary kind of temporary place.

British director John Schlesinger, quoted in the *New York Times*, 1975

Hollywood—loneliness by the swimming pool.

Swedish actress Liv Ullmann, in *Changing*

Hollywood is like being nowhere and talking to nobody about nothing.

Italian film director Michelangelo Antonioni, quoted in the *Sunday Times*, 1971

The Big Nipple.

Italian director Bernardo Bertolucci in his acceptance speech after being presented an Academy Award for his picture *The Last Emperor* in 1988.

★

British actor, novelist, and playwright Peter Ustinov often turned his sharp wit on Hollywood, where he has worked on numerous occasions:

Hollywood is like death—the great leveler.

Few Hollywood top executives seem sure of their friends, but they all seem absolutely sure of their enemies.

In Hollywood they say that there are only two things an actor can't get over—bad women and bad scripts.

Hollywood is full of men of fifty who look after themselves with such assiduous application that they look like a very healthy sixty.

From *The Wit of Peter Ustinov*

In late 1977 Franco Zeffirelli, the Italian director of film and opera, went to Hollywood at the request of MGM "to see whether there was a place for me at the centre of the American film industry":

My view of Hollywood may disillusion some people. I loved the place because it offered such a healthy, open existence. Beverly Hills is a suburb of spacious houses surrounded by large gardens bursting with flowers all year round. The rooms inside are nearly always filled with cut blossoms, which is a thing I adore. I also found it a wholesome place, for people exercise a lot and any myths about the *louche* lifestyle of the cinema world can be discounted; if you're working, you're up before dawn to get to the shoot. The only ones who live any sort of infamous night-time existence are those who are out of work, and in Hollywood terms that means failures. The truly big stars are never out of work and are very careful how they use their time and energy. When not involved in actual film-making, most of them have business interests that take up their time and are normal family people. Typical were Gregory Peck and his adorable wife, Veronique, who had a large, sunny English-style home. I was delighted to see that it was surrounded with columbines, one of my favorite flowers, and, when I saw how they cherished a dog that had lost a leg in an accident, I knew we were bound to become close friends.

From *Zeffirelli*

In her memoirs, Swedish actress Liv Ullmann recounted a date she had with a leading Hollywood star during her 1972 stay there:

The famous Movie Hero fetches me for dinner. He brings an enormous fir tree covered with artificial silver and imitation pearls. Unfortunately, he resembles my first love and when anyone does that, red warning lights switch on inside me. It is very difficult in America when those lights start blinking because American men say "I love you" as part of the conversation.

And when the man is one of the Famous you cannot laugh it off because they have such sensitive egos and think they never give better performances than when they half-close their velvet eyes over a glass of wine and whisper lines from the films in which they have acted.

The next day all the papers proclaim that the famous Movie Hero and I are lovers.

From *Changing*

★

During his 1986 visit to Hollywood, Adam Nicolson visited the aging matinee idol Stewart Granger:

He lives in a small apartment just off Sunset Boulevard in Pacific Palisades. (Aren't these names wonderful?) It is jammed with the carcasses of animals. He'd shot them all. Two pairs of elephant tusks scraped the ceiling. A table was covered by an Indian leopard, the floor carpeted in lion and zebra skins, the walls encrusted with the horns of various creatures. This was quite alarming, but worse were the guns—not in a nice glass case but leaning up against the furniture as if this was the Alamo. A huge revolver lay on the table between us as we talked. "This is a nice one," I said, stroking the head of a leopard. "I shot that one from the back of an elephant. Had trouble seeing it at first but then *boom*." He made a little pistol with his fingers and thumb. "Sixty or seventy yards. The elephant was shaking like a jelly."

Mr. Granger was sitting on a sort of high stool near the window overlooking the Pacific, but there was nothing else to sit on within about ten yards. I wasn't quite sure what to do. Should I sit down 30 feet away and shout questions across the room or should I come nearer and be forced to stand? I decided to stand, about four feet in front of Mr. Granger, with my hands in my pockets to show I was relaxed and quite used to talking to sitting-down film stars while standing in front of them. Mr. Granger felt ghastly but looked marvelous, ruddy with swept back silver hair. "You look marvelous," I said. "Yes, I know, with this colour, but I'm ashen underneath." It was a tricky start, but as he talked about his extraordinary life (Had I seen *King Solomon's Mines*? No. Had I seen *Scaramouche*? No. Had I seen the *Prisoner of Zenda*? Yes. Relief. "You were marvelous in that, Mr. Granger"), as he talked about all of this, his chaotic life, I warmed to him. He's only got one lung—the other was taken out by mistake when they thought he had cancer. He lost all his money in the property crash in the early seventies and he dreams rather sadly of becoming a big star again. He even had to say to me, "I was a very big star, once, you know." He feels sad that the glamorous romantic days, the swashbuckling and the really beautiful women, all that has gone. Woody Allen is not Errol Flynn. . . . Here was the past, once a beneficiary and now a victim of fashion.

From *Two Roads to Dodge City*

Shortly after the death of John Huston, British actor Robert Morley penned an affectionate recollection of this legendary film director:

I had taken a fancy to the winner of a small seller at Sandown. "Let's buy it," I urged him. "We go halves." Huston appeared to agree. I turned back to catch the eye of the auctioneer and the horse dropped dead. "Thank you, Bob" was Huston's only comment. It was not the first corpse we had examined together. The man lay dead on the pavement of the grand boulevard. John had knelt briefly, then taking my arm propelled me forwards. "He's going to be fine, Bob, just fine," he reassured.

The first time I worked for him [on the filming of *The African Queen*] I hadn't learnt the script. American actors always knew their lines, but in those days we British were more casual. With Bogart and Hepburn I should have known better. When Huston was asked that evening how I had fared, he replied that I had failed to turn up but had sent another actor instead. "But I think," he added, "he will come himself in the morning."

. . . To be directed by John Huston was always a privilege and often a pleasure. Film-acting, unless the director watches it, can be an excessively boring occupation. Nowadays most of them watch the budget and not the actor. As they say in television, we don't want a performance, we want it Thursday. . . .

One is tempted to ask what on earth D. W. Griffith, René Clair, and David Lean could have done in life if the profession of film director had not been invented for them. In Huston's case he could have become a preacher, an explorer, even perhaps a great political leader. He had the courage, the gift of leadership, the confidence, the charm, and the cheek.

From *The Spectator*, September 5, 1987

On February 26, 1983, Her Majesty's Yacht Britannia *glided into San Diego harbor. A few hours later Queen Elizabeth, wearing a navy-blue silk suit and hat, stepped ashore off the ship's red-carpeted gangway and set foot for the first time in the western United States. The highlight was a five-hundred-person bash on Sound Stage 9 at Twentieth-Century Fox hosted by Nancy Reagan. Australian Clive James filed this report for* The Observer:

[The several hundred] guests arrived by limo, stepping out under an awning while the shivering media, under nothing but the wet night sky, took notes and fired flashbulbs. "I've had the privilege," said Henry Kissinger, "of meeding the Gween before, but id's always a special oggasion." The limos being a block long each, it took a while for all the guests to be delivered. . . . Fred Astaire was one of the younger luminaries present. Some of them had risen from the grave for the occasion but they had more in common than mere immortality. Gradually it dawned that they were nearly all Republicans. The Democrats were at home, seething. When Nancy Reagan finally welcomed the Royal Couple, she was shaking hands with practically the only invitees who hadn't voted for her husband. . . .

The Royals were seated with the British film star colony all along one side of a long table on stage, like a Last Supper painted by Sir Joshua Reynolds. Before and below them stretched a sea of Americans all staring in their direction. It was a stiffening circumstance in which only Dudley Moore could possibly look cheerful, although Michael Caine was also trying hard. Jane Seymour looked very attractive, which was more than you could say for Anthony Newley. Rod Stewart, clad in a black and gold John Player Special pants suit, sported an extravaganza hairstyle that left his wife Alana's coiffure looking like a crew-cut, but facially he resembled an ant-eater who had run out of ants.

The Duke was talking to Julie Andrews. In between the Queen and the First Lady sat Tony Richardson, looking very calm. Later on it emerged that this was because, having not been apprised of the *placement* until he was about to sit down, he had died of fright.

To have expired was to be fortunate, because the Entertainment now began. Emcee of the Entertainment was Ed McMahon, Johnny Carson's straight man. It is conjecturable that Carson would be lost without McMahon, but there can be no doubt that McMahon is lost without Carson, who was not present, having stayed at home because of a wisdom tooth, or perhaps because of wisdom. McMahon introduced Dionne Warwick as a Great Song Stylist. For the benefit of the Queen and other strangers, he explained what a Great Song Stylist was. A Great Song Stylist was someone who was not only a singer with Style, but a stylish singer with Greatness.

Ed took so long over the introduction that Dionne felt compelled to deliver an extended set. She was breathtaking if your breath is taken away by a display of technique. She clapped her hands and swayed her hips. Gene Kelly, seated just in front of me, did neither of these things. Nor did the Queen, but she evidently quite liked George Burns, the next act on. George also went on too long, but at least he was himself. Frank Sinatra and Perry Como pretended to be Frank Sinatra and Dean Martin, doing that endless medley which is a good joke if the previous numbers have been kept short. They hadn't, so it wasn't.

The Entertainment had elephantiasis, like the evening in general. When Hollywood gets beyond energy without taste, it arrives at taste with proportions. Perry ruffled his hair to prove that it really grew on top of his head, even if it had started its life somewhere else. "You probably do *not* adore me," Frank sang at the Queen, who if she didn't nod her head, didn't shake it either. The big night out was a downer, but it wasn't her fault. They had put on the display.

In fact, she had been had. The evening was a pay-off for Ronald Reagan's financial backers, who would never have met the stars if the stars had not come to meet the Queen. Buckingham Palace had been hustled into bankrolling the next campaign wagon.

From *Snakecharmers in Texas: Essays, 1980–87*

6 ★ THE VIEW ★ fROM JAPAN

"FIFTEEN *years from now it is quite possible that the world's greatest industrial power, just after the United States and Russia, will not be Europe, but American industry in Europe. . . . As early as 1963 . . . American firms in France controlled 40 per cent of the petroleum market, 65 per cent of the production of films and photographic paper, 65 per cent of farm machinery, 65 per cent of telecommunications equipment, and 45 per cent of synthetic rubber, among others. . . . American corporations in Europe control: 15 per cent of the production of consumer goods; 50 per cent of semi-conductors; 80 per cent of computers; and 95 per cent of the new market for integrated circuits."*

Thus warned the French scholar Jean-Jacques Servan-Schreiber in 1967 in his best-selling book, The American Challenge. *Many European political and corporate leaders then shared his concern about the "American economic invasion" which threatened to reduce Europe to a mere subsidiary of the United States.*

Today, of course, the perceived threat is no longer the United States but Japan. And the economic battleground has shifted from Europe to America. For many American politicians, corporate heads, and labor leaders, Japan-bashing is the new sport. More and more Americans are convinced that the Japanese are taking unfair economic advantage of them while feverishly buying up many of America's prized assets with their surplus dollars, ironically echoing the same complaints that a generation ago foreigners voiced against America.

As much of the following chapter will suggest, the Japanese are a people preoccupied by their relations with the rest of the world, especially America. They very strongly feel put upon unjustly. Japan, in their view, succeeds by its own hard work and strict discipline. But this success is resented and punished abroad, particularly in an America which has grown weak while its competitive edge has been undercut.

"In the complex interaction between Japan and the United States over the past thirty-five years, it is clearly the Japanese who have profited the most," insisted Robert C. Christopher in his book The Japanese Mind. "And they have done so essentially because many of them have observed the United States in such minute detail. At times, indeed, the dogged manner in which Japanese scholars, journalists, and businessmen pursue even the most trivial piece of information about American life borders on the absurd. . . . [And yet it is] this tireless investigation of the tastes, habits, and needs of American consumers . . . that has so often enabled Japanese industry to outcompete American companies in their own market."

Perhaps the wisest words of caution came from Mike Mansfield, for years the American ambassador to Japan: "The next century will be that of the Pacific and what happens then will depend upon the foundations laid down by the United States and Japan in the rest of the century."

Akira Baba runs a sushi bar in Tokyo. He says of Americans:

American people challenge everything. They have the frontier spirit. Europeans are conservative, I think, and Americans are not. I was very impressed by that difference. I like Americans because Japanese are very inward looking and pessimistic. Americans are very open and optimistic.

Quoted in the *Dallas Morning News*, July 6, 1986

Satohiro Akimoto, a young executive with the giant Mitsubishi Trading Co., sees the United States as an alternative to the relatively strict hierarchy of Japanese society:

America is the closest place to paradise for people who want to be free, who want to do their very best. It's a great experiment for human beings. There are so many diverse people from different backgrounds.

Quoted in the Dallas Morning News, July 6, 1986

★

In 1988 the average price for a house in Tokyo was $823,000 and for a condominium $370,000, according to the private real estate research group Fudosan Keisai Kenkyusho. Yet the average Tokyo house measured 958 square feet on a 1,646-square-foot lot. In the United States the average house is nearly twice as large.

Yoshie Takahashi, a government worker who earns the equivalent of $1,300, lives in a one-room apartment the size of a small dormitory room at a U.S. college. She pays $424 a month rent and has no air conditioning or heat, no laundry facilities, and a 70-minute round-trip commute to work each day. She considers herself lucky that her commute is so short and her apartment so new.

Takahashi's small place is so packed with furniture and appliances—a color television, microwave oven, tape deck, electric rice cooker, and electric frying pan—that she often must give away gifts she receives because she has no room for them.

When she worked at the Japanese Embassy in Washington, she lived in an apartment three times larger. Her response is automatic when asked what she misses most about life in the United States:

"Space."

Quoted in a United Press International wire service story,
February 7, 1988

The Japanese Love Affair with American Culture

Junji Itoh, a young art critic and promoter in Tokyo, is excited by his vision of a world in which Japan and the United States blend together culturally. "A Pacific Internationale is being born," he says enthusiastically. "Tokyo is starting to share more with L.A. than New York. If you add up what's happening in Japan with California, China, and other Pacific countries, you can see a new cultural zone forming."

147

The Japanese fascination with American culture dates back over forty years to the early years of the occupation. Virtually every new twist of lifestyle and new trend of pop culture, no matter how bizarre, quickly finds imitators somewhere in Japanese society. In fact, so many of the externals of Japanese culture have become effectively Americanized that sometimes it would appear to the casual foreign visitor that Japan seems hell-bent on transforming itself into an ersatz America. Japanese drink more Coca-Cola than any other people in the world except Americans and Mexicans. The Japanese fast-food market is dominated by such familiar American giants as McDonald's and Kentucky Fried Chicken. Tokyo alone has more than 130 Dunkin' Donuts outlets. Japanese housewives buy over $100 million worth of Tupperware products each year. Japanese shoppers flock to two thousand 7-Eleven convenience stores. Schick has controlled such a major part of the Japanese market for razor blades (70 percent at its peak) for so long that many Japanese believe it is a Japanese company. Younger Japanese children watch American cartoons on their televisions while their older siblings tune in to the latest American rock music.

While our politicians and businessmen rant about the Japanese domination of some U.S. markets, few Americans appreciate the ironic fact that on average each Japanese spent $583 in 1988 on American goods, while each American spent only $298 on Japanese goods.

Now it turns out that many Japanese are closet "Marlboro Men" with a powerful hankering for the Great Outdoors, inspired by the lifestyle of their American counterparts. Newsweek reported on the phenomenon in an article called "Japan: The Call of the Wild":

It's Friday, the end of another workweek in Tokyo. Hiroki Uchiyama swings into the driver's seat of his four-wheel drive, rough-terrain vehicle, adjusts his cowboy hat and bandanna, switches on a Willie Nelson country-music tape and heads for the Wild West of his dreams. Awaiting at the foot of Mount Fuji, two hours away, is his weekend retreat—a huge log house, American frontier-style, complete with an electric-fired "wood stove" shipped from Arkansas and a mirror trimmed with a black leather horse collar he bought in Montana. In real life Uchiyama, 52, runs a specialized auto-parts business and lives in a posh Tokyo apartment. But comes the weekend, his craving for the wide-open spaces takes over, and he becomes . . . John Wayne.

Uchiyama isn't alone. . . . Countless Japanese, it seems, are closet Marlboro Men. Outdoor magazines, including the Japanese edition of

Field and Stream, are hot. More than 2,000 camping and sports-equipment stores have opened, 10 times the number a decade ago, and they're doing a land-office business in rugged wilderness gear: hiking boots, fishing rods, safari jackets, cowboy hats. *The Japan Sports Industry News* estimates sales of outdoor goods will total $1.5 billion this year, nearly twice as much as four years ago. And that doesn't include sales of such things as vacation homes and log houses (boom industries in themselves), or macho four-wheel drive vehicles (sales of which have nearly tripled over the last six years).

From *Newsweek*, April 25, 1988

Pico Iyer, an Indian citizen raised in Britain, found himself fascinated by the Japanese obsession with baseball:

When first I set foot in Japan, baseball fever was sweeping the country. Every radio in every cab, so it seemed, crackled with play-by-play commentaries. Blackboards had been set up outside electronics stores to provide passersby with inning-by-inning scoreboards. Huge Sonys in tidy blond-wood cases filled every departure lounge in Narita Airport with faultless images of the game of the moment. And the games and the moments never ended: from dawn to midnight, the screen was filled with one mega-montage of half-familiar images—high fives and hyperactive electronic scoreboards and the swaying of fans to caterwauling organ music, and men circling the bases, half-mythic figures, in many cases, from my boyhood, like Reggie Smith. "Baseball School for Children" was on one network at noon, pro baseball was on another at 7:04 P.M. and the All-Japan National High School Championship was being featured on the government station for nine hours each day. . . .

Baseball, indeed, was everywhere I looked in Japan. In the narrow streets of Tokyo. I saw children working and working to perfect their moves, and along the wide boulevards, businessmen were lined up in batting cages to refine their skills against pitching machines. Soft-drink machines incorporated games of baseball roulette, magazines offered readers in Hiroshima the chance to "meet your Carp." Half the little boys across the length of the country seemed to be sporting Giants caps, and every day brought seven different newspapers dealing with nothing—nothing—but sports. Earlier in the summer, a colleague told me, he had been on a photographic assignment in a Buddhist monastery outside Kyoto. Gradually, and patiently, he had won the trust of the head monk. Finally, once the sacred rituals were complete, the holy man had been moved to give his visitor, as a token of his appreciation, a poem. Oh, and one more thing, the monk had added: Were Yogi Berra and Mickey Mantle still playing in the major leagues?

"Baseball is the All-American sport," marveled Tina, a horse-trainer from Seattle who was bicycling through Japan. "But they're more fanatic about it here than they are at home." So indeed it seemed. In America, baseball was only the national pastime; in Japan, it was a national obsession.

From *Video Night in Kathmandu*

Yukiko Yoshida of Matsusaka, Japan, wrote the following letter which ran in the June 6, 1988, issue of Time:

Although J. D. Salinger was displeased with the photographers who took his picture while he was at the grocery store, I was happy to see his face because to do so has been one of my dreams. Since I live in Japan, there is little chance to know him. He may not be pleased to hear this, but I think it is natural to want to know something about a person who interests you. Now my heart is satisfied with having seen just one photograph of my favorite novelist.

★

In one poll, in which a group of Japanese were asked what had given them the most happiness in life, over half replied, "Disneyland." Chicago Tribune *writer Bob Greene visited the Japanese Disneyland during his 1988 trip to the country and filed the following column:*

The Japanese version of Disneyland—the only Disney park to operate outside the United States—celebrated its fifth anniversary this year, and it is a spectacular success. Since the park opened in 1983, more than 54 million people have passed through its gates. Located midway between Tokyo International Airport and downtown Tokyo, it has become a true phenomenon of the Far East.

This is not a business-page story, though. This is the story of one man—not a Disney employee—but a man named Yoshimi Yabe who is an accountant at a downtown Tokyo department store and who . . .

Well, let's just say it. Yoshimi Yabe, who is 38 years old, married and the father of two children, has visited Tokyo Disneyland 205 times during the five years it has been open. Think about it. The guy has gone to Disneyland 205 times.

"I go by myself, with my family, or with my friends," Yabe told me. . . . Yabe said that his wife, Kiyoko, 38; his son, Gohei, 10; and his daughter, Yuko, 7, are getting a little tired of accompanying him. "They think 200 times is crazy," he said. "But they understand. If I ask them to go with me, they go with me, but often I go alone."

I was trying to imagine what it was that drew Yabe to Tokyo Disneyland time after time. Was it the feel of America which has become faddish in this country—a country that competes fiercely with the United States economically but passionately embraces American popular culture? Was it the lovable Disney characters—Mickey, Donald, Goofy, and the rest? Was it the food and the rides?

Nope.

"I love Walt Disney himself," Yabe said.

I thought perhaps the translation was a little off. So I asked again.

"I love Mr. Disney," Yabe said. "I love him personally, and I love his philosophy. When I go to Tokyo Disneyland, I feel the full realization of Walt Disney's philosophy."

Walt Disney, of course, has been dead for some years now. Has Yoshimi Yabe seen old movies that feature Disney's likeness on the screen?

"No," he said, "but I have read a great deal about Mr. Disney." Japan is an almost totally literate society; that made sense.

Still, though . . . going to Disneyland because of a reverence for Walt Disney?

"Yes," Yabe said. "I go for the person."

I asked him what his favorite part of Tokyo Disneyland was. Did a particular ride thrill him? A beautiful exhibit?

"My favorite thing is the parking lot," Yabe said.

Again, I thought I might be getting the translation wrong.

"The parking lot is the best part of Disneyland for me," Yabe confirmed.

But why would anyone go to Disneyland for the parking lot?

"It considers safety in the way it is constructed and the way it operates," Yabe said. "I like the way the cars are parked."

He gave me a complex explanation of the Disneyland way of parking cars, compared with the normal Tokyo way of parking cars. Tokyo may be the most congested city in the world—it makes Los Angeles freeway traffic seem like a deserted country road—and apparently parking is difficult.

The Disney people have made a science out of safe and efficient parking, and Yabe spent a good 10 minutes marvelling out loud for me about the wonders of that parking lot.

On some days when Yabe knows that the crowds will be heavy and he is a little short on cash, he will ride the train from his home for an hour and a half just to wander around the parking lot. "The spirit of Mr. Disney is in that parking lot," he said.

He is somewhat annoyed with certain Japanese reporters who have written about him. They always demand to know how much total time and cash he has spent at Tokyo Disneyland. (Admission is the equivalent of around $30 in American money.)

"The reporters don't understand me," Yabe said. "For me, Mr. Walt Disney is like a religion. If a Christian goes to church 200 or 300 times, no one says anything. But they poke fun at me."

He said he is aware that some negative things have been written about Walt Disney, but "I don't want to listen." Even though Tokyo Disneyland officials know of his 200-plus visits, he does not want free tickets because "I don't think I would enjoy it unless I paid my own way." His dream is to take his family to Disney World in Florida, but he does not have the money.

He knows that people have a tendency to chuckle at all of this; I was tending toward that myself, especially with the parking-lot stuff.

But then he said:

"What better way to spend a life than the way Mr. Walt Disney spent his? To make people happy and to fill them with joy. The warmth of the family in *Mary Poppins,* the beautiful story of *Snow White,* the happiness of *Pinocchio* . . . Can you not see why I feel the way I do about Mr. Disney?"

We spoke different languages, but I thought I understood.

★

New York City is now the most popular foreign destination for a broad spectrum of Japanese tourists. Sara Rimer filed this story for the New York Times News Service:

Twelve young women from Tokyo came to New York for the first time last week, to eat American steak, shop at Tiffany's and listen to jazz at the Village Vanguard.

They spoke only a few words of English, but they had more reason to feel at home than most foreigners. Everywhere they went, they were surrounded by other Japanese tourists. At their midtown hotel, the New York Hilton, half the 1,000 registered foreign guests were Japanese.

New York is once again awash in foreign tourists—record numbers of them, by all indications. And it is especially awash in Japanese tourists, who in the last few years have replaced the British as the most frequent foreign visitors to New York. . . .

Asked what they wanted to do in New York, the women from Tokyo smiled and answered in Japanese. Their guide, Kondo Masahiro, gave a rough translation: "Eat steak and go to Tiffany's."

When they descend on Tiffany's, it will be ready for them. All the sales-people have been instructed in basic Japanese, including counting, according to Pierce MacGuire, the store's director of Far East sales. MacGuire said the single most popular item among Japanese customers is Elsa Peretti's medium-sized, 18-karat-gold heart necklace, which costs $350.

Tiffany's jewelry and other American products are sold in Japan at prices inflated by high import taxes. The staggering import taxes and cost of living . . . combine with a strong yen to make New York a bargain for Japanese tourists. And New York has become the most fashionable destination, particularly among younger travelers.

"There is a strong sense of rivalry in Japan," Masato Ikeda, director of international and leisure markets for the New York Hilton, said. "If my neighbor has a car, I have to have a car. If my neighbor has an air conditioner, I have to have an air conditioner. If he's been to New York, I have to come to New York."

Even so, New York is still portrayed in Japan as a place where danger and drugs lurk on every corner. Masahiro delivered his standard introduction speech to the 12 Tokyo women whom he was guiding around New York. "Don't ride the subways, don't go to Harlem, don't go west of Eighth Avenue, don't board a helicopter," he said. "Please enjoy New York City."

★

Few Americans make any effort to learn the specifics about Japanese culture. For years this ignorance of Japanese culture, language, history, and society has handicapped American businessmen attempting to set up shop in that country. In sharp contrast to their American counterparts, a growing number of Japanese businesspeople travel to the United States for seminars and workshops which guarantee them total immersion in American culture. This sort of extra effort may help explain why Americans consistently end up on the short end of the trade balance. Reporter Jon Funabiki described one such popular program which takes Southern California for its classroom:

At topside aboard the *Zumbrota*, a 103-foot luxury yacht once owned by Mae West, the sun was shining, sea gulls soared, and the landmarks of the San Diego skyline scooted by on the starboard side.

But Yamaguchi Naoko, a 27-year-old Japanese woman who hopes to become an international newscaster, and Masuda Mitsu, a 39-year-old Japanese man who sells fancy teas, were below deck, locked in concentration as they listened to a lengthy and detailed thesis on American business etiquette.

They were getting tips on why a warm handshake, cocktail party small talk, and a look-you-straight-in-the-eye demeanor help you "look successful and be credible" in American business circles. Even lunch, served by a white-jacketed waiter, turned into an Emily Post–style lesson on dining manners.

It may seem like an odd way to spend five hours aboard a chartered yacht on San Diego Bay, but to Yamaguchi, Masuda, and their Japanese traveling companions, it was just day No. 2 in a grueling but eye-opening introduction to American culture.

"It's like a shock treatment," said Utsumi Tora, president of TOLA, Inc., which owns the private language firm in Tokyo that organized the program. "I don't want people to *sight-see*. I want people to *experience* California."

In a six-day trip to San Diego and Los Angeles, the Japanese travelers faced:

•Daily drills in English, at a pace so fast that the words "Hollywood and Vine" disintegrated into a tangle of tongue and giggles.

•Seminars, also given in English, in not only business etiquette, but also American fashion and real estate—the latter including a tour of the ritzy Los Angeles district of Bel Air.

•A Los Angeles cocktail party with American guests to put some of their lessons into actual practice.

•A dinner party and concert with Nancy Wilson, a singer with the rock group Heart.

•One day of rest to do what tourists ordinarily do: visit Disneyland, Universal Studios, or shop in Malibu Beach.

Cost? About $4,000 per traveler.

Purpose? To force clients to speak English and to teach them to become more "international."

Internationalism has become the buzz-word of Japan in the 1980s. Though Japan often is described as having an inward-looking society, its rapid economic development, growth in overseas investment and new, yen-charged affluence have stimulated overseas travel and a desire to become more in touch with global affairs. And for many Japanese, that means learning about America.

"I want to know what's going on in America," said Dobashi Kyota, a 43-year-old housewife who left her husband, a golf-shop owner, at home. "I want to see how they act, how they eat, and what they are talking about. And I want to see it with my own eyes."

From the *San Diego Union*, January 18, 1989

Shigeo Minabe is a professor of economics at Hiroshima University. After spending several years on the faculty of American universities, he penned this account for the newspaper Chugoku Shimbun *contrasting his lifestyle in America with that in Japan:*

Everybody who lives in a foreign country has some adjustment problems, but many Japanese experience severe reverse culture shock when they return to Japan. Poor housing and sky-high food prices make you wonder why you came home again.

I've lived in the United States on six different occasions, spending about half of the last three years in Texas and California. My cultural reentry to Japan last autumn was the most difficult ever.

I suffered spatial disorientation, a psychological consequence of spending two academic semesters in Texas, where the wide open spaces stretch to the horizon. Even during a three-month stay in California, which is about the same size as Japan, I felt hemmed in compared to the Lone Star State. Back in Japan's crowded cities and my own tiny house, I feel claustrophobic.

The high cost of food here is infuriating. Everything is expensive—meat, fish, vegetables, fruit, rice—whether you eat at home or in a restaurant.

I thought my eyes were playing tricks on me when I saw a head of lettuce advertised for $3.27 at a local supermarket. Rainy weather in Japan last summer is blamed for high produce prices, but in Texas you could buy 12 heads for that price. The $150 that some Japanese pay for one fancy melon would purchase several crates of canta-loupes in Austin.

In Osaka, I paid the equivalent of more than $10 for a pork-cutlet lunch made from tough, tasteless frozen meat. I wanted to heave that greasy mess into the kitchen.

You can get a great meal in Japan for $50 a person but the portions are so small you want a second or third helping. For $50, four or five Texans can eat and drink in a neighborhood bar for hours.

The recent meat scandal in Japan—beef from diseased cows was sold as hamburger—was the final insult. Maybe Japanese athletes did so poorly at the Seoul Olympics because they couldn't afford good steak.

After living in Texas, where people dress casually, and Berkeley, where intellectuals are indifferent to how they look, it's hard to understand middle-aged Japanese who spend a small fortune on designer-brand clothes. Dressed like Beautiful People, they live in unbearably cramped quarters.

Gasoline in Japan costs four times what it does in the United States, despite the drop in oil prices. And the exorbitant toll fees here are officially sanctioned highway robbery.

For $30 in San Francisco music lovers could attend a 10-concert symphony series commemorating the 200th anniversary of Mozart's death. In Hiroshima a ticket for one concert costs $40 or $50. In Texas I paid $3 for a haircut, but here barbers get 10 times as much.

Because of the yen's appreciation, Japanese per-capita income has nominally surpassed that of Americans. In real terms, however, our living standards are still less than half of those in the United States.

The expensive and inferior lifestyle of the Japanese is caused by protectionism, the multilayered distribution system, and bureaucratic obstructionism.

Southern hospitality is ingrained in Texans, and they are friendly and kind. But in Japan affluence has taken a toll on civility. Seeing what materialism and status-seeking have done to our values was the saddest part of my homecoming. Japan is not becoming a gentler society.

We have yet to learn the truism that "Man doth not live by bread alone." Unless we seek spiritual and cultural fulfillment, Japan's Gilded Age will turn out to be made of fool's gold.

But many Japanese businessmen assigned to the United States do not share Professor Shigeo Minabe's acceptance of our culture. For them their time in America becomes a painful ordeal, as reporter Frank Green's investigations revealed when he interviewed Japanese businessmen living in San Diego:

Seiki Shimizu is a stranger in a strange land. At work, the Japanese businessman—who runs a local electronics plant for a Tokyo-based company—often clashes with American workers he believes are not sufficiently industrious or loyal.

Home life is equally stressful. Shimizu's wife, who speaks only Japanese and who can't drive, has been a virtual recluse in the family's Bonita home during their two-year stay in the United States. Both worry that the "bad, bad" education their son and daughter are receiving in public schools will leave them ill-prepared to compete in Japan. "I will be happy when my company calls me back home," Shimizu said.

As Japanese investment in the American economy continues to swell, so do the ranks of Japanese executives assigned overseas by their companies to manage new holdings. At least 300 Japanese work at 60 San Diego County firms owned by Japanese companies, from Sanyo and Sony to Kyocera and California First Bank. Most are stationed here for two to three years; many are accompanied by their families.

For some, life abroad can be beneficial and enjoyable.

Others, however, have trouble coping with cross-cultural differences. Leisurely American lifestyles are regarded by some as slothful.

And many sense a suspicion—even racism—directed toward them by Americans alarmed at the increasing Japanese encroachment on U.S. economic turf.

"To go from living in a very homogeneous society like Japan to a diverse country like the United States is a very big leap to make," said Yoko Fujita, a Chula Vista–based social worker who counsels Japanese families. "The problems encountered can be insurmountable."

In addition to their culture shock is the fear that they have been banished by their bosses, possibly because their work was less worthy than that of their peers.

"Your fellow workers stay and earn promotions, while you are sent away," said one Japanese executive, in a rare display of anger and frankness. "It's like being in the service."

. . . What makes the Japanese businessman's experience in the United States more unsettling than that faced by other foreign executives assigned overseas, though, is the disparity between conditions often found in the Japanese and American work places.

Japanese workers typically spend their entire careers with one company. To jump from one firm to another for more money or a better position, as American workers often do, is considered the mark of a disloyal individual. Additionally, Japanese businessmen often work 10-hour days, six days a week.

"Japanese people live to work, while Americans work to live," said Milton Chen, a business professor at San Diego State University who is a specialist on Japanese business practices. "The realization that American workers have more independence is a difficult concept for Japanese managers to accept. Intellectually, they understand, but emotionally, no."

Some are unable to make the transition from overseeing a homogeneous, largely male work force, to managing ethnically mixed American companies, where women are supposed to enjoy equal footing with men.

In some Japanese executives' eyes, blacks, Hispanics, women and some Caucasians are intellectually inferior. . . . In one of the largest settlements of its kind, the Sumitomo Corp. of America was fined $2.6 million last year after losing a federal lawsuit that accused the Japanese-owned company of favoring males—both Japanese and American—over American women. . . .

Even at Japanese businesses where cultural friction is minimal, the work place can be imbued with Oriental traditions and attitudes, oftentimes causing communication breakdowns. For example, Japanese bosses seldom like to use the word "no," or to make snap judgments.

"Their top priority is saving face," said Nissan's Gerald Hirshberg. "So you have to be careful when phrasing questions. A lot of American workers misread signs—like the positive nodding of the head—as acquiescence for what they're saying. But they may learn later that it merely meant they were understood. Some Americans read this as flat-out lying."

. . . While Japanese expatriates struggle to get through their workday, they may find that their real troubles may be just beginning when they get home. Wives often blame husbands for the lonely lives they now lead in the States. Some are professional women who left budding careers back in Japan. "They suddenly find themselves unable to function, and it's devastating," said Yoko Fujita.

Couples with children sometimes are burdened with more acute worries, as their youngsters adopt the relatively lax study habits and disrespectful attitudes towards elders of their American friends. Many Japanese families send their children to weekend schools to offset what they consider the poor schooling here, and to keep them academically fit for their return to the rigorous ways of Japanese schools.

. . . Most expatriate families adjust to their new home in America by clinging to Japanese culture. For entertainment, they subscribe to their country's daily newspapers and watch Japanese movies rented from specialty video shops. . . . Seiki Shimizu, for one, dines at the Katzra restaurant on Convoy Street whenever he feels homesick. In a setting tailored to Oriental tastes, Japanese waitresses converse with customers in their native tongue, the music softly playing in the background includes the latest hits from Tokyo—"I Missed the Shock" by Akina Nakamori, among others—and chopsticks are the mandatory place setting.

"This is quite nice," Shimizu said, "but it isn't quite the same as the real thing."

From the *San Diego Union*, December 13, 1988

Shape Up, America!

"Despite their readiness to adopt foreign ideas, institutions, and techniques, most Japanese don't welcome too much personal contact with foreigners and, in their hearts, feel superior to the rest of the world,"

Robert Christopher observed in The Japanese Mind. *"As is frequently true with individuals, Japan's national sense of vulnerability and fear of being regarded as inferior go hand in hand with a certain arrogance—the kind of arrogance which holds, to paraphrase an old U.S. Army saying, that there are three ways to do things: the right way, the wrong way, and the Japanese way."*

For all the intensity of their love affair with American culture, many Japanese find themselves increasingly contemptuous of many aspects of that same culture. Japan-bashing in prominent American circles has led inevitably to a similar sort of America-bashing in Japan.

Thirty years ago the label "Made in Japan" on a product signified in most American eyes cheap junk. Then twenty years ago the Japanese started making things that were both cheaper and better, and Americans began to worry. Japanese cameras, calculators, and cars were no longer junk; they were competition. But Americans decided not to worry. After all, we told ourselves, the Japanese were essentially copycats. We had our creativity, our Nobel Prizes, and our new ideas that would keep us ahead in the race for high-tech. No longer is that true. Today Japan is challenging us even here, in the field of new ideas, new innovations, and new technologies. On every front, Japan is struggling to be Number One. And because of their extraordinary achievements, the Japanese are less disposed toward humility now than they were thirty years ago.

Important changes in the Japanese attitude toward the United States were signalled in an April 1980 speech in Hiroshima by the late Prime Minister Masayoshi Ohira, who stated: "The United States has changed from a superpower to just another power."

Europe is a boutique, and America is a farm.

Popular Japanese saying

Yasuko Kurachi Dower is a faculty wife of an American professor of political science at the University of Wisconsin in Madison. She grew up in a college town on the west coast of Japan before meeting her American husband. One of the most striking changes she notes on her return trips to her homeland is the different attitudes that many Japanese now have toward the United States:

For several years, America was paradise in Japanese eyes. The Occupation was considered wonderful. Americans were fair, kind, generous, and rich. More than anything, rich. Students who came to the United States didn't want to go back. Coming here was a dream for many of us.

Now it's completely changed around. America is no longer considered paradise. To common Japanese people, it is a place of crime, violence, and unemployment. In 1980 when I was in a Tokyo taxi-cab, I told the driver I lived in America. He was shocked, He said, "My brother went to Los Angeles last spring and he had to drive half an hour to find a Japanese restaurant." (Laughs.) I was reminded of Americans in Tokyo in 1955, frantically looking for a steak house. (Laughs.)

> Quoted in Studs Terkel's *The Good War: An Oral History*
> *of World War II*

★

Shiro Inoue, a former senior executive at the Bank of Japan, recalls the change in different terms:

At the beginning of my career, we were still under occupation and had practically no foreign exchange. Japanese mills needed to buy American cotton, but the Americans told us no commercial bank was creditable enough to borrow the $40 million needed. The Bank of Japan, our central bank, was in this case the only bank creditworthy enough to borrow money from the Export-Import Bank in the U.S.

The negotiations were difficult. I commuted to the Exim Bank in Washington so often that thirty-five years later, I still remember their address: 811 Vermont Avenue. Eventually, we got the loan. The text of the agreement was in English, and the currency was U.S. dollars.

At the end of my career, our foreign exchange reserve was increased sharply. We wanted to use a part of our wealth for the benefit of the world. We decided to make what was then the biggest single loan to the World Bank—100 billion yen. Mr. Brochas, general counsel for the World Bank, flew to Tokyo and signed the agreement written in Japanese, not a word of which he understood. The currency was, of course, Japanese yen.

> Quoted in Daniel Burstein, *Yen! Japan's New Financial Empire*
> *and Its Threat to America*

Iida Tsuneo is a professor of economics at Nagoya University. He began a recent article entitled "Decline of a Superpower" with this thought:

Japan appears to be rising swiftly from the status of a mere major economic power to that of an economic superpower just as America slides from its position as an economic superpower to that of a mere major economic power. This may sound like monstrous conceit, and of course it does not become us to be arrogant, but neither is there anything to be gained from false humility or servility. When two nations are trading places in this way, frequent and severe outbursts of trade friction are only to be expected, and a comprehensive solution to the problem is in all likelihood an impossibility.

From *Japan Echo,* Autumn 1987

In an important speech former Japanese Foreign Minister Saburo Okita insisted that Japan's concern is for American economic, rather than military, strength:

In my view a strong U.S. economy is even more important in the long run than U.S. military power. Because without a strong economic foundation your military power may not be very effective.

Quoted by Robert Christopher in *The Japanese Mind*

★

Kenichi Ohmae, the manager of McKinsey Securities' office in Tokyo, made these observations about the collapse of the dollar against the yen, which has turned America into one enormous K-Mart for Japanese shoppers:

Toshi Sato's 1,500-square-foot apartment in downtown Tokyo, which cost him a half-million dollars five years ago, has a market value today of $8 million. Earlier this year Mr. Sato talked with a Tokyo bank, which offered to loan him $6 million. So off he flew to Southern California, where for $1 million, a small fraction of his lending limit, he bought a five-bedroom house on the waterfront.

Half the appreciation of Mr. Sato's Tokyo apartment is real, but the other half comes from the devaluation of the dollar. Indeed, the dollar-yen exchange rate, which has moved to 120 from 260 in the past several years, has declined to the point of making America a bargain basement. . . .

Some of America's most competitive "exports" today are land, houses, and companies. But they are becoming too cheap. To realize how out of balance things are, consider this: If you collateralized a good-sized Tokyo office building, you could buy a $1 billion company in the U.S. In fact, the real-estate value of Tokyo at $7.7 trillion is so high that, once collateralized and borrowed against (at 80% of current value), it could buy all the land in the U.S. for $3.7 trillion, and all the companies on the New York Stock Exchange, NASDAQ, and several other exchanges for $2.6 trillion.

American concern about the trade deficit with Japan has created the false idea that the dollar must depreciate further for the U.S. to become competitive. If that happens, investment in the U.S. will increase. But if the U.S. wants to slow the pace of foreign investment, then it must keep up the value of the dollar.

From the *Wall Street Journal*, November 30, 1988

In a 1982 article, an exasperated Tetsuya Ozaki of the Jiji Press wrote:

Every moment the U.S. delays in putting its house in order inconveniences the entire world. Shape up, America! Japanese used to regard Americans as teachers, but now we see them as equals. So these days, when the United States complains or makes demands upon us, Japanese want to say, "Look, in economics we are both students. Your marks are bad; my marks are better. So don't tell me what to do!"

Quoted by Robert Christopher in *The Japanese Mind*

By the end of 1988 Japan had clearly established itself as superior to the United States in several critical areas. A single Japanese company—Nippon Telegraph & Telephone—had become the world's most valuable corporation, its shares worth more than IBM, AT&T, General Motors, and General Electric combined. Nomura, Japan's leading securities firm, was twenty times bigger than Merrill Lynch. Eight of the world's largest banks were now Japanese. With half the population of the United States

and a land mass just the size of California, Japan boasted more billion-aires than America. Japanese investors financed one-third of Washington's budget deficit. With the new affluence came an arrogance and a barely concealed contempt for the United States on the part of many Japanese, as the following anecdote suggests:

Consider, for example, the casual discourse of Ichiro Yamanouchi, one of Nippon Telegraph & Telephone's top executives in North America, just before NTT's stock offering made it the world's largest corporation. Over lunch one day, Yamanouchi mentioned that he really wanted to bring some American products back to Japan as gifts for friends and business associates. This would be his own personal gesture to help alleviate the trade deficit. But he couldn't find anything in the United States that could measure up to the scrutiny of a quality-conscious Japanese. At long last he had found one perfect item: Vermont maple syrup, a high quality product suitable to the Japanese taste—in this case, Japan's national sweet tooth.

Without the least self-consciousness that an American listener might find it an overstatement to imply that maple syrup was America's only exportable product, Yamanouchi continued on to talk about how America could get more competitive in trade. The United States should market its national parks more aggressively as tourist attractions. Nature-loving Japan had nothing to compare with Yosemite or Yellowstone. Bringing more tourists across the Pacific would bring more Japanese dollars back to the economy.

Finally, he said, NTT had learned much from AT&T years ago. But it was disappointing that AT&T wouldn't listen to *his* advice, now that NTT had become the world's biggest telephone company. AT&T should stop trying so hard to sell their telephone switching systems and other advanced technology in Japan, since the Japanese have the capability to make all these things themselves. But he had an idea about what AT&T *could* export successfully. At AT&T headquarters in New Jersey he'd seen displays of sweatshirts and baseball caps made by company employees for sale as charity fund-raisers. These products, he said, would be a big hit in Japan.

Yamanouchi, an extraordinarily polite man, was certainly not *trying* to be offensive. He was simply expressing an image of the United States he'd developed as his country catapulted ahead of it. Some Japanese had begun to see America the way some Americans see exotic countries in the Third World: beautiful game parks, delicious indigenous agricultural products, and workers capable of turning out sports clothing at low cost.

From Daniel Burstein, *Yen! Japan's New Financial Empire and Its Threat to America*

★

Recently, researchers learned that only half the students at a California state college were able to locate Japan on a map. However, at a Tokyo junior high school in a working class neighborhood 100 percent of the students knew exactly where to find the United States. Kenichi Ohmae, the managing director of McKinsey & Co., Tokyo, suggests that the failure of modern American education is a major factor behind the country's fall from economic supremacy:

Today, the basis of the world's wealth is shifting from natural resources to advanced technology. The natural resource superpowers are watching the relative worth of their assets dwindle while nations with intelligent human resources are expanding their trade and accumulating surpluses. . . . The population of the United States is now twice that of Japan, but both have a roughly equal number of engineers. The United States has a higher illiteracy rate and more citizens on welfare. . . . In America it is apparently possible to earn a high school or even college diploma and still not be able to read a map or a menu.

From *Beyond National Borders*

★

What about the invasion of tens of thousands of Japanese tourists who fill the streets from New York's Fifth Avenue to Santa Monica's beachfront? What view of America do they take home when their guided tours are over? On assignment for Condé Nast Traveler, *American Daniel Burstein, the author of* Yen! Japan's New Financial Empire and Its Threat to America, *joined a Japanese tour group. He discovered that the local guides were all Japanese, not natives of the countries as employed by American tour groups, and each had definite opinions on contemporary America. Burstein's experiences in San Francisco were typical:*

165

The local guide, Mr. Horiuchi, was an opinionated fellow who imparted his ideas as we drove. First were the requisite warnings we would get in every city—a set of admonitions so dire as to scare anyone out of a latent desire to wander alone or explore beyond the confines of the tour: "Don't trust anyone. People steal passports here. People steal everything here. Don't even trust Japanese people who live here. Some have been living here too long—they will steal too." As for the neighborhood around the St. Francis Hotel, where we would be staying, "Don't go more than two blocks from the hotel," Mr. Horiuchi warned. "It's very dangerous."

He further advised the group not to drink tap water in restaurants and to order bottled water in restaurants throughout America. Storekeepers, he said, would probably try to cheat them when making change, but he conceded this might not always be intentional: "Americans are not as good as Japanese at calculating. Many American youngsters smoke marijuana, so they cannot learn much in school."

Mr. Horiuchi had a lot of theories about the differences between the United States and Japan. American prisons are so full, he explained, that no one bothers to arrest criminals anymore. "We have a better system in Japan. We teach children what is right and wrong from the beginning. Americans try to teach criminals they have done wrong only when it is too late."

. . . The tourists were surprised to discover how many Japanese cars were on California's roads. One member of the group tried counting the Toyotas and Nissans until it became obvious that keeping track would be impossible. "The technology of the Japanese auto industry is ten years ahead of America," Mr. Horiuchi explained bluntly. But the Japanese, he opined, could continue to learn valuable lessons from America's "frontier spirit." As for learning from American industry, those days were over. . . .

As our bus wended its way through the streets of San Francisco, we crisscrossed an unending procession of other Japanese tours. At each stop we jumped out of the bus, took pictures frantically for a few minutes, and jumped back in. Posing for our official group portrait in front of the Golden Gate Bridge, I began to sense that the purpose of this trip was not to see America at all. Rather, our itinerary was designed as a series of backdrops for the posed quick clicks of point-and-shoot cameras. Presumably, back at home, the photos would be evidence that tour members had become that suddenly envied new kind of human being: the oh-so-international Japanese.

From "Yen and the Art of Package Travel,"
Condé Nast Traveler, May 1989

A Japanese businessman who has studied American business practices on his many trips to the United States makes the following complaints about his counterparts across the Pacific:

American executives are too aristocratic. Very few of them have ever worked on a production line themselves, and they have little or no contact with their workers, whom they treat as interchangeable parts. Here in Japan it's routine for the president of a big department store, if he has no other engagement, to have lunch in the company cafeteria, mingling with the salesclerks and other employees. And that's not just a gimmick. All of us—every one of us in Japan— believe that the rise or fall of our organization rests on the individual shoulders of each one of us.

Quoted in Robert Christopher, *The Japanese Mind*

★

The Japanese typically express a two-part theory on the origins of the trade imbalance. First, Japan can make most products better than anyone else, so there's very little for it to buy besides raw materials. Second, Japan's markets are already open, so if American products do not sell there that only confirms America's lack of will. Karatsu Hajime, a professor in electrical engineering at Tokai University and a former technical advisor to Matshushita Electric Industrial Co., made both these arguments in his article "Japanese Know-how for American Industry":

"American auto-parts makers are hard to deal with," former Honda Motor President Kawashima Kiyoshi complained to me recently. "They tell you that GM and Ford have no problems with their supplies, so Honda shouldn't have any problems either. If we don't make a purchase, they claim that we're trying to shut them out." The American suppliers, one is inclined to think, may have a point. But as anyone involved in actual production is aware, different automakers have different requirements. As long as American industry assumes that what is good for General Motors is good for the world, it will never regain its competitive strength.

. . . In the case of electronic parts, for instance, Japanese manufacturers insist on no more than one defective part per several tens of thousands. Few suppliers can meet such an exacting requirement. . . . However, zero-defect quality control is critical for Japanese automakers because their factories are almost totally automated. In such plants defective parts cause production lines to grind to a halt.

The September 1985 agreement to guide the dollar to a lower level was based on a belief that a strong yen would undercut Japan's international competitive power and restore trade to a more equitable balance. One year has passed, and still there are no signs that an avalanche of manufactured American goods is about to overwhelm the Japanese market. Although there has been an increase in imports of German automobiles, even the smaller American models are not selling. About the only American products being promoted in Japanese television commercials are cigarettes—and this at a time when the United States itself has decided to ban promotion of tobacco products from the screen. . . . Are the Americans really serious about selling to Japan? Or do they expect Japanese charity to solve their trade problems?

The reason for the passive approach of U.S. manufacturers is obvious. The deindustrialization of the American economy has progressed to the point where practically no domestically made products can be successfully exported to Japan. Indeed, American products are increasingly unable to compete even in the United States. As the mighty yen squeezes Japanese imports out of the American market, they are being replaced not by domestic products but by imports from South Korea, Taiwan, Hong Kong, Singapore, and more recently, Mexico. To make matters worse, U.S. manufacturers continue to move production facilities offshore despite the success of devaluing the dollar. The time is right, one might imagine, for stepping up investment in domestic industry. Yet American management, which is concerned only with short-term profit, thinks differently.

Here is an example of the attitude of corporate America: When the climbing yen forced Japanese automakers to hike the dollar prices of their cars, Detroit jumped on the bandwagon, marking up its own prices. The truth, it seems, is that Detroit has no intention of expanding its share of the Japanese market; hiking prices at home is a much easier way to rake in profits.

From *Japan Echo,* Winter 1986

Takashi Ishihara, who became president of Nissan Motor Corp. in 1977, has always taken a bleak view of American workers and factories. In a confrontation with Doug Fraser of the United Automobile Workers Union, he shouted: "Your problem in America is of your own making. It is your work force—it is your whole American system. Nobody wants to work."

Quoted in David Haberstam, *The Reckoning*

★

Economist Shimomura Osamu argued that the American insistence that all bilateral trade problems are caused by Japan's ruthless export drive is misplaced, hypocritical, and dangerous. He gave the following example:

Recent demands that Japan deregulate rice are a good example of America's inconsistent stand on free trade. The United States is telling Japan that it should buy American rice because the United States produces a lot of rice and can supply it cheaply. The United States rejects the argument that it should buy Japanese cars because they are cheaper than American cars, yet it brazenly uses the same argument to try to sell its rice to Japan.

Shimomura then offered his explanation of the origins of "Japan-bashing" on the part of American politicians, journalists, business leaders, and workers:

Under free trade conditions, for every winner there must be a loser. But the United States cannot bear to be the loser, and so it concludes that free trade means arranging things so that it cannot lose. Doubtless this attitude reflects the U.S. belief in excellence—its own excellence. America believes that by rights it ought to be stronger than Japan; since it cannot be, it tries to hold Japan back.

From "The 'Japan Problem' Is of America's Making," in *Japan Echo,* Autumn 1987

★

In late 1986 Shotaro Ishinomori's full-length comic book, Japan, Inc., *appeared and quickly sold over 600,000 copies. Its story involves a giant trading company, whose executives grapple with some of Japan's major economic problems—trade conflicts, the rising yen, and an aging society.* Japan, Inc., *suggests the extent to which the Japanese are preoccupied by their relations with the rest of the world, and the degree to which they see themselves as victims. The book opens with a graphic depiction of an America caught up in an orgy of violent Japan-bashing:*

After the second oil crisis, sales of gas-saving Japanese cars took off in the U.S. In 1980 there was a recorded growth of 17.6% over 1979, and automobile friction rose.

Meanwhile, Kudo, an executive at the big Mitsutomo Automobile Corporation, worries about the unwillingness of Japanese government and corporate officials to stand up to unfair and unreasonable American demands:

★

Hiroshima has long been a rallying point for peace campaigners. But some Japanese resent America's victory. So argues British author Ian Buruma in this dispatch for The Spectator *about more extreme Japanese reactions to foreign pressures:*

In a curious new book, readers are offered the following curious theory: the two tragic symbols of the second world war are Auschwitz and Hiroshima. The Jews were clever enough to make sure nobody touched Auschwitz, so this monument to Jewish suffering could serve as a boost to their "racial renaissance." The Japanese, however, on orders from General MacArthur, rebuilt Hiroshima and, under the influence of the Tokyo Trials, mistakenly believed that Hiroshima was bombed because the Japanese started the war. So, while the Jews now rule the world, the Japanese have lost their "racial confidence." If only they had left Hiroshima in ruins, as a permanent appeal to the world, the Japanese would have regained their "identity." The book, by a former economist called Uno Masami, and entitled *The Day the Dollar Becomes Paper,* is a best-seller. . . .

The war, Uno says, was forced on Japan by Jews in Shanghai, who supported Chiang Kai-shek, and Jews in America, who put pressure on Roosevelt—a Jew himself, of course—to get into the war with Germany. Jews built the nuclear bomb and Jews drew up a democratic, egalitarian "peace constitution" which emasculated Japanese power and pride. . . .

There is no evidence that [Prime Minister] Nakasone believes any of this, and if he does, he is clever enough to keep it to himself. Instead Nakasone's rhetoric, a mixture of prewar national myths and postwar theories about the Japanese national character, is more peaceful, despite his fondness for discredited wartime symbols. Indeed, it is all about peace. The Japanese should not feel guilty about the war because Japanese culture, and what Japanese like to call the Japanese spirit, are inherently peaceful. Japanese culture, according to Nakasone, is a "wet, monsoon culture," based on mutual trust and social harmony, while Western culture, born of the arid desert, is based on power, wars, and contracts.

This is a popular theory in Japan. The philosopher Umehara Takeshi, who has become a popular guest on television chat shows, wrote a book entitled *Theory of Japanese Culture.* He holds that

European civilization is threatening mankind because it is by nature vengeful and belligerent. Zeus and "the Christian god" are angry gods of vengeance; Japanese gods are all uniquely peaceful. Thus another thinker of the new Right, Hasegawa Michiko, can argue that the Japanese war was a temporary aberration which took place because Japan was forced by Western imperialism to join the aggressive outside world, ruled by bellicose European nations. . . .

Japan's geographical and linguistic isolation makes it fairly easy to convince the great television-watching public that they are constantly threatened by an unfriendly world—idiot American Congressmen bashing Japanese cassette recorders with hammers help to confirm this belief. Criticism from the outside, uniformly labelled "Japan-bashing," is seen as a result of natural Western aggression and misunderstanding of Japanese culture. Toshiba, for example, did not seriously threaten the security of Japan and her allies by selling sensitive technology to the Soviet Union, but is simply the victim of Japan-bashing by jealous, aggressive Americans, or so it would seem from the Japanese popular press.

From *The Spectator,* August 22, 1987

A much more constructive view of American criticism of Japan comes from Saeki Shoichi, a professor of American literature at Chuo University. In 1987 he spent a semester teaching at the University of California in Berkeley and returned with these perceptive observations on some critical differences between the two cultures:

Berkeley may not be a typical American campus, but the difference between it and any college campus in Japan is like night and day. It seems utterly unfettered, all its denizens free to do as they please. Call it frivolous if you will, but it has an order of its own, and few genuine disturbances occur. I would not hesitate to tell anyone who asked that American college campuses have far more vitality than their Japanese counterparts, and in general offer a more congenial environment.

A major reason is the atmosphere in the classrooms, the way students respond. At Berkeley I gave a course on Japanese literary theory using works translated into English. The lively, direct response of my American university students puts to shame anything one could expect in Japan. Questions, comments, arguments, and counterarguments flew. In Japanese universities even considerable effort on the teacher's part usually fails to elicit any response or reaction. When the teacher solicits the students' opinions, they sit in stony silence, many of them casting their eyes downward lest they be called on. . . .

Since returning to Japan, I have run across the term "Japan-bashing" constantly. To be sure, the United States seems to be leveling an unending barrage of complaints against Japan on a wide range of issues, from alleged semiconductor dumping and Toshiba Machine's violation of COCOM (Coordinating Committee for Export Control) regulations to the domestic rice and beef markets and participation in construction of the new Kansai International Airport. . . . What I wish to point out is that this sort of repeated confrontation is typical American behavior.

Make no mistake, demolishing a Toshiba radio cassette player with a hammer is embarrassingly childish behavior for any politician. But even this can be interpreted as a somewhat extreme manifestation of American-style directness. I would venture to add that it is probably preferable to allowing one's irritation and discontent to seethe within.

I am reminded of the classroom behavior of my Berkeley students. In America college students bring all their gripes and grievances right out into the open and confront the instructor with them. It is almost expected for students to complain about the marks they receive on papers and tests. "I don't see why you gave me this grade," they insist. "Why did you give me a B? Show me where the problem is." And the teacher has to respond clearly to each of these queries and complaints.

Because it is unthinkable for a student to complain to a professor about test scores or grades in Japan, I was initially taken aback and even somewhat offended by this behavior. However, when I sat down and talked with the students, I found them neither emotional nor intractable. A few got a bit worked up, but once they heard my explanation and their doubts were dispelled, they would generally say "O.K." with a relieved expression and depart cheerfully. Once they have received an explanation they can accept, the problem is solved. The direct approach, in other words, allows for a quick solution—provided, that is, that the instructor's explanation is frank and clear. It would probably never occur to most American students that their actions and reactions might provoke the professor to anger.

I believe that the enviable vitality of the American classroom relates directly to this sort of thinking.

This attitude, this basic premise, is what Japanese classrooms sorely lack. Japanese teachers are apt to bristle at any comment or question that challenges their authority. The students, for their part, doubtless think long and hard before speaking up. They worry that if they ask too simple a question they will be written off as dull-witted. They fear not only the professor's disapproval but also the disgusted looks of classmates.

At Japanese universities this tendency holds even in seminars and small classes. These days you find a surprising number of students who do such a faultless job of preparing and presenting their reports that you are tempted to pat them on the head. Yet something is lacking. Their personations are too conventional, too tidy. They research diligently and itemize all the different opinions and theories on a given theme or problem in an effort to compile a report with which no one can take issue. But they take too much care over each detail and end up with a presentation that lacks character. This seems to be the result of a powerful defense mechanism that urges them to avoid mistakes and thus prevent the teacher and classmates from finding fault or asking searching questions. . . .

The marked difference between the look and feel of classrooms in Japan and those in the United States comes to mind when I hear complaints of Japan-bashing. Washington says whatever it pleases with brash assertiveness, while Tokyo responds with passive, defensive, evasive mumbling. That the behavior of college students should echo the rhythms of Japan-U.S. trade friction is perhaps less amusing than frightening.

From "Rediscovering America's Dynamic Society,"
in *Japan Echo,* Spring 1988

Yuji Hirayama, a professor of economics at Shinshu University, came to similar conclusions regarding the differences between American and Japanese research scientists. His remarks first appeared in the newspaper Shinano Mainichi *of Nagano:*

When biologist Susumu Tonegawa received the Nobel Prize in 1987, Japan's scientists were chagrined, for his research was conducted mainly at the Massachusetts Institute of Technology in the U.S. Japan has earned only five Nobel Prizes in science since the awards began in 1901. Recently, I spent three months visiting U.S. universities and research institutes to discover why American scientists and scholars are so much more creative than their Japanese counterparts.

The key to America's high-powered intellectual performance is motivation. U.S. scientists are driven by more than personal ambition. Imbued with a strong sense of mission, they try to live by their ideals and take the pursuit of scientific truth seriously. Moreover, the society encourages and rewards outstanding effort. In Japan, by contrast, the social ideal is the hard-working, low-key craftsman. To maintain group harmony, we are encouraged to downplay individualism. Japanese society frowns on people who stand out from the crowd, who disrupt the status quo.

In the U.S. individuals are expected to take charge of their own lives. Self-expression is highly valued. And Americans, for better or worse, are aggressive. Quiet, self-effacing Japanese cut a poor figure in U.S. labs.

U.S. institutions subject every scientist to ruthless scrutiny. The theme must be relevant, the methodology reliable, the conclusions valid. Scholars who do not measure up to these exacting standards get less responsibility and are politely ignored. The competition to get to the top of any scientific field is severe, and many fall by the wayside. In Japan a scientist is virtually assured of tenure merely by landing a job. You can work hard or coast along; no one really cares. . . .

Recently team efforts in both countries have made major breakthroughs in basic research. This team approach often utilizes facilities more efficiently than individuals can. But individuals, not groups, come up with new ideas, the sine qua non of research. Group work—the norm in Japan—stimulates good minds, but most team members exert a leveling influence on their members and thus stifle individual creativity.

My trip to the U.S. forced me to re-examine my own research methods and motivation. I realized that only by unleashing society's creative forces can we make claims on the future. That means restructuring academic and research institutions to maximize individual initiative. To fail in that challenge is to accept being second-best.

Quoted from *World Press Review*, January 1989

★

Jiro Tokuyama, a senior adviser to the Mitsui Research Center, insists:

The U.S. is a land of opportunity and Japan is a land of lack of opportunity. We close our market because opportunities are scarce and we don't want to share them with others. Already our college graduates don't have the same opportunities as those twenty years ago. But being closed is a weakness. This is our dilemma.

Quoted in the *Wall Street Journal,* January 30, 1989

Masataka Kosaka, a professor of economics at Kyoto University, also has an optimistic appraisal of America's future in the world:

It is probably a mistake to believe that the United States will blithely choose the path to ruin by allowing its debt to grow without bound. The United States makes great jumps forward every ten or twenty years and it may well be able to take advantage of this national characteristic to raise productivity and regain its position of leadership in the world economy. The Japanese have tended of late to view the United States as an ailing giant, but this is more a reaction to Japan's worship of the United States over the past three or four decades than an accurate appraisal of the situation.

From "Can Japan Cope?" in *Look Japan,* January 1987

And finally Seizaburo Sato, a Japanese political scientist and advisor to former Prime Minister Nakasone, is even more emphatic, predicting:

The 20th century was the American century. And the 21st century will be the American century.

Quoted in the *Wall Street Journal,* January 23, 1989

7 ★ AMERICAN
★ POLITICS
★

"POLITICS *is the only pleasure an American knows,*" *Alexis de Tocqueville observed in 1832. Few aspects of the American scene have proven more perplexing to foreign observers than the dynamics of our politics. The British, who are reared to strict party loyalty, look upon the undisciplined competition for individual power in the U.S. House of Representatives, where "leaders" cannot confidently promise to deliver the votes of their own party members, as impossibly anarchic. And the structured and hierarchical nature of Japanese democracy, in which individual ambitions are always submerged beneath an identification with the group, represents yet another democratic process far removed from the American system. At the other extreme, the Marxist approach reduces American politics to a manifestation of economic forces and interests in which all political leaders are puppets of the monopolists and foreign policy is bound to be imperialistic.*

Americans often pride themselves on practicality and skepticism about ideology. But in fact, we are a people who are deeply ideological on certain basic matters. Our national ideology, for example, insists that adversarial methods and free-market competition together produce efficient solutions to the problems of contemporary society. And yet in the European Community, governments take an active role in directing indus-

trial research and promoting projects too vast or too expensive for individual countries. Private money under governmental direction is building the Channel Tunnel. Other examples are the European Space Agency, the Airbus consortium, and numerous high-technology military programs. Foreigners often find infuriating the sense of inevitability that most Americans have about the way the United States does things, assuming that this must be the best, even the only, way.

British journalist and author Alistair Cooke made the following observation in his BBC broadcast of October 19, 1969:

There's just one point I'd like to make to people who despair of American society—and I have to confess it's a point I often forget myself. In a self-governing republic—good government in some places, dubious in others—3,000 miles wide, 1,800 miles long, with fifty separate states which in many important matters have almost absolute powers; with 200 million people drawn from scores of nations; what is remarkable is not the conflict between them but the truce. Enough is happening in America at any one time—enough that is exciting, frightening, funny, brutal, brave, intolerable, bizarre, dull, slavish, eccentric, inspiring, and disastrous—that almost anything you care to say about the United States is true. You can make a case for thinking this the best, the worst, the most abject, the most alert democracy ever invented.

On the eve of the 1988 presidential election, visiting Soviet human rights activist Andrei Sakharov told reporters at a press conference:

I respect in America her democracy. I respect her dynamism, her self-criticism. It is a very rare quality in the world arena. In most countries public opinion is structured to support the image of that country.

Britisher David Frost observed during the 1988 election:

In England people *stand* for office. In America they *run* for office—It's more vigorous there.

From *The Today Show*, September 6, 1988

Hanna Roditi, the director of a Tel Aviv school, visited America and came away a strong supporter:

With all the problems, what impresses me the most about America is that there's no gap between ideology and reality. In most countries they talk about freedom and justice and a chance for everybody, but the reality is so far away from that. In America they don't just talk about those principles, they really apply them.

Quoted in the *Dallas Morning News,* July 6, 1986

Wan Di offered the following thoughts on the 200th anniversary of the American Constitution in the Beijing Review:

Although the U.S. Constitution has been flexible enough to survive 200 years, it may be time to have another look at this historical masterpiece. The increasing power of the government, particularly of the White House, often encroaches on areas reserved for others and can create more opportunities for the abuse of powers. At the same time, the U.S. government sometimes seems unable to act efficiently. In the year of the Constitution's bicentennial, it seems that there is a need for a realistic assessment of the document with a view to its continual evolution.

★

British actor and author Peter Ustinov has written often and wittily on American politics. After observing the political developments of the mid-seventies, he noted:

I'm depressed about America. It's going through a crisis within itself. It is something like Palestine must have been before Christ appeared, a country of minor prophets. Unfortunately, America is also highly concerned with major profits.

And on another occasion Ustinov scoffed:

In America they interpret American democracy as the inalienable right to sit on your own front-porch in your pajamas drinking a can of beer and shouting out, "Where else is this possible?" Which doesn't seem to be freedom, really, so much as licence.

From *The Wit of Peter Ustinov*

British observers in the sixties and early seventies sometimes worried about the growing threat of an imperial presidency. "The U.S. Presidency is a Tudor monarchy plus telephones," novelist Anthony Burgess commented during the darker times of the Johnson and Nixon administrations. T. H. White, the British author whose novel The Once and Future King *yielded the popular Broadway musical* Camelot, *had come to a similar conclusion shortly before his death in 1964:*

America is a bit like ancient Rome. She has her senators and presidents from families of power and riches. Roosevelts and Kennedys might just as well be Claudians or Acilians. We are their cultured Greeks, they our powerful Romans. So why not introduce slavery too? It worked very well under Hadrian, whose laws for slaves were enlightened. Why not solve the labor shortage by importing Costa Ricans, etc., without hindrance and using them to solve the problem of porters and room service? . . . I foresee a time when the President of the United States will be as powerful and vicious as Caligula. We are in the Republican Rome at present; the Emperors of America have yet to seize power.

From *America at Last*

Vladimir Bukovsky, a dissident political activist who spent eleven years in Soviet prisons and psychiatric hospitals before being sent to the West in 1976, expressed a common view among Russian exiles:

The United States is in its political development something like a handicapped adolescent.

Quoted in *U.S. News and World Report*, August 17, 1987

★

Anthony Burgess commented in a 1971 article in the New York Times:

American politics, at both the state and federal levels, is too much concerned with the protection of large fortunes, America being the only example in history of a genuine timocracy. The wealth qualification for the aspiring politician is taken for granted; a government system dedicated to the promotion of personal wealth in a few selected areas will never act for the public good. The time has come, nevertheless, for citizens to demand, from their government, a measure of socialization—the provision of amenities for the many, of which adequate state pensions and sickness benefits, as well as nationalized transport, should be priorities.

★

"In one sense, virtually everyone in America is THE ESTABLISHMENT with the possible exception of migrant workers and people on welfare," Jane Walmsley observed in Brit-think, Ameri-think. However, she did concede the development of a "Super Establishment," what she called the "Power Elite," and offered this tongue-in-cheek guide on how to recognize the people who have the money and influence to make the elected political leaders responsive to their needs:

AMERICA'S HAUTE ESTABLISHMENT—ANYONE WHO:
1. is unduly preoccupied with the latest rulings on tax shelters.
2. has stopped *buying* "how to" books and started *writing* them.
3. has ever played in the Bob Hope Classic.
4. buys drugs at regular price.
5. toys with the food at yet another $1,000-a-plate fund-raising dinner, then eats an omelette at home.
6. has homes and cars on both coasts.
7. is racking up "frequent traveler miles" with three separate airlines.
8. has a nutritionist, a broker, an accountant, a lawyer, a shrink, a housekeeper, and a personal "trainer," and is considering a press agent.
9. owns several furs, but spends half the year in hot climates.
10. operates a McDonald's franchise.
11. has personal and corporate AMEX Platinum Cards and gets letters of congratulations for frequent use.
12. lost money with John DeLorean.

Russian novelist Vassily Aksyonov is one who cheerfully accepts the disparity between the classes in America:

If there was such a thing as an American Millionaires' Club, it would represent the heart and soul of the country. Social demagoguery has no place in a society where everyone wants to be a millionaire, where inequality encourages people to pull themselves up by their boot straps and earn more, spend more. The consumer society offers a new kind of equality, an equality based on the marketplace rather than on Marxism or other social theories. A rich man buys a Rolls-Royce for $100,000, a poor man buys a Honda for $5,000. The inequality, the social injustice of it all! But wait. Is the Civic so inferior to the Silver Shadow? It will light your cigarettes and play your tapes; it has a heater and an air-conditioner, first-rate shock absorbers, and comfortable seats. And even if those seats are plastic instead of morocco, it will take you wherever you want to go. As far as actual transportation is concerned, therefore, the rich man and the poor man are all but equal. Though not quite. Many parking garages refuse to take Rollses: the insurance rates are too high. There you have it: discrimination against the rich.

From *In Search of Melancholy Baby*

Polish visitor Leopold Tyrmand joked:

At home in Warsaw, I'm going to repeat that the American working class is deprived of roofs over their heads. Chiefly when they sit in convertibles.

From *Notebooks of a Dilettante*

Three foreign observers, a South African, Indian, and Russian, comment on the American racial situation:

You in America are very efficient. You killed your King. But we still have this Mandela. We can't get rid of him.

A white used-car dealer in Johannesburg, South Africa

Arun Gandhi, the grandson of the martyred leader in India's hard-won struggle for independence, visited Oxford, Mississippi, in 1988 to conduct

research for a book comparing discrimination in the United States with that in South Africa and India. Although he acknowledged that blacks had scored impressive gains in civil and economic rights over the past two decades, he still insisted that racial hatreds bitterly divide American society. He told reporters:

I see both sides—whites and blacks—just barely tolerating each other and not being fully understanding or accepting. There is no real integration. Whites have taken a hard position; blacks are taking a hard position. There is no dialogue between them. Tensions are building and confrontations are inevitable.

The Mississippi Delta is a very sorry situation. You see these white plantation owners in their big mansions and right next to them are black people who work for them living in shacks that are ready to fall apart.

Quoted in the *Los Angeles Times*, May 23, 1988

Yelena Hanga is a young journalist for the Moscow News agency. In early 1988 she toured the United States on assignment to examine the plight of black Americans. What made her unusual was the fact that she is the granddaughter of a black-American communist cotton farmer who emigrated to the Soviet Union with his white wife in the 1930s. Toward the end of her trip she told representatives of the American media:

I made an investigation about the attitudes of blacks and whites to the Soviet Union. I think that well-to-do blacks are more conservative toward the Soviet Union than well-to-do whites. But among average people, the blacks are more progressive. I talked with young black college students in Los Angeles. Among them, they have much more favorable feelings about the Soviet Union than white Americans because the American press feeds people with stereotypes. That's not a secret to anybody.

If you say to a white person, "Communists are going to take everything from you," he will believe it because that is what he reads. If you say the same thing to a black person, he'll think about whether it's true or not because so many bad things have been written about blacks. Also, black people relate better to the Soviet Union because they know there is no racism there.

Quoted in the *Christian Science Monitor*, February 19, 1988

Grass-roots American politics have fascinated two visitors as diverse as Polish writer Malgorzata Niezabitowska and the British correspondent Alistair Cooke. Niezabitowska, who crossed the States in the summer of 1986 on assignment for National Geographic, *was strongly impressed by the hundreds of American flags she saw everywhere, a sight that carried powerful political overtones for her:*

It happened at the very beginning of our journey across America. On a July morning we were driving through small Massachusetts towns. Flags were hoisted on many houses, stores, banks, and gas stations along the way. I said to Tomek, "It must be a national holiday."

When we stopped for gas, however, we found out that the day was no different from any other. Only later did we realize that Americans fly the flag for no other reason than patriotic sentiment.

We Poles are also greatly attached to our white-and-red flag, but its public use apart from official holidays is forbidden. Any violation of this state monopoly is in Poland a symbol of resistance. That is why the famous Solidarity emblem shows the Polish flag defiantly streaming in the wind. We were startled, delighted, and a bit envious to be among a people who so freely use their flag to express their feelings.

From National Geographic, January 1988

★

In 1968 Alistair Cooke visited New Hampshire to cover the forthcoming presidential primary elections and found himself, one cold and blustery winter evening, in the overheated basement of a church, observing his first New England town meeting. Later he wrote the following account of that experience:

There were, I should guess, a hundred, a hundred and twenty people in there. Farmers in knee boots, leather jackets and plaid shirts, overalls, jeans, snow boots, galoshes. Road men in peaked caps and check shirts. Women in cloth coats and bandannas and hats that had served through two wars. Young girls in ski pants and windbreakers. Tradesmen and a teacher or two in coats and ties. They all sat on rows of folding chairs facing the stage, some of them picking their teeth and wiping their mouths and making discreet sucking sounds. . . .

The business was all set down in a fat little booklet, which had just gone out to every family by mail and which now rested on their laps. It was the annual report of the Town of Boscawen (pronounced Boskwine). A handsome print job of a hundred glossy pages, containing an accounting of every nickel spent in the past year, beginning with "Property Tax, current year $76,659.84," going on to $1,172 to the railroad and $300 for dog licenses and down to "Ezekiel Webster, $300 for fuel for the grange hall."

What they were doing was nothing less than the annual business of the town meeting, which is called in every big and small town of the six states of New England, and in many places in the Midwest originally settled by New Englanders; so that every man and woman who lives there shall have a voice in how the town's moneys are to be spent.

Shall they build a new hospital? It will go to a vote. Shall the bounty paid to every boy who brings in a dead hedgehog (porcupine, to be exact) be reduced to twenty-five cents or maintained at fifty cents? The porcupine is a pest in these parts and ruins floorboards, sewers, and the family's sleep. There was a tense issue here. Some boys had been fetching in only the tails, which can be ingeniously manufactured. The moral question was whether they ought not to have turned in also the nose and whiskers. While this was being debated, an old bald man in knee boots got up and hurled three logs on the stove in the middle of the room. The temperature had been easing down to a chill eighty-five or so. The old man went out and soon the pipes started sizzling again, and it was back to a comfortable ninety-five. There was a hound dog somewhere which occasionally heckled the proceedings with a long low whine. When it heard a motion passed with a reverberating "Aye," it let loose with a short, high yelp. . . .

There were some perfunctory questions about various items in the booklet, and these explanatory exchanges gave you a chance to catch up on the agenda. $14,362.09 for road maintenance. That might sound like a lot for a small village but in winter the snow can pile up to ten feet and in summer the roads groan and crack with the heat. The snowplows guzzle gasoline and there is the matter of repairing their scoops and brushes after every snowfall.

$4,288 for old-age assistance. $315 for Memorial Day "and other patriotic celebrations—fireworks for Independence Day, a new flag for Washington's birthday." The flagpole in Boscawen had cracked last year, and it took $50 to mend it. . . .

The New England town meeting grew out of the English vestry meeting, but it grew very fast into something else because in the eighteenth century landowners with royal grants were always trying to run the town. It was the majority vote of the town meeting, made up of everyone from the parson to the street sweeper, that hand-cuffed their power. In 1774, two years before the American Revolution, London caught on a little late to the subversive content of this humble institution. The Parliamentary Act of that year banned it throughout the colonies as a "revolutionary and powerful force." Which it was and can be, wherever the people have the wit to preserve it. For it is the original backbone of local government and local initiative in the United States. To the sophisticated visitor it is now, of course, merely quaint and delightful. To the people who take part in it, it is the Parliament of Man.

From *Talk About America*

However, John Blundell, the British-born executive vice-president of the Institute for Humane Studies at George Mason University, was appalled at the extent to which Americans surrendered their individual freedoms when they moved into some communities:

One of the more bizarre aspects of life in America is local government. The United States has a written constitution to "secure the Blessings of Liberty"; the United Kingdom's [is] unwritten. The U.S. does not have hard-left Marxist local authorities, the U.K. does. Yet otherwise sane local council members in the United States daily exercise horrendous powers that megalomaniac Brits can only dream about.

In Palo Alto, California, you can't hang out the wash or build a child's treehouse. In nearby Atherton, a fascist planner's heaven, residents can't rent out a room in their home, and there are *no* businesses. In Fairfax, Virginia, no more than three unrelated people may share a house, and basketball hoops on free-standing poles are tightly regulated and closely monitored by local officials. You're not free to dribble in Fairfax driveways.

Without specific legislation authorizing such nonsense, no British judge would hesitate to throw it out. The dark side of American local government and of the, to me, totally foreign neighborhood associated system cannot weather a test of reasonableness.

From "What About Drug Stores?" in *Reason*, January 1988

America's Foreign Policy

"Living next to the United States is like sleeping with an elephant," Pierre Trudeau, the former prime minister of Canada, once observed. "You are very aware of every twitch and grunt." Far more controversial than America's domestic politics are her foreign policies, which impinge directly or indirectly upon hundreds of millions of people abroad.

French novelist André Malraux observed:

The United States is the first nation in history to become a dominant world power without trying to do so.

Quoted in *Life*, October 1987

French actor Yves Montand is one who believes that America is a potent force for good in the world:

You want to criticize America? *Bien.* America is not perfect. But be careful when you criticize America's political institutions. They are the safeguard of freedom on this planet. In our world without America there would be no France!

Quoted in *People*, May 16, 1988

Polish author Leopold Tyrmand saw a correlation between America's size and her global responsibilities:

It takes but a glance to notice that tomatoes and billiard tables, highways and the lust for life are unquestionably larger here than in Europe. But the consequences are not always obvious, either to Americans or to us. We, for example, tend to overlook what great literature, great idealism, and great determination are derived from this scale of distance and streets. Americans sometimes seem to forget what grave responsibilities towards the world weigh upon them and what great skill is necessary to fulfill great obligations.

From *Notebooks of a Dilettante*

Chinese editor Liu Zongren spent two years in Chicago and afterward concluded:

The Chinese have a proverb: "A rich man talks louder." America had long and arrogantly tried to keep power over others with its economic strength. Won't obey? Well, we won't give you grains, machines, or technology. They were trying to play God. Carter had used this kind of pressure and Reagan is now using it. The motto of Sun Yat-sen, the pioneer of the modern Chinese revolution, was, "Fight to stand equal among the nations of the world." I hoped that American politicians would someday learn from the words of this great world leader.

From *Two Years in the Melting Pot*

Two more observations by Peter Ustinov:

At times the United States are about as elegant as an elephant dancing on its points in their attempt to avoid hurting the sensibilities of smaller nations and allies in the vast expediency which makes up the various Atlantic and Pacific alliances.

American democracy is like that of a rich man who hails the porter in his apartment block. "Hi, Tom!" (His name's really Jack.) "How are the kids, Tom?" (He has no children.) Yet both parties are pleased with this friendly transaction.

From *The Wit of Peter Ustinov*

★

Some expressions of contempt from world bankers and economic advisors concerned with the burgeoning American trade and budget deficits:

193

When you are the world's greatest debtor, it's hard to pay attention to you.

Australian banker, Melbourne

★

In this world money is power. And America no longer has the money.

Japanese banker, Tokyo

★

One way to look at the financial condition of America in the summer of 1988 is to imagine the country as one vast leveraged buy-out. Like a company, it has built up huge debts, outpacing its equity. As is by now familiar, the United States has become the world's largest debtor and is selling off its assets (factories, property, bonds) to foreigners in order to service its debts. Unlike most LBOs, however, the United States has continued to borrow as if there is no tomorrow. Which, if it carries on borrowing, there may not be.

From *The Economist,* June 11, 1988

★

The following exchange took place in the "Letters to the Editor" section of the San Diego Union *on January 20 and 23, 1988:*

[Americans call their military] service in Germany a supplied service, costing American taxpayers enormous amounts, and suggest that Germany help foot the bill.

I, as a young German citizen, never before realized how fortunate we are. We are honored to be allowed to house your nuclear warheads in our country! What fun it is to relax in our Alps and listen to the American war machine raging below and overhead. Of all the more deserving countries, why is it that we get so much military protection? Could it be that the location of my country is, in fact, essential to the defense of America?

Your conflicts with the Soviet Union will be jousted out, in, on, and over the population of Europe. Germany is ground zero. Expecting us to foot the bill for this is an insult!

Looking at the American war machine trampling across Germany frightened me as a child and it still frightens me now. I don't feel safe. I feel occupied!

Karoline Keesling

I would like to answer the "young German citizen's" question. "What fun it is to relax in our Alps and listen to the American war machine raging below and overhead."

I am an older, naturalized German-American citizen who listened to the "American war machine" for months on end when these machines, during Stalin's brutal attempts to subdue West Berlin, kept the citizens of Berlin alive and free.

I listened to their "raging" with the same rapture as I listen today to Beethoven's Ninth Symphony, and have not forgotten the American lives lost in this "joust."

Karoline Keesling should ask the Poles, East Germans, Hungarians, etc., etc., if they would have felt insulted when asked to "help foot the bill for an American war machine" which could have kept them free.

The answer will help her to relax in her Alps.

Hellmuth Fleige

The following story appeared in the "Humor in Uniform" section of Reader's Digest, *July 1988:*

As a U.S. Army company commander conducting armored maneuvers in Germany, I was careful to minimize the impact on our host nation's civilians. One morning as our tanks rattled over the cobblestone streets of a small village, I noticed a group of elderly Germans covering their ears from the deafening roar. I sent my radioman over to apologize for the inconvenience.

The private returned shortly, hands filled with gifts of cheese, bread, and coffee. "Sir!" he shouted above the din. "They said our vehicles are very noisy, but Russian tanks would be much louder."

Contributed by Capt. Thomas T. Smith

An older generation of Europeans remembers the Nazi occupation and continues to harbor strong feelings of gratitude toward their American liberators, as American columnist Richard Reeves discovered on a 1988 trip to Normandy, where almost two million young Americans fought and thirty-one thousand of them were killed in seventy-six days in 1944:

"We are eternally grateful to the United States for having given us back our liberty and dignity," said Jean-Marie Girault, the mayor of this city in Normandy, last Monday during the dedication ceremonies for the city's museum of the D-Day landings and the Battle of Normandy of World War II.

On June 6, 1944, Girault was 18 years old. He worked as a Red Cross volunteer tending the wounded when the Americans, the British, the Canadians, and their allies came ashore that day. The museum, on top of a German command bunker, was his idea. But he really didn't begin to work on it until 1983, when the city was finally rebuilt; 80 percent of it was rubble after the battle of Normandy.

In the nearby city of Lisieux, a man had once asked me what I thought of the place. "Quite nice," I said. "No," he said. "No more. But it was beautiful before the bombing."

"Who did the bombing?" I asked stupidly.

"You did," he said. . . .

"You are American, yes?" a woman a little older than I said, coming up to my wife and me in a café. "I am from Caen. I was just a little girl when we ran to the fields and lived out there because of the bombings. We will always be grateful to you for coming. All those boys. I realize now they were so young."

. . . It seems to me that there are very few ugly Americans abroad these days. There are, however, more than a few stupid ones at home. Or, at least that is how it seems to friendly foreigners, who find us almost awesome in our openness and generosity, but can't understand why we seem so determined to destroy or diminish ourselves with deficits and drugs and demonic anti-communism.

Oscar Arias Sánchez, the president of Costa Rica and a Nobel Peace Prize winner, was asked by reporter Tad Szulc what would be the most fruitful approach for the United States to take toward Central America. He replied:

Be nice. Stop being the ugly American. There are so many ways of obtaining the support, affection, and gratitude of the people of Latin America through U.S. help and understanding that I think you should concentrate on a dialogue with us—not the use of force.

Quoted in *Parade* magazine, August 28, 1988

Honduran Manuel Acosta Bonilla, a prominent lawyer and politician, resents American policy toward his country:

Honduras has been like the circus dog that jumps through the hoops when its master tells it to. There has been a complete submission to the United States, and people are tired of it.

Quoted in a *New York Times* News Service story, April 13, 1988

Directly opposite the U.S. Special Interests Section in Havana, a branch of the Swiss embassy staffed by twenty Americans, rises a neon sign featuring a caricatured version of Uncle Sam and a Cuban guerrilla. It flashes the message: MR. IMPERIALIST! WE HAVE ABSOLUTELY NO FEAR OF YOU.

On the back wall of a large warehouse in southern San Diego, near the border with Mexico, someone has painted a series of political slogans in Spanish:

Migra Asesinos! Rompemos la Frontera. Bajo con la Ley Simpson–Rodino. Revolución Mundial, No Guerra Mundial. ("Immigration Murderers! We are tearing apart the border! Down with the Simpson-Rodina Law! World Revolution, not World War.")

Aquí Estamos. Aquí nos quedamos. No nos Vamos! ("Here we are. Here we'll stay. We will not go!")

A Cuban government worker in Havana dreams wistfully of an escape to Florida: "If ever I get to the U.S. I could get a job in

Hollywood. All my life I have learned how to act. Sometimes I smile inside, it is so crazy."

Quoted in *Time*, September 21, 1987

★

After American naval pilots shot down two Libyan fighters on January 4, 1989, Muammar Gaddafi warned in Tripoli:

If America has prevailed because it is a superpower in the air and the sea, it will inevitably be defeated on land. We, as well as the fishes, are awaiting them.

Quoted in the *San Diego Union*

★

In 1982 American Mark Salzman arrived in Hunan Province in China, where he spent over a year teaching English to adult instructors and studying the martial arts. One day he engaged his students in a discussion of World War II, which produced unexpected results:

Five minutes after the bell rang for afternoon class, the Middle-Aged English Teachers gradually trickled into the classroom and argued with each other for a few minutes. It seemed that the blackboard had gone unerased the night before, and they were trying to determine who among them had been responsible for erasing it. I saw that the discussion could easily fill the two hours, so I asked them to put it off until after class and to open their textbooks to Chapter Thirteen. That chapter was entitled "War" and contained two pages of photographs of World War II destruction, including a shot of the atomic bomb explosion over Hiroshima.

After they had settled down, I had them read passages from the text and do a few grammar exercises. As usual, we finished up with "free talk" on the chapter. Since China and the United States fought on the same side during World War II, I did not think this would be an offensive or controversial subject.

"Teacher Zhu, you were a Navy man, can you tell us something about your experiences during the war?"

Teacher Zhu, an aspiring Party member, stood up and smiled.

"Yes." He hesitated. "This is a picture of the atom bomb, isn't it?"

"Yes."

He smiled stiffly. "Teacher Mark—how do you feel, knowing your country dropped an atom bomb on innocent people?"

My face turned red with embarrassment at having the question put so personally, but I tried to remain detached.

"That is a good question, Teacher Zhu. I can tell you that in America, many people disagree about this. Not everyone thinks it was the right thing to do, although most people think it saved lives."

"How did it save lives?"

"Well, by ending the war quickly."

Here, Teacher Zhu looked around the room at his classmates.

"But Teacher Mark! It is a fact that the Japanese had already surrendered to the Communist Eighth Route Army of China. America put the bomb on Japan to make the world think America was the . . . the . . ."

"The victor!" shouted Fatty Du.

"Yes—the victor," said Teacher Zhu.

I must have stood gaping for a long time, for the other students began to laugh nervously.

"Teacher Zhu," I asked, "how do you know this is a fact?"

"Because that is what our newspapers say!"

"I see. But our newspapers tell a different story. How can we know which newspaper has told the truth?"

Here he seemed relieved.

"That is easy! Our newspapers are controlled by the people, but your newspapers are owned by capitalist organizations, so of course they make things up to support themselves. Don't you think so?"

My mouth opened and closed a few times but no sound came out. Fatty Du, apparently believing that the truth had been too much for me, came to my aid.

"It doesn't matter! Any capitalist country would do that. It is not just your country!"

My head was swimming. I asked her if she thought only capitalistic countries lied in the papers.

"Oh, of course not! The Russians do it, too. But here in China, we have no reason to lie in the papers. When we make a mistake, we admit it! As for war, there is nothing to lie about. If you look at history, you can see that China has never attacked a nation, it has only defended its borders. We love peace. If we were the most powerful country in the world, think how peaceful the world would be!"

From *Iron and Silk*

★

*Films about what the Vietnamese government calls "the American War"
have become a staple of that country's movie industry. Since 1975 the Ho
Chi Minh City Film Company has produced over seventy movies, one
third of which treat the war. Most are shot in black and white with
budgets of less than $500,000. Murray Hiebert covered this aspect of
postwar Vietnam in an article for the* Far Eastern Economic Review:

Thousands of Vietnamese have flocked to theaters in recent months
to see *Platoon,* the 1987 Academy Award–winning movie about the
experiences of American soldiers fighting in Vietnam. *Platoon* is the
first American-made movie about the Vietnam war shown in Ho Chi
Minh City since communist forces defeated the U.S.-backed government in 1975 in what was then South Vietnam.

Vietnamese interpret the showing of an American movie as a
symbol of the cultural relaxation launched by Vietnam's Communist
Party in late 1986. But *Platoon* is not the first Vietnam war movie
shown in the city's theaters. Like the Americans, the Vietnamese have
been making their own movies about how the war was won—and
lost—for the past 13 years.

One popular Vietnamese film, *Desert Field,* ends with a peasant
woman defiantly approaching a burning American helicopter, which
she helped shoot down after its gunners killed her husband. As she
nears the wreckage, she sees that the dead American pilot has
dropped a picture of his wife and son.

Desert Field, which won a gold medal at the Moscow Film Festival,
depicts the struggle of a peasant, his wife, and their baby to survive
against the onslaught of sophisticated U.S. military technology. Heli-
copters come almost every day and disrupt the family's life in the
southern Mekong River delta. Often the parents have to put their
baby in a plastic container and hold him under water to protect him
from gunfire. "We wanted to tell people that during the war Vietnamese
suffered as well as Americans," said Hong Sen, the movie's producer,
who was born in South Vietnam but spent the war years in the
north. "I try to make people understand the unjust cause of the U.S.
war against the Vietnamese people and the spirit of our people—
their heroism—in fighting the Americans."

From *World Press Review*

From Russia with Love

In May of 1988 the New York Times and CBS News conducted the first Western-style poll ever taken in the Soviet Union. The Institute for Sociological Research of the Soviet Academy conducted a telephone survey of 939 Moscow residents, asking questions prepared by the two American sponsors. A number of these dealt with the United States. A majority of the Moscow residents saw in the United States a country richer and more hardworking than their own, but one less humane. Seventy-nine percent of the young said they had a positive attitude toward America, compared to sixty percent of the older generation. The young were also more likely to believe that life is better under the American system.

However, the gap between the views of the Russian people and their officials on America has always been profound. The Soviet leadership has historically viewed world politics in Manichaean terms, insisting the United States must bear all the blame for the cold war and the arms race.

General Secretary Mikhail Gorbachev rarely departed from the official party line toward America in his book, Perestroika: New Thinking for Our Country and the World, *asserting that the tensions between the two superpowers are strictly the result of reckless American policies and denying that his government has ever manufactured anti-American propaganda or possessed imperialistic aims:*

For our part the Soviet Union has no propaganda of hatred toward Americans or disregard for America. In our country you won't find this anywhere, neither in politics nor in education. We criticize a policy we do not agree with. But that's a different matter. It does not mean that we show disrespect for the American people. . . .

Yet some people in the United States, it turns out, "need" the Soviet Union as an enemy image. Otherwise it is hard to understand some films, the inflammatory American broadcasts from Munich, the spate of articles and programs full of insults and hatred toward the Soviet people. . . .

I would not idealize each step in Soviet foreign policy over the past several decades. Mistakes also occurred. But very often they were the consequence of an improvident reaction to American actions, to a policy geared by its architects to "roll back communism."

... Pondering the question of what stands in the way of good Soviet-American relations, one arrives at the conclusion that, for the most part, it is the arms race. I am not going to describe its history. Let me note that at almost all its stages the Soviet Union has been the party catching up. ... The U.S. sets the tone in this dangerous, if not fatal pursuit.

I shall not disclose any secrets if I tell you that the Soviet Union is doing all that is necessary to maintain up-to-date and reliable defenses. This is our duty to our own people and our allies. At the same time I wish to say quite definitely that this is not our choice. It has been imposed upon us.

Anatolii Andreievich Gromyko, the son of Soviet Foreign Minister Andrei Gromyko and the head of the Foreign Policy Section in the U.S.A. Institute of the U.S.S.R. Academy of Sciences, voiced the official position on American foreign policy in his 1973 book Through Russian Eyes: President Kennedy's 1036 Days:

The principal aims of the American reactionary politicians and ultra-rightists in the foreign policy sphere were and still are: rejection of peaceful coexistence with socialist countries, suppression of the national liberation movement by military force, magnification of international tension through the arms race, preservation of the military-political imperialist blocs throughout the world, reliance on German militarism and revanchism, renunciation of even the smallest steps in Soviet-American relations, and support of decaying reactionary regimes in the international arena. To conceal their aims, the reactionary circles in the United States constantly utilize frantic anti-communist propaganda.

As might be expected, Soviet textbooks reflect a bias and distortion because of undue emphasis on particular facts, statements, or events taken out of context and given more significance than they deserve. A good example can be found in a grade-eight world-history textbook. Commenting on the attitude of white settlers toward American Indians, the author writes:

The American bourgeoisie and the slave-owners tried to seize as much foreign land as possible. First of all they began with the extermination of the Indians, in order to seize their lands. "The only good Indian is a dead Indian," said American generals. One means of exterminating the Indians was the following: Blankets were strewn about near an Indian settlement. The Indians, not suspecting anything, gathered them up and covered themselves with them. Then they began to die in masses from smallpox. It turned out that the Americans had wrapped up those who were sick with or had died from smallpox beforehand in the blankets. Thus, by the 19th century the American military was already using methods of monstrous bacteriological warfare.

Quoted in Robert English and Jonathan Halperin,
The Other Side: How Soviets and Americans Perceive Each Other

★

Despite glasnost, Soviet propaganda often lampoons Uncle Sam as a fiendish charlatan responsible for one global atrocity or another. The themes of repressed minorities, chronic unemployment, epidemics of crime and drugs, and the homeless are endlessly repeated. Much of this clumsy propaganda ends up as grist for the famous Soviet political joke. Serge Schmemann, who was the chief of the Moscow bureau of the New York Times, *recalls two classic jokes:*

There's the one that asks, "What is the difference between the Soviet Constitution and the American Constitution?" Reply: "The Soviet Constitution guarantees freedom of speech and of gathering. The American Constitution guarantees freedom after speech and freedom after gathering."

Or there's the old one about an American and a Russian debating who has more freedom. The American says, "I can walk in front of the White House and shout, 'Down with Reagan,' and nothing will happen to me." The Russian retorts: "I can walk in front of the Kremlin and yell 'Down with Reagan,' too, and nothing will happen to me either."

From "The View from Russia," in the *New York Times Magazine,*
November 10, 1985

Arkady N. Shevchenko, the United Nations Under Secretary-General, a former advisor to Soviet Foreign Minister Andrei Gromyko, and one of

the highest-ranking Soviet officials ever to defect to the West, warned in his best-selling book, Breaking with Moscow:

The U.S. sometimes lacks the steadiness needed to deal persuasively with the Soviets. Its policy toward the Soviet Union seems to jump from extreme to extreme. Yet I have never doubted that America's strength makes it the one power capable of forcing Moscow to restrain itself. This is something that can be achieved if American leaders do not forget an old and true lesson: what the men in the Kremlin understand best is military and economic might; energetic political conviction; strength of will. If the West cannot confront the Soviets with equal determination, Moscow will continue to play the bully around the globe.

Edward Lee Howard was the first CIA defector to the Soviet Union. Trained by the CIA to be a spy in Moscow, Howard sold the agency's most sensitive information—the secrets of its Moscow operation—to the KGB and then eluded an FBI surveillance team. He surfaced a year later, on August 7, 1986, in Moscow, and was granted Soviet citizenship. Later he conducted a television interview at which he stated: "I fled to the Soviet Union because I felt that the Soviet Union was the only force able to stand up to the CIA. After more than a year and a half in the Soviet Union, I think much about my future, where shall I live permanently, what kind of work I shall do permanently. I want to continue working in economic research and not only in the Soviet Union. I feel at home in the Soviet Union, and today I must say I feel that I shall stay here. I have good creative work, and the only wish I have is to have more friends."

What does Howard miss most about the country he betrayed? "I miss Skippy peanut butter, chunky style," he confided to David Wise, American journalist and author of The Spy Who Got Away. *Why not have his wife mail him a jar? "When she was here, a friend in Moscow warned her the peanut butter might be poisoned by the CIA. My parents heard that, and now they won't mail me any food."*

American Innocence Regarding Communism

A common theme among observers from Russia, Eastern Europe, and Communist regimes in Latin America and Asia is the political naiveté of many Americans regarding the true nature of communism and the threats it poses to the world order. Jean-François Revel, the great French philosopher and author of a dozen books on culture, science, philosophy, history, and social criticism, found himself in the American Midwest during one particularly tense moment:

When the KAL flight was shot down by the Soviets in 1984, I happened to be here in the United States at a university in Indiana for a few days. I was very struck by hearing conversations among students and faculty in which the great danger posed was not the Soviet's military power and the extraordinary arrogance of their crime, but Reagan's reaction! Most of them seemed to be greatly relieved, however, when the president said that there would not be any kind of violent retaliation. How can we expect such citizens to exert themselves in defense of democracy?

From "The Crisis in Western Democracy," in *Imprimis,*
April 1988

★

José Sánchez, a refugee from Nicaragua living in San Diego, has strong feelings about American supporters of his country's communist regime:

I fled Nicaragua in 1985, due to the barbarism of Tomás Borge and the other Sandinistas. My brother lost his left hand when a Sandinista chopped it off for working as a messenger for the freedom fighters. He was fortunate to escape to Honduras with his testicles still attached to his body. He has since lost his left leg due to stepping on a Soviet-made "foot popper" on a trail near the border.

The Sandinistas plant these mines because it *costs* more for the U.S.A. to give a *contra* a prosthesis than to bury him or her—about ten percent of the freedom fighters are female, from eight to eighty years old.

[For a time] I believed all of San Diego wanted to ruin my country more by helping the cruel and anti-people Sandinistas.

I have seen these American Sandinistas carrying the most ridiculous signs saying "Reagan is Hitler," "Nicaragua did not invade Honduras," "U.S. drug trade funds *contra* war," and "Reagan is the number one world terrorist." They should talk to millions of now-Americans who fled Vietnam, Cuba, Czechoslovakia, Hungary, Afghanistan, the Ukraine, Armenia, El Salvador, Cambodia, Nicaragua, and everywhere else the Soviet-Sandinista Communists have ruined people's lives.

God bless Ron Reagan and Ollie North for trying to save my country.

From the "Letters" section of the San Diego Reader,
April 21, 1988

★

Polish author Leopold Tyrmand was in New York City in the summer of 1968 when the Soviet army invaded Prague to crush the new democracy blossoming there. In his Notebooks of a Dilettante *he recorded the following conversation with a young American college girl whose left-wing ideology blocked her from grasping the enormity of the developing crisis:*

"But they cannot arrest a whole nation that doesn't want them in its country!" exclaimed a young, attractive Manhattan girl. "Everybody is against them, and they can't arrest everyone!"

We walked down Second Avenue; pubs, bars, and sidewalk coffee houses were filled with her mini-skirted, paisley-covered, pajama-trousered sisters. It was a warm, gregarious, New-York-in-the-East-Sixties evening, the fourth in a row of the most cynical violence staged by one nation against another during the last twenty years and called, officially, the Czech crisis. News had just reached us that the Russians intended a mass arrest of all Czechs suspected of being liberal-minded or, at least, reluctant about the Russian invasion and occupation of their country.

"Why not," I said. "Of course they can. We've seen events like that in Europe, especially in Russia."

"But . . ." she smiled incredulously, "suppose they do arrest them? What do they do with them? Who's going to watch such a mass of people? How will they be fed?"

"Small worry. Feeding is no problem where political prisoners are concerned. They are expected to starve. The proletariat works hard and is not obliged to feed its foes, even if they are its members. Russia is a very congenial country for such undertakings; its gigantic, deadly emptiness allows perfect discretion. In the thirties, Russians exterminated some four million Ukrainian peasants who opposed the agricultural collectivization. No one even knows where their collective graves are. After the last war the entire ethnic minority of

Crimean Tartars and nearly half of the population of Lithuania—some three million people altogether—were subjected to the same treatment on grounds of alleged hostility towards the Soviet Union's principles. A few million Czechs and Slovaks won't make much trouble for experienced specialists."

"You're infatuated with your hatred of the Soviets, and you can't be trusted." She was apparently vexed. "No normal person would believe that!"

"I know," I said melancholically. "It's much harder to believe that Marines kill little children in Vietnam."

"This we can see with our own eyes on every TV news program," she said triumphantly.

"Certainly, you're right," I sighed with more melancholy. "I'm always overlooking the American access to so-called free information."

"And who could execute an operation arresting several million people?" she asked bitingly. "Russian soldiers? Why, soldiers do not arrest people just because they do not like them very much."

"American soldiers don't. But Russian soldiers have other manners. During the first day of their invasion, the Slovaks in Bratislava bombed Soviet tanks with paper balls. I found it groovy, indeed, a remarkable manifestation of ingenuity, peaceful intentions, and well-marked rejection as well. The Russian soldiers didn't share the same sense of humor; they fired into the crowd and killed many. But I doubt that they would be burdened with arresting balky Czechoslovaks—they came to liberate them from eventual imperialist subjugation, as the formal Soviet statement worded it, so it would somehow be inconsistent to arrest them. The task will be turned over to the KGB which, I can assure you, will perform a flawless job. You know what the KGB is?"

"Of course," she said proudly. "The Russian CIA."

"Not exactly. There are significant differences between the two institutions."

"Differences?" She resorted to open mockery. "Might you, perhaps, point them out to me?"

"Easily. I don't know how many people work for the CIA, but according to official Soviet statistics there are two million special KGB troops, and seemingly a corresponding number of civilian employees, which amounts to nearly three percent of the entire Soviet population. There are whole towns populated exclusively by KGB members and their families, whole branches of industry producing, for example, electronic equipment for bugging, that are restricted to the KGB's control. A network of prisons and concentration camps exists, exclusively under the KGB's sway and supervision, which no regular Russian may look into, let alone intervene in. KGB members have a much higher standard of living than the rest of the population; they have their own shops where they get better goods for less money than the average citizen, and they have their private, luxurious seaside resorts that a man from the street is forbidden to enter. They are uniformed; they can arrest anyone without giving a reason and hold him in detention many years without a trial. They can shoot people without facing the consequences for causing death and injury. Insulting a KGB man, on the other hand, is considered a crime against the state, and punching him in the nose during street unrest results in the death penalty. Can you imagine someone in America sentenced to death because he kicked a CIA man in the bottom? Or imprisoned because he insulted the institution? The majority of United States universities would have to hold their classes in jail, not to mention the excruciating hilarity caused by the idea of an exclusive CIA department store. Hence, for the KGB taking care of and disposing of a few million Czechoslovaks destined to disappear would be child's play."

She walked, silent, for a while. Then she said, "Then why don't we protest? As loud as possible."

"That's what I want to ask you as a representative of American youth and a loquacious speaker for the so-called American political conscience. Where are the huge crowds of protest marchers against injustice and inhumanity that so eagerly burn the American flag? Where are all the valiant, bearded freedom fighters? Where are the ebullient Brooklyn writers and the Upper Manhattan novelists? Where are the sensitive-to-every-suffering Chelsea playwrights, the distinguished but social-minded Boston poets, the fierce pacifist-pornographers, and the well-born, radical clergymen? Where have all the flowers of the brilliant anti-war demonstrations gone? Where, these days, is the praised, combative, shining spirit of the American intellectual, and where is his sense of social morality?"

Anti-Americanism

"Always blame the Americans," advises a character in Costa-Gavras's leftist political film thriller, Z. "Even when you're wrong, you're right."

In both the public and private sectors, America-bashing has become a kind of national sport around the world. For the past thirty years the

United States has been a nearly universal scapegoat symbol. No other country in history has experienced more hostile demonstrations in front of its embassies, had its flag burned on more occasions, been denounced more frequently in the United Nations and other world forums, and been blamed so completely for the ills of the world and the misfortunes of individuals. Few parts of the world are free of anti-Americanism, which is now so universal that most people, including Americans, seem to take it for granted.

"Anti-Americanism is one of the most significant, widespread, and intellectually neglected cultural, political, and social-psychological phenomena of the last few decades," sociology professor Paul Hollander, one of the few scholars to study the subject, observed in "Reflections on Anti-Americanism in Our Times" (Worldview, June 1978). He attributes this to several factors, including the fact that so much is known about the United States; our affluence, which excites many negative responses, including simple envy; our pervasive global cultural presence, much of which presents an unflattering picture of our country; the anti-Americanism of many Americans, especially intellectuals and opinion leaders; and the combination of great power with the weakened will to use it. "America appears as the big, bumbling country that can be taunted, teased, and abused with relative impunity," he noted in his article.

Two foreign observers who have thought long and provocatively on the causes and nature of anti-Americanism are British author Paul Johnson and Russian novelist Vassily Aksyonov. In his highly acclaimed history, Modern Times: The World from the Twenties to the Eighties, Johnson explored the theme of anti-Americanism, especially in the context of the seventies:

The attacks on America during the 1970s were so venomous and for the most part so irrational as to merit the description of an international witch-hunt. One might say that the most ubiquitous form of racism during the decade was anti-Americanism. The adage, "to know all is to forgive all," does not work in international affairs. One reason why America was attacked so much was because so much was known about her, chiefly thanks to the American media and academia, which poured forth a ceaseless torrent of self-critical material. But a more fundamental reason was that America as a great power and still more Americanism as a concept stood for the principle of individualism as opposed to collectivism, for free will as opposed to determinism. The spirit of the late Sixties, and still more of the early and mid-Seventies, was strongly collectivist and deterministic.

★

Vassily Aksyonov perceives other factors at work:

Even now, after living in America for more than five years, I keep wondering what provokes so many people in Latin America, Russia, and Europe to anti-American sentiment of such intensity that it can only be called hatred. There is something oddly hysterical about it all, as if America were not a country but a woman who has hurt a man's pride by cheating on him.

Let us forget (for the time being) the role of anti-American propaganda in the strategy of the opposition, which, in the case of the Soviet Union, is managed by the anything but friendly people at Agitprop. In the international arena this "war of ideas" exists on a par with bacteriological warfare and the anthrax bomb. Let us limit our discussion to feelings, complexes, and unconscious hostility.

A Soviet poet once asked the revolutionary Ernesto "Ché" Guevara why he hated America with such a passion, and Ché launched into a tirade against Yankee imperialism, the enslavement of economically underdeveloped nations by rapacious monopolies, expansionism, the suppression of national liberation movements, and so on. The poet, to give him his due, found Ché's lesson in political literacy less than satisfactory and inquired whether there wasn't perhaps something personal behind his feelings. After a few moments of silence, during which the ever-present daiquiri turned slowly in his fingers, Ché cast a glance in the direction of Florida and launched into a curious story. Since I'm not sure the story has made it into the biographies adorning leftist bookshop windows these days, I will retell it as I heard it from the poet.

As a teenager in Argentina, Ernesto made a cult of the United States. He was wild about Hollywood westerns and the latest jazz. One day, riding his bike past the airport, he saw a plane being loaded with racehorses for America. Instantly the revolutionary in him took over. Think of it—a free ride to the land of virile cowboys and forward blondes. All he had to do was to stow away. No sooner said than done: on to America, and here is he in America.

In Georgia to be exact. A hundred degrees in the shade. When the ground crew discovered the Argentine adventurer, they beat him black and blue and locked him back up in the empty plane. For three days they left him there to bake without food or water. Then they sent him home.

"I'll never forgive them that airplane," Ché whispered to the poet. And flaring up again: "I hate all gringos, their easygoing voices, insolent struts, confident leers, obscene smiles."

Other Latin American anti-American revolutionaries—the Sandinistas in Nicaragua, for instance—may have just such a "plane" in their backgrounds. And even if it was not quite so burning an issue as Ché made it, even if it was incidental and short-lived, it was still a blow to their self-esteem, a humiliating slap in the face. How to deal with it? Blame the fair-haired colossus of the North. Provincial inferiority complexes have played an enormous part in the spread of Marxist doctrine.

Simplistic as it may sound, many if not most of these "planes" can be chalked up to misunderstandings. Americans take no pleasure in humiliating people. Their "pushy voices" reflect the intonation patterns of American speech, their "insolent struts" the way generations of American bodies have learned to propel themselves from one place to another. As for "confident leers" and "obscene smiles," they are not commonly found among the populace, and when they do occur they generally represent an innocent attempt to copy the latest TV or movie look. Besides, the image of the American superman is quickly becoming a thing of the past. Take the sad and instructive case of the American marines entrenched on the outskirts of Beirut in 1983. Soviet propaganda raised an international hue and cry about American invaders and rapists, but if you had taken a good look at them you would have seen they were just a bunch of kids, young working-class kids. The "insolent struts," "obscene smiles," and "confident leers" belonged to the more-American-than-the-Americans Arab terrorists roaming the streets of the devastated city and surrounding hills. Anti-American sentiment is essentially hatred for an outdated stereotype, a celluloid phantom.

From *In Search of Melancholy Baby*

John Kennedy

The assassination of President Kennedy in Dallas on November 22, 1963, was as traumatic a shock for the people of the world beyond America as it was for Americans. In almost every country there was mourning. Americans learned how many people of other lands considered Kennedy their President. The loss they felt was the loss of one who seemed a personal

friend as well as a world leader. "Everything in one cried out in protest,"
Sir Alex Douglas-Home said to the press. "This young, gay, and brave
statesman, killed in the full vigor of his manhood when he bore on his
shoulders all the cares and hopes of the world."

British author T. H. White learned of Kennedy's death while lying
seriously ill in an American hospital room in New Orleans. At the time he
penned the following moving observations:

Americans are young, inexperienced, idealistic, sentimental, longing
for culture, confiding, lovable, wanting to be loved. They are sweet
in this way as boys at puberty, as touching, as protectable. They long
to be grown-up, "correct."

After killing their President, they looked upon me uncertainly,
blushing, guilty, fearing *and hoping* that I would scold them for doing
wrong.

It was a deep shock to them. The people of Dallas are going about
saying doubtfully, We are not really wicked?

This voluntary acceptance of blame, this innocent ambition to be
an adult civilization, moved me very much.

Fortunately, in the sunlight of late fall, it was a perfect funeral.
There were no visible journalists, no crowding, no need for policemen, no vulgarity, no hysteria. Thousands upon thousands of people
conducted themselves with silent dignity, sorrow and reflection in a
wonderful, daylong purgation of emotion which brought the act of
horror under control again.

Kennedy's death will probably do more good for the cause of
integration than his life.

I watched the four-day serial on a beat-up TV set in the hospital. It
was odd to see the dead President's demagogic cares being shifted
from his simple and restful grave to the shoulders of his successor.

Well, death may be what life is for.

From *America at Last*

On November 25, Moscow Radio broadcast the following tribute by Yakov
Viktorov:

For the American people this has been a day of mourning for
President John Kennedy, whose death came so tragically and un-

timely. The Soviet people and Soviet press share the American people's sorrow at this severe loss. They share the American people's anger and indignation at the criminal activities of the repugnant reactionaries who incited and engineered the brutal assassination of the President.

John Kennedy will go down in history as one of the outstanding U.S. statesmen. In the short period that he held office, he displayed great broadmindedness and a sober appreciation of political realities and of contemporary development.

Quoted in Robert D. English and Jonathan J. Halperin,
The Other Side: How Soviets and Americans Perceive Each Other

Anatolii Andreievich Gromyko, a top Soviet specialist on America, voiced the official Soviet position on the Kennedy years in his book Through Russian Eyes: President Kennedy's 1036 Days. *He argued the Marxist orthodoxy that Kennedy was a representative of Eastern financial and industrial interests and served those same interests through his domestic and foreign policies. The views in Professor Gromyko's book are still widely held in the Soviet Union today. He offered the following explanation of the assassination:*

The question of who killed the President may never be answered accurately and precisely. On the other hand, the question of why Kennedy was killed remains. To this an answer may be offered.

The "murder of the century" could have had numerous motives which, woven into a tight and ominous tangle, prompted the assassin or assassins to commit this crime. It is common knowledge, for instance, that the various groups of American monopoly capital engage in a furiously competitive struggle, which often produces tragic consequences for the individual—even if he is rich and powerful. Kennedy, as a member of the Boston financial grouping, with his close ties to Wall Street, doubtlessly displeased numerous rival monopolists. They not only envied him, but also feared him. Indeed, while he was in the White House, Kennedy could frequently give the "green light" to some business tycoons, and, in so doing, jeopardize the financial fortunes of others.

This whirlpool of ruthless, competitive struggle (which engulfs everyone and everything in capitalist America) aroused in some people initial feelings of envy and discontent toward the young, energetic and generally successful President. Later, to the extent that Kennedy began to display political realism, feelings of malice emerged, which rapidly degenerated into hatred. . . .

In the last year of his Presidency, Kennedy began to depart from the "cold war" dogmas with regard to several foreign policy problems and Soviet-American relations. And though this was a barely noticeable step, many among the American ruling elite considered it dangerous. "Better to be on the brink of war than to be chicken," many Texas newspapers cried out during the summer and fall of 1963. . . . Clearly, forces existed in the United States which were ready to remove Kennedy from the White House by any conceivable means.

The reevaluation of Kennedy's place in history by American historians over the past fifteen years has had its counterpart among foreign commentators. One of the harshest reassessments came from the prominent French historian and political thinker, Jean-François Revel, in his influential How Democracies Perish. *For Professor Revel, August 1961 marked a critical turning point in East-West relations when the new American President failed to defend Allied rights in Berlin:*

It is arguable that the missile crisis, which brought the world, say the experts, to the brink of nuclear war, might not have happened at all if the Allies, led by the United States, had not surrendered in East Berlin the year before and so convinced the Soviet Union that they no longer even had the energy to claim their rights or manifest their instinct of self-preservation. . . .

The Communists built the wall to prevent East Germans from emigrating to the West via Berlin, the only point of free access between the two Europes. . . . Under the terms of the quadripartite agreement governing Berlin, all four occupying powers were responsible for the *entire* city; the Soviet occupation zone no more belonged to the Russians than the French zone to France or the American zone to the United States. East Berlin was never included in the Soviet "sphere" by any Yalta agreement, not even a fictitious one. The demarcation line between East and West Berlin was not a frontier between two states. Forcibly isolating one section of the city, therefore, was a treaty violation by one of the occupants. Which meant that an Allied military reaction would have raised none of the problems that stopped us from intervening in Hungary five years earlier and which would also apply to aggressions committed elsewhere later. Moreover, we now know that if the West had sent a dozen tanks to disperse the East German soldiers building the "wall of shame" (under a rain of insults from their fellow Germans), who were not even armed, these masons in uniform would have scattered. They had been ordered to do so by their Soviet masters had such an eventuality arisen. . . .

In June 1963, standing before the wall, Kennedy uttered his famous *"Ich bin ein Berliner."* It is edifying that, after our deliberate capitulation, the detail that history chose to remember was the American President's pompous proclamation that "I am a Berliner" —one who had allowed the Communists to amputate part of Berlin to satisfy their imperial needs. It had a fine sound, this hollow phrase, worthy of the events that produced it and a fitting postscript to the sad farce of the Berlin wall.

Kennedy's handling of the Cuban missile crisis was widely praised at the time and for many years afterwards. On the other hand, Khrushchev was blamed by his own colleagues for a course of action that was both inept and dangerous and cost the Soviet Union enormously in terms of international prestige. The most complete and authoritative account of the Cuban missile crisis as viewed from the Russian side comes from Arkady N. Shevchenko, a high-ranking official in his country's foreign service who defected in 1978. In his book Breaking with Moscow, *he confirmed Revel's observation that Kennedy's failure of will in Berlin was a major factor behind Khrushchev's decision to move medium-range nuclear missiles into Cuba. And he also deflated the popular notion that the world stood on the edge of a nuclear exchange during that fateful encounter in October of 1962:*

The idea to deploy nuclear missiles in Cuba was Khrushchev's own; many years later he admitted as much in his memoir. Beyond a defense for Cuba, the more important gain would be a better balance of power between the United States and the U.S.S.R. Khrushchev's plan was to create a nuclear "fist" in close proximity to the United States, and at first glance it seemed seductive. The Soviet Union could get a "cheap" nuclear rocket deterrent, and accomplish much with very little. . . .

Khrushchev's calculations were based upon the assumption that he could dupe Americans by installing the missiles rapidly and secretly. Then he would confront the United States with a *fait accompli*. He believed that after successful implementation of the plan, the United States would not dare strike a blow, since this would threaten to unleash a nuclear world war.

To a substantial degree, such premises were based on Khrushchev's assessment of Kennedy's personal qualities as President and statesman. After the Vienna summit, Khrushchev concluded that Kennedy would accept almost anything to avoid nuclear war. The lack of confidence the President displayed during both the Bay of Pigs invasion and the Berlin crisis further confirmed this view.

I saw what Khrushchev's attitude was at the end of 1961, when I attended a meeting in the office of his personal assistants. Someone had remarked that Khrushchev, to put it mildly, didn't think very highly of Kennedy. At that moment, the Premier himself entered the room and immediately began to lecture us about Kennedy's "wishy-washy" behavior, ending with the remark: "I know for certain that Kennedy doesn't have a strong backbone, nor, generally speaking, does he have the courage to stand up to a serious challenge." Khrushchev's impression of Kennedy was a prevalent one among Soviet leaders generally. . . .

Once the crisis developed, Khrushchev had only two options if he decided on confrontation: a nuclear war, for which the United States was much better prepared, or a war limited to the area, also advantageous to the United States. Given the American geographical position and strength in the area, the Soviets would find it costly to penetrate the blockade or defend their ships. Moreover, Vladimir Buzykin, head of the Latin American Department in the ministry, told me that there were no contingency plans in the event the Cuban operation failed. By establishing the quarantine, Kennedy had pressured Khrushchev with a *fait accompli* instead of the other way around.

In the aftermath of the crisis, it was plain that we had not been on the brink of nuclear war. At no moment did Khrushchev or anyone else in Moscow intend to use nuclear weapons against the United States. When the crisis broke, our leaders were preoccupied almost exclusively with how to extricate themselves from the situation with a minimum loss of prestige and face.

In his popular book Modern Times, *British historian Paul Johnson argued that Kennedy botched the military and diplomatic advantages the Americans enjoyed during the Cuban missile crisis and thus allowed Khrushchev to turn a devastating defeat into a major triumph:*

In fact both Castro and Russia did very well out of Khrushchev's brinkmanship. Before Russia started arming Cuba on a big scale in September 1962, Castro was an easy target for American intervention. No American president was under any contractual restraints in handling the danger. Properly considered, Khrushchev's installation of strategic missiles was tantamount to a major act of aggression. When Kennedy called Khrushchev's bluff, he had Russia at a disadvantage. As de Gaulle rightly perceived, Russia really had no alternative but to back down completely. Khrushchev admitted this himself: "Cuba was 11,000 kilometres from the Soviet Union. Our sea and air communications were so precarious that an attack against the United States was unthinkable." The missile crisis took place at a time when the strategic nuclear equation was still strongly in America's favour, and in a theatre where America enjoyed overwhelming advantage in conventional power. Kennedy was thus in a position to demand an absolute restoration of the *status quo ante*. He could have gone further; he could have insisted on punishment—on Soviet acceptance of a neutral, disarmed Cuba: the Finnish analogy. As Dean Acheson rightly observed: "So long as we had the thumbscrew on Khrushchev, we should have given it another turn every day."

Instead, Kennedy, while winning a public relations victory, rewarded the aggressive Soviet act with two substantial concessions. The minor one was the withdrawal [from Turkey] of the Jupiter missiles, supposedly on the grounds of their obsolescence. Far more important, however, was Kennedy's acquiescence in the continuation of the Communistic regime in Cuba, in open military alliance with Soviet Russia. On the practical issue of Cuba and Caribbean security, Kennedy lost the missile crisis. It was an American defeat: the worst it had thus far suffered in the Cold War.

Richard Nixon

Richard Nixon has long enjoyed much greater respectability and esteem abroad than in America. His political career stretches back to 1947, longer than any other Western leader except François Mitterand. Since

1953 he has been intimately involved in shaping major affairs of state, which puts him second only to Andrei Gromyko in length of service as one of the world's primary statesmen. He continues to write prolifically, while his political advice is eagerly sought by those in public office. And yet he remains in a fundamental sense the most enigmatic of the American presidents. Perhaps no event in modern American political history has so perplexed foreign observers as Watergate and Nixon's subsequent resignation. The Soviet leadership, in particular, was puzzled at the bizarre unfolding of events. In Breaking with Moscow, *Arkady N. Shevchenko described their reactions:*

Soviet leaders never properly understood the enormous effect of such a "trivial" thing as Watergate. "Watergates" are routine and permanent features in the Soviet Union from top to bottom. Bugging, taping, intimidation, bribery, lying, cover-ups—these are the standard measures taken by the KGB, with the leadership's blessing, wherever it wishes and without restriction. . . .

Nonetheless, if the Soviet leadership was unable to understand Watergate, what it did realize almost immediately was that presidential authority in the United States had been weakened; and the Kremlin quickly began to exploit the situation. The Politburo decided to deploy the new medium-range SS-20 missiles in the western U.S.S.R. in violation of détente, in an effort to alter the military balance in Europe. There was no fanfare over this; it was all done under the guise of "replacing" old missiles. The peace movements around the world seemed to have missed this move completely. Only later did NATO members fully understand the dimensions of the Soviet threat and take responsive measures.

For Vassily Aksyonov, the ordeal of Watergate suggested the strengths of American democracy:

It doesn't ever seem to occur to Americans that their democracy could fail or even falter. To those of us who come here from Eastern Europe, however, American democracy at first seems fragile, as vulnerable as Little Red Riding Hood in the forest. Accustomed as we are to the brute lawlessness of our former governments, we tend to look upon democracy as weak. We fear for it.

Take Watergate, for instance, when the American press took advantage of its right to criticize any individual, including the president, and the *Washington Post* all but ran him out of office. Many Russian émigrés maintain that the crisis in the American presidency led to the establishment of totalitarian regimes in several countries of Asia and Africa, the annihilation of three million Cambodians, and a global drop in the prestige of the democratic system. They are afraid of what will happen if history repeats itself. Will it be the "last and decisive battle" prophesied by the Soviet Communist party anthem? Will the United States come tumbling down?

It is hard for former Soviets to see the other point of view; it is hard for us to see Watergate as one of the cataclysms essential to the *consolidation* of American democracy. And it is hard for us to understand that as patriotic as the great majority of Americans are, they do not identify their country with its government.

From *In Search of Melancholy Baby*

British historian Paul Johnson took a much bleaker view of those events in an article in the October 1988 issue of Commentary:

Although the events which led up to Watergate and Nixon's abdication are extremely complicated, one salient fact must be borne in mind. The Eastern liberal establishment never really admitted the legitimacy of the Nixon administration. From the start, the media interests which spoke for the establishment treated the Nixon presidency as in some metaphysical sense an outlaw regime whose true, unconstitutional character would eventually be exposed. The powerful barons of the Eastern press and TV felt themselves morally and constitutionally entitled to snatch back the power he had secured from the voters by (as they saw it) chicanery. All they needed was a pretext.

Nixon played into their hands. His deep sense of insecurity, reinforced by what was now almost a paranoid hatred and fear of the press, led him to confuse a perfectly justified desire to prevent the media from publishing state secrets—as they had done in the case of the Pentagon Papers and other documents—with the routine skulduggery of party-political espionage. The result was the Watergate mess.

In essence, Watergate *was* a mess and nothing more. The Nixon administration's record of misuse of power and *raison d'etat* was no worse than that of Truman and Eisenhower, and considerably better than Franklin D. Roosevelt's. There was none of the personal corruption which had marked the rule of Lyndon Johnson, let alone the gross immoralities and security risks of John F. Kennedy's White House. Nixon's sins were venial and sprang mostly from misplaced loyalty. The notion that he plotted an assault on the Constitution and the rule of law is a malicious invention.

Indeed, the way in which the opportunities offered by Watergate were exploited by the Eastern media, aided by a hostile Congress—a key element in the story—and by a section of the legal establishment to whom Nixon was anathema, is a frightening example of how the will of a popular majority can be frustrated and overturned by the skillful manipulation of press and TV. This was the first media *Putsch* in history, as ruthless and anti-democratic as any military coup by bemedaled generals with their sashes and sabers.

So great was the inequity of Nixon's downfall that future historians may well conclude he would have been justified in allowing events to take their course and in subjecting the nation to the prolonged paralysis of a public impeachment, which at least would have given him the opportunity to defend himself by due process of law. But, once again, his patriotism took precedence over his self-interest, and he cut short the national agony by a voluntary abdication.

In defeat he was dignified and not at all disposed to recriminate. The episode wrecked his official career, but going through the fire strengthened and refined his moral character. By a curious paradox, Richard Nixon was one of the very few people who emerged from the Watergate affair with credit. But he remained, and remains, as mysterious as ever.

Jimmy Carter

The Russians made no secret of their preference for Richard Nixon, whom they understood and with whom they had established a working relationship, over Jimmy Carter, whom they distrusted from the start. In Breaking with Moscow, Arkady Shevchenko summarized the Soviet reaction to Carter's presidency in the early years:

On November 2, 1976, Jimmy Carter was elected President. Carter's selection of Zbigniew Brzezinski as his National Security Adviser put into the White House a man the Soviets regarded as an unrelenting enemy. The new President's campaign declarations on human rights, including a telegram of support to a noted Jewish activist in Moscow who had been denied permission to emigrate, persuaded the Soviets that Carter sought to promote subversion in the U.S.S.R. Finally, his inaugural address, expressing the hope that "we will move this year a step forward toward our ultimate goal—the elimination of all nuclear weapons from this earth," was taken as a signal that America's new leader intended to shatter the existing framework of SALT negotiations.

Carter's unpredictability, as much as the substantive shifts in his approach to the superpower relationship, disturbed the Soviets. Americans take change for granted. Its rapidity may disturb them briefly but in general they find ways to adjust quickly to new circumstances. Soviets lack such flexibility. It took them time to come to terms with the Carter administration. There was an extended period when the momentum of cooperation diminished further, and misunderstanding accumulated before a working relationship was achieved.

Ronald Reagan

Like that ancient wonder of the world, the Colossus of Rhodes, Ronald Reagan loomed larger than life over American politics for eight years. Right up to the end he was the center of attention as he bade farewell to supporters and detractors alike. He had arrived in Washington on the confluence of many streams. Liberalism and dissent were sharply out of favor with the American people. The Democratic Party had collapsed under the stewardship of Jimmy Carter. The political winds blew strongly from the right. Reagan soon established himself overseas as the most popular president since Kennedy, as American columnist Richard Reeves found on his trips abroad:

There is nothing like being away from America to realize how American you are. I understand that best when I try to explain Ronald Reagan, not my favorite president, to foreigners. I usually end up defending him, or at least rationalizing his ideas and actions within the context of the American experience, our history, and ideas.

Reagan, in fact, has not needed that much defense around the world. This president has been extraordinarily popular in the countries I have reported from these last seven years. Most Europeans and Asians I have talked with find this president ideologically alien. The normal American commitment to freedom and individualism in politics and economics is almost *sui generis*—to say nothing of Reagan's enmity to just about all central government. But they tend to like this old right-winger because he has generally shown a confident and strong American face. When the United States vacillates, as it seemed to during the Carter presidency, much of the rest of the world trembles.

Column of June 11, 1988

Britisher Bill Thomas observed wittily from Washington:

Americans may have finally grown disenchanted with Reagan's policies, but a sizeable portion of the population still loves what Reagan stands for: God, Country, and Long Vacations.

From the *Illustrated London News,* October 1988

A more critical view was voiced by British novelist Graham Greene in an interview for The Spectator. *The magazine's reporter asked, "What do you think about the state of the world? Is this the worst time you can remember?" Greene replied:*

The worst time? You mean the horrible state that Reagan's got us into? Well, it's certainly the most dangerous for many years, and that's entirely due to Reagan. I think the attack on Libya was absurd and unjustifiable. I mean, they talk about self-defence and all because of the death of one American soldier! Reagan's behaviour in Nicaragua? He's certainly caused the deaths of more innocent women and children than Gaddafi could ever be blamed for. But I suppose Reagan's hand is forced, to some extent, by his constituency. The only bright spot I can see is that I have every confidence in Gorbachev. He seems to have a great deal of common sense.

From *The Spectator,* June 14, 1986

Alexander Yakovlev studied at Columbia University, worked in various Soviet Communist Party schools and publishing houses, and served as the Soviet ambassador to Canada from 1973 to 1983. Today he sits at Mikhail Gorbachev's right hand, advising him on American affairs. In 1985 he published On the Edge of an Abyss: From Truman to Reagan, the Doctrine and Realities of the Nuclear Age, *in which Yakovlev showed himself to be unremittingly hostile and contemptuous toward American culture, politics, and foreign policy. Of Reagan he wrote:*

All of Ronald Reagan's actions are steeped in fanaticism and personal hatred for socialism and all progressive changes. . . . The Republican Platform [of 1984] confirms that Reagan's peace rhetoric was nothing but shameless hypocrisy and primitive demagoguery.

Trevor Fishlock, the long-time correspondent in New York City for The Times *of London, penned a perceptive appraisal of Reagan's strengths and weaknesses at the end of his fine book,* The State of America. *He wrote:*

To an extent Americans see in their presidents a representation of themselves, a diary of their fortunes. Kennedy was cut short, Johnson broken, Nixon besieged, Carter troubled. The images of these men were a shorthand for difficult and disappointing years. But Reagan was optimistic, and optimism is like a vital chemical secretion to Americans. They feel they deserve good things: their Declaration of Independence holds the pursuit of happiness to be an inalienable right. And while "Have A Nice Day" is phatic, it has an edge of American optimism to it. Reagan's gift was to communicate the optimism in a strong and physical way, and to package it brightly on television. . . .

Reagan was plain and people could understand him. He did not have many ideas, but people thought they knew what he stood for. Much of his popularity lay in his presidency being a repudiation of the immediate past and his appeal as repository of hope. He talked frontier, free enterprise, and "traditional values," sizzle rather than steak. He suggested that Americans could stop worrying about the poor, and channelling money to them, because in America everyone was free to make it to success, to swim as well as sink.

In the final weeks of the Reagan administration, Jan Krauze summed up the president's achievements in the French paper Le Monde:

After a series of presidential failures—Lyndon Johnson, Richard Nixon, Gerald Ford, and Jimmy Carter—that left a bitter aftertaste, Reagan is already being placed among the success stories. He is often compared to John F. Kennedy, whose memory glows warmly in the hearts of many Americans. "Like John Kennedy, Ronald Reagan fought hard, with remarkable success, to enable Americans once again to feel good about their country." This compliment comes from New York Gov. Mario Cuomo—a Democrat.

It may seem strange to compare the young, martyred president to the old man who, a quarter of a century later, is ambling toward a peaceful exit. Their ideas—aside from a powerful faith in America—are truly different. But both men knew how to win over their countrymen, and both left a lasting mark: Kennedy by the grace of the myth he became and Reagan because his presidency has been crowned by the election of his faithful teammate, Vice President George Bush.

The Election of 1988

Americans visiting Europe for the first time during an American election year are often surprised by the great attention given to U.S. politics there. Television commentators are fully conversant with the intricacies of America's political caucuses and primaries. The names of leading politicians are household words. And newspaper editorials freely instruct the candidates as to what will be expected of them once in office. Seth Lipsky reported on the interest generated during American presidential campaigns:

More than 2,500 paying guests swamped the American community's election-night party [in Brussels]. The crowd got so big, three times over the course of the evening, sales of tickets had to be halted. Probably 80% of the crowd was Belgian. In Paris, when at Ambassador Joe Rodgers's post-vote breakfast an interview was hooked up with one of the president-elect's pollsters, French guests started lobbing questions about the details of the Senate races.

All this may seem a bit surprising at the end of a race that cynics have set down as uninspiring. It may seem improbable at a time when American influence in the world is supposedly on the decline.

"They don't look upon this as an American election, as we do," Frank Shakespeare, U.S. ambassador to the Holy See, said. "They look upon this as the choosing of the leader of the Western world."

... The attraction of the American presidential election goes beyond spectacle. It comes from the fact that, at the end of the day, the world has found that for all its length, its cost and occasional oppressive demands on one's attention, the campaign is emerging as a global debate. ... The power of the American election on the world's imagination grows steadily, year by year, a fact in which both the winners and the losers can take enormous pride.

From the *Wall Street Journal,* September 11, 1988

★

Although officially the Russian government maintained a stance of impartiality, privately most Soviet leaders clearly favored George Bush. Paul Quinn-Judge filed the following report from Moscow:

Most Soviets expect George Bush to be the next United States president.

Most apparently like the idea. And the Soviet establishment, both official and unofficial, is rooting for the Republicans.

For Soviet foreign-policy makers, Vice-President Bush promises continuity with the Reagan administration's approach to Moscow.

Many radical reformers here, for very different reasons, also turn out to be fervent Republicans. And members of both groups say that they view the Democrats as unpredictable partners in world affairs.

Soviet foreign specialists came away from the Moscow summit last spring convinced that they could work with the Republicans. The road to the summit has been long and hard. They say they do not want to start over again. ...

U.S. Democrats suffer here from the image of being unreliable partners in foreign policy. It's harder to negotiate treaties with them, Soviet observers say, and they are more likely to feel the need to prove their anti-communist credentials.

From the *Christian Science Monitor,* November 8, 1988

★

After a sex scandal ended Gary Hart's run for the presidency, the editors of the French paper Le Quotidien de Paris *observed:*

225

When we hear this kind of story in France we cannot help but smile. A woman? Is that so bad? In France his image would probably improve.

British reporter Alexander Chancellor commented in The Spectator:

The Americans are a little embarrassed about the Gary Hart affair, because they feel it is an un-American sort of scandal. Their scandals are more often to do with money than with sex, and their newspapers are not given to snooping on political leaders. Indeed, the whole thing has a disturbing British feel to it. This was pointed out on one of the main television networks which showed old footage of Christine Keeler and John Profumo . . . to illustrate the fact. The *Miami Herald* is conspicuously shifty about finding itself behaving like a British tabloid. Its spokesmen keep insisting that its reporters behaved in a "professional" manner by keeping watch on Mr. Hart from legal parking places at a respectable distance from his house. Nevertheless, snooping was what they were doing, and this is considered here to be a new phenomenon for a "responsible" newspaper. Presidents Roosevelt and Kennedy were spared any publicity for their extra-marital liaisons, although these were well known to journalists at the time. But it was perhaps the Edward Kennedy incident at Chappaquiddick, which, because it involved a death, could not be ignored, that made sexual conduct seem a legitimate subject for journalistic inquiry. If this is Senator Kennedy's legacy, then his influence on American politics will be an enduring one.

From *The Spectator*, May 9, 1987

British observer Bill Thomas began an article about religious leaders who ran for the presidency with this look at Congress:

Unlike Britain, America has no official religion, although in Washington politicians and their spiritual advisers do not let that stop them from praying for special favours at election time. U.S. Senate chaplain Rev. Richard Halverson, D.D., recently opened a session of that pious body with this timely request: "Sovereign Lord of history and the nations, we pray for the Senators running for reelection. . . . Give wisdom to those who direct their campaigns. Give the Senators persuasiveness in speech . . . and provide wherever needed adequate campaign funds. We pray in His Name through whom Thou dost promise to supply all our needs according to Your riches in glory. Amen."

I asked Rev. Halverson if his prayer for extra contributions might give unfair advantage to incumbents, most of whom have already collected millions. His reply: "Well, I *do* work for them." So much for serving two masters.

From the *Illustrated London News*, October 1988

Later Viktor Linik in Pravda, *the big Communist Party newspaper, complained:*

One is amazed at how much buffoonery Americans inject into what would seem to be such a serious matter as the election of the country's top official. Today, much is being said about compassion for the humble, about everyone's right to the "American dream," and about justice. But where do these words go after the elections?

Quoted in *World Press Review*, September 1988

Writing in Izvestia, *the big government newspaper in the Soviet Union, Aleksandr Shalnev observed:*

George Bush is not well suited to the television age. A graduate of privileged Yale University, he does not always find a common language with the average American. He affects poses, tries to fine-tune himself to his audience, and, by overdoing it, arouses irritation.

Quoted in *World Press Review*, November 1988

★

British observer Ambrose Evans-Pritchard offered the following thoughts on Democratic candidate Michael Dukakis:

Dukakis is a first generation Greek. His wife, Kitty, is Jewish. It is a sign of how much America has changed that these ethnic ties are not thought of as a significant liability. In fact Dukakis's staff has been pushing him to talk about his family much more in order to put some feeling into his cool, impassive speeches. He tells how his father came over from Asia Minor before the first world war, worked his way through Harvard Medical School, and became the first Greek obstetrician in Boston.

Dukakis inherited this work ethic, but not a trace of Mediterranean excitability or extravagance. He drives a Chevrolet Celebrity—the social equivalent, perhaps, of a Cortina—takes the subway to work, and carries his lunch in a brown paper bag. He talks numbers and percentages with clockwork precision and likes to discuss photovoltaics. On the campaign trail he is attentive, affable in a quiet way, and thoroughly unlike an old pol.

From *The Spectator*, November 14, 1987

As election day neared, Chukwuemeka Gahia noted in African Guardian, a newsmagazine published in Lagos:

It is clear that the Democrats seriously underrated the Republican candidate. . . . Bush has shown himself to be quite good at understanding and using symbols, nuances, and emotions that easily find a resonant chord in the minds of ordinary voters.

After the voters had cast their ballots and made George Bush the next president by a wide margin, Werner Holzer wrote in the German newspaper Frankfurter Rundschau:

In the benevolent shadow of the still-popular Ronald Reagan, George Bush has become the first man in 152 years to reach the White House directly from the vice presidency. His victory over Massachusetts Gov. Michael Dukakis reflected the voters' desire to stick with the familiar. In this respect, they resembled the governments of many nations around the world. After two terms in office, what Bush's current boss, President Ronald Reagan, had to offer was known in both East and West, and there seems to be a tacit assumption that as president, Bush will not change Reagan's policies in any fundamental way. For the foreseeable future, turbulence on the international stage is unlikely. With the Democrat Dukakis, the world was not so sure. It must have hurt the loser to hear a certain note of relief in the congratulatory notices that Bush received from around the globe— from Moscow and Beijing, Israel and the Palestinians, Europe and Japan.

From *World Press Review,* December 1988

Vitaly Korotich is the assertive editor of the popular Russian weekly magazine Ogonyok (Little Flame). *He attended the inauguration of George Bush. Afterward he gave a lengthy interview to the* World Press Review, *during which he expressed his thoughts on American democracy:*

I was very impressed—and pleased—by how the transfer of power from Reagan to George Bush was accomplished. I attended the inauguration, and later when Reagan waved farewell, two women near me began to cry. They were very upset; they wanted Reagan to stay on. I am sure that many people in the U.S. felt the same way, but he could not stay. Democracy is a strict affair. I like that very much, and I thought that if we had had that same procedure, Stalin would have left in 1932, and he would not have had time to do anything. Brezhnev would have left in 1972. Democracy is a wonderful thing.

What I sensed most keenly in the U.S. is that people make demands on their president because they elect him by a relatively direct ballot. America has a great many shortcomings and a great many difficulties, but Americans have elected a new president, and instead of hanging up his portrait everywhere, they demand that he make America better.

When I saw those women crying over Reagan, I recalled that I had never seen a single leader of the Soviet Union leave office of his own accord. Everybody died, except for Khrushchev, who was overthrown.

From *World Press Review,* May 1989

★

The newspaper Jornal do Brasil *in Rio de Janeiro warned the new president:*

It will not be an easy period for Bush. The Soviet challenge has been replaced by the Japanese challenge. If the U.S. does not take steps,

229

Japanese supremacy, already apparent in several high-technology areas, will expand. The country that controls high technology controls the world.

From *World Press Review*, December 1988

★

From Johannesburg, South Africa, the financial newspaper Business Day *offered the following optimistic appraisal of the election:*

Bush is an experienced public official bred to power, and he is likely to be a better president than people think. But even if he proves to be an indifferent president, his election helps consolidate the victory of the free individual over the state, which is the dominant theme of our times.

★

Yakov Smirnoff, the Soviet-born comedian who emigrated to America and became a U.S. citizen, enjoyed his first opportunity to vote in the 1988 election. On the eve of the election, he set down his thoughts:

I was sworn in as an American citizen on the Fourth of July. That's a national holiday. As a matter of fact, it was a national holiday *before* I was sworn in, but to me it has become my own personal national holiday—which, of course, I don't mind sharing with everybody else.

I have one other national holiday I'd love to share with my fellow citizens. It's called Election Day. Most of you have been celebrating it for years, but for me Nov. 8, 1988, will be the first time.

Now, of course, I've voted before. In Russia we used to vote regularly—very regularly. They told us when to vote, where to vote and whom to vote for. No problem. There are advantages that way—you don't have to compare candidates, follow campaigns, listen to debates. . . .

When it was explained to me that in America my voice would be heard, I was confused. America is such a big country, and I have such a little voice. How will anyone hear me? Then I learned there is one place where everybody's voice speaks volumes. It's the voting booth—a wonderful invention, and definitely not Russian in origin.

In the Soviet Union, I and my fellow citizens had nothing to say about big decisions, like who represents us in and out of government, what quality of life we can provide for our children, what our country stands for, and what our country stands against. Here, in the voting booth, I control all that. So do you—as long as we do it together.

So when I step into the voting booth for the first time on Tuesday, it will be no less memorable a moment than that Fourth of July when I took my Oath of Allegiance to the United States of America.

I'll always remember that, right after I had been sworn in, I felt like I had been given a life membership in the greatest country club in the world.

Next Tuesday, I pay my dues.

What a country!

Parade magazine, November 6, 1988

ACKNOWLEDGMENTS

A number of people graciously helped to solicit responses from foreign observers of America. Dr. Margaret Posey, Helen Merchant, Donald Morse, John Reardon, Sherilyn Mentes, and Evelyn Kieran all provided invaluable assistance. And special thanks go to my agent, Howard Morhaim, for first suggesting this project.

Grateful acknowledgment is made for permission to quote from materials listed below:

Adhikari, Gautam. "A Dry Martini and Double-Nut Mocha," from the *New York Times,* January 15, 1988. Copyright © 1988 by the New York Times Company. Reprinted by permission of the author and the *New York Times.*

Aksyonov, Vassily. *In Search of Melancholy Baby.* Translated by Michael Henry Heim. Random House, New York; 1987. Translation copyright © 1985, 1987 by Random House, Inc. Reprinted by permission of the publisher.

Barzini, Luigi. *Americans Are Alone in the World.* Random House, New York; 1953. Copyright © 1953 by Luigi Barzini. Reprinted by permission of the publisher.

Bethell, Tom. *The Electric Windmill.* Regnery Gateway, Inc., Washington, D.C.; 1988. Copyright © 1988 by Tom Bethell. Reprinted by permission of the publisher.

Blundell, John. "What About All Those Drug Stores?" *Reason,* January 1988. Copyright © 1988 by The Reason Foundation. Reprinted by permission of the publisher.

Burstein, Daniel. "Yen and the Art of Package Travel," in *Condé Nast Traveler,* May 1989. Copyright © 1989 by Daniel Burstein. Reprinted by permission of the author.

Burstein, Daniel. *Yen! Japan's New Financial Empire and Its Threat to America.* Simon & Schuster, Inc., New York; 1988. Copyright © 1988 by Burstein & O'Connor, Inc. Reprinted by permission of the publisher.

Christian Science Monitor. "A Soviet Star Is Born," by Linda Feldman, February 19, 1988; "Soviets Hope for Continuity—They're Pulling for Bush," by Paul Quinn-Judge, November 8, 1988. Copyright © 1988 by The Christian Science Publishing Society. All rights reserved. Reprinted by permission of the publisher.

Christopher, Robert C. *The Japanese Mind.* Simon & Schuster, Inc., New York: 1983. Copyright © 1983 by Kriscon Corporation. Reprinted by permission of Linden Press, a division of Simon & Schuster, Inc.

Conrad, Peter. *Imagining America.* Routledge & Kegan Paul, London; 1980. Copyright © 1980 by Peter Conrad. Used by permission of Peters Fraser Dunlop and Routledge.

Contreras, Raoul Lowery. "Mama, Where's Poppa?" and "Cousin, What a Country!" Copyright © 1988 by Raoul Lowery Contreras. Reprinted by permission of the author.

Cooke, Alistair. *The Americans.* Alfred A. Knopf, New York; 1979. Copyright © 1979 by Alistair Cooke. Reprinted by permission of the publisher.

Cooke, Alistair. *One Man's America.* Alfred A. Knopf, New York; 1952. Copyright © 1952 by Alistair Cooke. Reprinted by permission of the publisher.

Cooke, Alistair. *Talk About America.* Alfred A. Knopf, New York; 1968. Copyright © 1968 by Alistair Cooke. Reprinted by permission of the publisher.

Costa, Elena Alexandra. *Stepping Down from the Stars: A Soviet Defector's Story.* G. P. Putnam's Sons, 1986. Copyright © 1986 by Elena Alexandra Costa. Reprinted by permission of the publisher.

Dallas Morning News. Kerry Gunnels, "The World's View of Us," July 6, 1986. Copyright © 1986 by the *Dallas Morning News.* Reprinted by permission of the publisher.

De Beauvoir, Simone. *L'Amérique au Jour le Jour.* Editions Gallimard, Paris; 1954. Copyright © 1954 by Editions Gallimard. Reprinted by permission of the publisher.

English, Robert and Jonathan J. Halperin. *The Other Side: How Soviets and Americans Perceive Each Other.* Transaction Books, New Brunswick, N.J.; 1987. Copyright © 1987 by Transaction Publishers. Reprinted by permission of the publisher.

Fishlock, Trevor. *The State of America.* John Murray, London; 1986. Copyright © 1986 by Trevor Fishlock. Reprinted by permission of the publisher.

Fotheringham, Allan. "Canadians Cope, Americans Conquer," in *Financial Post,* Toronto, Canada, 1989. Copyright © 1988 by Allan Fotheringham. Reprinted by permission of the author.

Glick, Edward B. "English Only: New Handicaps in World Trade." From *Los Angeles Times,* May 17, 1988. Copyright © 1988 by Edward B. Glick. Reprinted by permission of the author.

Glowacki, Janusz. *Hunting Cockroaches.* Translated by Jadwiga Kosicka. 1985. Copyright © 1985 by Janusz Glowacki. Reprinted by permission of International Creative Management, Inc.

Gorbachev, Mikhail. *Perestroika: New Thinking for Our Country and the World.* Harper & Row Publishers, Inc., New York; 1987. Copyright © 1987 by Mikhail Gorbachev. Reprinted by permission of the publisher.

Greene, Bob. "A Disney's Fan Theme: Parking," from the *Chicago Tribune,* July 17, 1988. Copyright © 1989 by John Deadline Enterprises. Reprinted by permission of Sterling Lord Literistic, Inc.

Gromyko, Anatolii Andreievich. *Through Russian Eyes: President Kennedy's 1036 Days.* International Library, Inc., Washington, D.C.; 1973. Copyright © 1973 by the International Library Law Book Publishers, Inc. All rights reserved. Reprinted by permission of the Board of Directors.

Haas, Charlie. "The King and, Well, I," from *Trips,* Spring 1988. Copyright © 1988 by Charlie Haas. Reprinted by permission of the author.

Hassan, Ihab. *Out of Egypt: Scenes and Arguments of an Autobiography.* Southern Illinois University Press, Carbondale, Illinois; 1986. Copyright © 1986 by the Board of Trustees of Southern Illinois University. Reprinted by permission of the publisher.

Hirayama, Yuji. "America Is Still No. 1 in Creativity." Translated from the Japanese newspaper *Shinano Mainichi* by The Asia Foundation's Translation Service Center. San Francisco, 1988. Copyright © 1988 by The Asia Foundation. Reprinted by permission of The Asia Foundation.

Illustrated London News. Richard Ingrams, "Stars and Gripes," September 1987; Nick Davies, "Brandywine Street," August 1988; Iain Finlayson, "New England Roots," September 1988; Bill Thomas, "Massachusetts Avenue," October 1988. Copyright © 1987 and 1988 by *Illustrated London News*. Reprinted by permission of The Illustrated London News.

Ishinomori, Shotaro. *Japan Inc.: Introduction to Japanese Economics (The Comic Book).* Translated by Betsy Scheiner. University of California Press, Berkeley, 1988. Copyright © 1988 by The Regents of the University of California. Reprinted by permission of the publisher.

Iyer, Pico. *Video Night in Kathmandu and Other Reports from the Not-So-Far-East.* Alfred A. Knopf, New York; 1988. Copyright © 1988 by Pico Iyer. Reprinted by permission of the publisher.

Jacobson, Mark. "Greetings from South Africa," from *Trips,* Spring 1988. Copyright © 1988 by Mark Jacobson. Reprinted by permission of the author.

James, Clive. *Snakecharmers in Texas: Essays, 1980–87.* Jonathan Cape Ltd., London, 1988. Copyright © 1988 by Clive James. Reprinted by permission of Peters Fraser & Dunlop and Sterling Lord Literistic, Inc.

Japan Echo. Karatsu Hajime, "Japanese Know-How for American Industry," Winter 1986; Shimomura Osamu, "The 'Japan Problem' Is of America's Making," Autumn 1987; Iida Tsuneo, "Decline of a Superpower," Autumn 1987; Saeki Shoichi, "Rediscovering America's Dynamic Society," Spring 1988. Copyright © 1986, 1987, and 1988 by *Japan Echo*. Reprinted by permission of the publisher.

Johnson, Paul. *Modern Times: The World from the Twenties to the Eighties.* Harper & Row Publishers, Inc., New York; 1983. Copyright © 1983 by Paul Johnson. Reprinted by permission of the publisher.

Johnson, Paul. "Nixon," in *Commentary,* October 1988. Copyright © 1988 by American Jewish Committee. Reprinted by permission of the publisher.

Le Corbusier, Eduard. *When the Cathedrals Were White.* Translated by Francis E. Hyslop, Jr. Harcourt Brace Jovanovich, Inc., New York; 1947. Copyright © 1947 by Harcourt Brace Jovanovich, Inc., and renewed 1975 by Francis Hyslop, Jr. Reprinted by permission of the publisher.

Look Japan. Masataka Kosaka, "Can Japan Cope?" January 1987. Copyright © 1987 by *Look Japan.* Reprinted by permission of the publisher.

Los Angeles Times. David Treadwell, "Gandhi's Grandson Finds Racial Bitterness in U.S.," May 23, 1988. Copyright © 1988 by the *Los Angeles Times.* Reprinted by permission of the publisher.

Minabe, Shigeo. "An Ungentler Japan." Translated from the Japanese newspaper *Chugoku Shimbun* by The Asia Foundation's Translation Service Center. San Francisco, 1988. Copyright © 1988 by The Asia Foundation. Reprinted by permission of The Asia Foundation.

Moorhouse, Geoffrey. *Imperial City: New York.* Henry Holt and Company, New York; 1988. Copyright © 1988 by Geoffrey Moorhouse. Reprinted by permission of the publisher.

Murray, William. "Muscular Milan," from *Condé Nast Traveler,* October 1988. Copyright © 1988 by William Murray. Reprinted by permission of Sterling Lord Literistic, Inc.

New York Times Company. Anthony Burgess, "Is America Falling Apart?," *New York Times,* November 7, 1971; Serge Schmemann, "The Views from Russia," *New York Times Magazine,* November 10, 1985; "Soviet Pans *Rocky* and *Rambo* Films," January 4, 1986; Marlis Simons, "Interview with Gabriel Garciá Márquez," *New York Times,* February 21, 1988; Sara Rimer, "Japanese Tourists Have Yen for New York City," *New York Times,* July 18, 1988. Copyright © 1971, 1985, 1986, 1988 by the New York Times Company. Reprinted by permission of the New York Times Company.

Newsweek. "Japan: The Call of the Wild," April 25, 1988. Copyright © 1988 by *Newsweek.* All rights reserved. Reprinted by permission of the publisher.

Nicolson, Nigel and Adam Nicolson. *Two Roads to Dodge City.* Harper & Row Publishers, Inc., New York; 1987. Copyright © 1987 by Nigel Nicolson and Adam Nicolson. Reprinted by permission of the publisher.

Niezabitowska, Malgorzata. "Discovering America," from *National Geographic,* January 1988. Copyright © 1988 by Malgorzata Niezabitowska. Reprinted by permission of the publisher.

Nordlund, Rod. "How to Speak Baksheesh," in *Trips,* Spring 1988. Copyright © 1988 by Rod Nordlund. Reprinted by permission of the author.

Ohmae, Kenichi. *Beyond National Borders.* Dow Jones-Irwin, Homewood, Illinois 60430; 1987. Copyright © 1987 by Kenichi Ohmae. Reprinted by permission of McKinsey & Company, Inc., New York.

Pern, Stephen. *The Great Divide: A Walk Through America Along the Continental Divide.* Viking, New York; 1988. Copyright © 1987 by Stephen Pern. All rights reserved. Reprinted by permission of the publisher.

Polovchak, Walter, with Keven Klose. *Freedom's Child.* Random House, New York; 1988. Copyright © 1988 by Walter Polovchak and Keven Klose. Reprinted by permission of the publisher.

Raban, Jonathan. *Old Glory: An American Voyage.* Simon & Schuster, Inc., New York; 1981. Copyright © 1981 by Jonathan Raban. All rights reserved. Reprinted by permission of the publisher.

Reader's Digest. Capt. Thomas Smith, "Humor in Uniform," July 1988. Copyright © 1988 by the Reader's Digest Association, Inc. Reprinted by permission of the publisher.

Reeves, Richard. "French D-Day Memorials." Syndicated column of June 1988. Copyright © 1988 by Universal Press Syndicate. Reprinted by permission of Universal Press Syndicate.

Revel, Jean-François. "The Crisis in Western Democracy," from *Imprimis,* April 1988. Copyright © 1988 by Hillsdale College. Reprinted by permission of Hillsdale College.

Revel, Jean-François. *How Democracies Perish.* Translated by William Byron. Doubleday & Company, Garden City; 1984. Translation copyright © 1984 by Doubleday & Co. Reprinted by permission of the publisher.

Salzman, Mark. *Iron Silk.* Random House, New York; 1986. Copyright © 1986 by Mark Salzman. Reprinted by permission of the publisher.

San Diego Union. Exchange of Letters to the Editor, January 20 and 23, 1988; Vu Thanh Thuy, "One Refugee Woman Tells Her Story of Survival," January 31, 1988; R. H. Growald column for August 15, 1988; Frank Green, "Lost in America," December 13, 1988; Jon Funabiki, "For These Visitors from Japan," January 18, 1989. Copyright © 1988 and 1989 by the *San Diego Union.* Reprinted by permission of the *San Diego Union.*

Wagner, Geoffrey. *Another America: In Search of Canyons.* George Allen & Unwin Ltd., London; 1972. Copyright © 1972 by Geoffrey Wagner. Reprinted by permission of the publisher.

Wall Street Journal. Seth Lipsky, "America's World-Wide Election," September 11, 1988; Adi Ignatius, "Chinese Monopolies Hate to Pass Go," October 4, 1988; Michael Ledeen, "Those Fun-loving Pranksters at NASA," January 23, 1990. Copyright © 1988, 1990 by Dow Jones & Company, Inc. Reprinted by permission of the *Wall Street Journal.* All rights reserved.

Walmsley, Jane. *Brit-Think, Ameri-Think.* Viking Penguin, Inc., New York; 1986. Copyright © 1986 by Jane Walmsley. All rights reserved. Reprinted by permission of the publisher.

White, T. H. *America at Last: The American Journal of T. H. White.* G. P. Putnam's Sons, New York; 1965. Copyright © 1965 by International Authors, N.V. Reprinted by permission of Harold Ober Associates, Inc., and David Higham Associates, Ltd.

Wise, David. *The Spy Who Got Away.* Random House, New York; 1988. Copyright © 1988 by David Wise. Reprinted by permission of the publisher.

World Press Review. Viktor Lishchenko, "Down on the Farm Near Coon Rapids," February 1987; Murray Hiebert, "Vietnam Looks at the U.S. War," September 1988; Interview with Vitaly Korotich, May 1989. Copyright © 1987, 1988, and 1989 by *World Press Review.* Reprinted by permission of *World Press Review.*

Zeffirelli, Franco. *Zeffirelli.* Weidenfeld & Nicolson, New York; 1986. Copyright © 1986 by Interfilm Finance, S.A. Reprinted by permission of the publisher.

Zongren, Liu. *Two Years in the Melting Pot.* China Books, San Francisco; 1984. Copyright © 1984 by China Books. Reprinted by permission of the publisher.

ABOUT THE AUTHOR

James C. Simmons is the author of six books and over two hundred magazine articles on history, travel, and wildlife. Raised in Cincinnati, he received his bachelor's degree from Miami University, Ohio, and a doctorate in British literature from the University of California at Berkeley. Before becoming a free-lance writer, he taught courses on British and American literature at Boston University and San Diego State University. He lives in San Diego.